02·13·05

For Barry,

In celebra[tion]

After reading [it]

look at relationships the same way again.

Best wishes for steady · unfolding

growth along your path.

Xo, Anne

THE SCIENCE OF LOVE

By

John Baines

Edited by Judith Hipskind

1993

Published by
JOHN BAINES INSTITUTE, INC.
Box 8556, F.D.R. Station, New York, NY 10150

This book was originally published as <u>La Ciencia del Amor.</u>
It was translated from Spanish by Josephine Bregazzi.
Cover design by John Costa.
Statue of "The Victory of Samothrace" by courtesy of the Louvre Museum.
Printed and bound by Edwards Brothers.

ISBN 1-882692-00-4

Library of Congress Catalog Card Number: 92-97419

The author and publisher welcome any comments and inquiries regarding the Teachings set forth in this book. You may address your letters to:

THE DARIO SALAS INSTITUTE
for HERMETIC SCIENCE
P.O. Box 8549
FDR Station
New York, NY 10150
U.S.A.

For more information about Hermetic Science, or for current schedules of Spanish and English language talks and instructional meetings held in New York City, or to request a brochure about correspondence courses or books written by John Baines, please write to the above address.

TABLE OF CONTENTS

PART TWO

LETTER TO THE READER

Dear Reader:

You are about to embark on a journey which could be compared to one across a vast expanse of seemingly perilous terrain. At the beginning, you see or imagine before you the oasis that awaits you. In order to reach it, you will need to create your own road map on the way, discarding the invisible excess baggage that could slow down your journey. The weight of the emotional baggage and the fantasies that you carry with you unawares, and the obstacles that seem to spring up out of nowhere, in fact, are your road signs and will dictate the nature of your journey.

The passage to real love obliges one to go through an arduous process of self-discovery, similar to Dante's descent into Hell in The Divine Comedy *and his subsequent passage through Purgatory to reach the Heavens. In **The Science of Love**, you will be lead through a meticulous examination of everything that is distorted with the current approach to love, revealing its darkest elements, in other words, what love is not. Then you will be lead through a profound exposition of fundamentals which will direct you towards perfection and deepest fulfillment, in other words, what real love is. This work synthesizes thousands of years of human behavior, therefore you will often experience uncanny recognition of your own emotional landscape or behavior unfolding on its pages.*

If true love be the goal, then reaching it will be the result of a process of profound comprehension, not the accumulation of simple information or techniques, nor the result of the piercing of Cupid's arrow. Instant love, instant enlightenment and instant solutions do not exist and to look for them can be self-deceiving.

If you recognize yourself in this book and are willing to earnestly and courageously look deeper within, you are halfway home. Each idea set forth is a sentinel which points the way to self-knowledge and fulfillment in love, and for many may be the doorway to a new life.

We wish you well on the rest of your journey.

INTRODUCTION

TO HERMETICISM

In the animal kingdom, there is a *"collective soul"* for each species, which acts as an invisible directing force that manages the instinctive behavior of its members, i.e. regulating reproduction, seasonal migration, territorial demarcation, etc. To the extent that man (*homo sapiens*) is a species of the animal kingdom, his psyche is implanted with the intention of the *"collective soul"* or central computer, which maintains the status quo of his species, limiting and/or prohibiting free will, individual thought and individual evolution. This *"collective soul"* has been described by Jung as *"the collective unconscious"* and through it, the individual receives an inheritance which governs his behavior, appearance, feelings, actions and thoughts. Man believes that his acts are a result of his own volition, but in reality, he is only acting out the directives of the collective soul and therefore must resign himself to sharing the common fate of his fellowmen, unless he is lucky enough to reach a Hermetic School. Through the study and practice of Hermeticism, man is reminded that he has also inherited another part, the "divine spark" or "spirit," which lies latent in the deepest recesses of his being.

The science of Hermeticism has been passed onto us through the teachings of Hermes Trismegistus, the wisest sage of ancient Egypt and being both practical and modern, it is as relevant today as it was in its genesis. The author succinctly defines the science of Hermeticism as "the wise use of natural powers," that is, the conscious use of the laws of Nature. Man, as a microcosm of the Universe, is subject to and cannot escape the laws of Nature. Thus, reinserting himself within the context of Nature's laws, which up till now he has tried to bypass, ignore or dominate, will lead him to knowledge of his inner world. Despite the vast technological and scientific advances of recent years, man himself, has not significantly changed. His brain essentially works in the same manner as it did over 2,000 years ago. His fear, hatred, passion and anxiety still dominate all his actions. While science has brought us some knowledge of matter and energy, it has not shed any light on understanding the spirit and power which generates and maintains life. The conquest of the outer world has been successful, but the conquest of the inner world has been null, therefore very few can state with certainty, "I know myself."

Hermeticism is the masterly science of the Universe, which is based upon seven Hermetic principles or Laws of Nature, as follows:

I.   *THE PRINCIPLE OF MENTALISM*
II.   *THE PRINCIPLE OF CORRESPONDENCE*
III. *THE PRINCIPLE OF VIBRATION*
IV. *THE PRINCIPLE OF POLARITY*
V.   *THE PRINCIPLE OF RHYTHM*
VI. *THE PRINCIPLE OF CAUSE AND EFFECT*
VII. *THE PRINCIPLE OF GENDER*

These principles are pivotal as they clearly and simply affirm man's relationship to all, as a microcosm of the Universe. The principle of Correspondence, "As it is above, so it is below," states that there is a correspondence or similarity among all cosmic phenomena and the study of this analogy enables us to read the unknown, commencing from that which is known. The laws of Nature dictate that if one throws a pebble into a lake, this simple act will some day influence the boundaries of the Universe in some way. Similarly, the negative behavior of an individual may inseminate hatred and rejection around him or her, while the conscious and positive behavior of another can affect the integral transformation of the human race. Each act, made consciously and constructively, has the potential to change one's psyche and the psyches of others. The principle of Polarity shows us that what is not desirable can be slain simply by changing its polarity and states: "Everything is dual; everything has poles; everything has its pair of opposites; like and unlike are the same; opposites are identical in nature, but different in degree; extremes meet; all truths are but half-truths; all paradoxes may be reconciled." For example, it is possible to change the vibration of hate into the vibration of love in one's own mind and in the mind of others; stress can be polarized by conscious relaxation, intolerance by comprehension and compassion, inertia by activity. In short, the art of polarization becomes a phase of mental alchemy or transmutation, known and practiced by ancient and modern Hermeticists.

The power to transform, which results from the profound understanding and harnessing of the laws of Nature, is the magical power of Hermeticism. It's practical application is tangible and should not be lost in intellectual theory or mysticism. In fact, our physical reality and daily experiences are the perfect arena for practicing these principles and seeing the results. Hermeticism gives the neophyte the keys to accomplish the transcendental act of raising oneself over one's animal instincts and of activating and manifesting the higher intelligence of true human beings.

Transcending oneself. This is the key of Hermeticism.

PROLOGUE

This book addresses the current impoverished condition of the act of loving, of the general ignorance of the meaning of love and of the unhappiness of those who fool themselves about their ability to love. The inability to love brings spiritual bankruptcy, rather than the rewards of genuine love.

Love has two sides; one born of darkness, called for the purposes of this book, Corrupt Love, and another born of light, called Divine Love. Through the achievement of true love, man can realize the divine side of his nature and through the practice of corrupt love, man can only know emptiness.

The aim of this book is to define the elements of true love, by illuminating the darkness for those lost on the path to true love, restoring what has been sullied in man's nature, enlightening the dark side of feeling and passion and putting the corrupt side of love to flight. Love must be reinvested with its lost purity, and freed from the effects of what religion terms Original Sin, dispelling immorality.

This book is meant to free those who yearn for love but who are held back by fear and hypocritical standards of morality. It is meant to train men and women to become masters and mistresses of love by transcending the limits of purely physical love, to achieve mental, emotional and spiritual union. As sex is approached without fear or reservation, the couple's path goes beyond marriage for convenience, money and other accepted behavior.

Highly evolved men and women can stop poor imitations of love and find fulfillment through the spiritual dimension of physical intercourse. This book will train couples to enter the spiritual dimension of love and present the couple as a luminous example for the future. The perfected couple must be born in the present to counteract the critical state of couples today.

Marriage is not undergoing a crisis today so much as the human couple itself. It is the couple who lives out a comedy of love limited by custom and habit, based on convenience and dollar signs and maintained by the physical side of love. It is a pathetic love that is limited to the body, lacking in warmth and content, without affection or tenderness. It is a dark and loveless coitus that chills the bones and subdues the intelligence and the spirit. Those who cannot rise above this condition and who are unaware of a higher type of union are most unfortunate.

The contrasting concepts of corrupt and divine are quite simple: the divine is the natural and the corrupt is the unnatural, or, the natural corrupted and perverted. This concept will be treated in greater depth throughout this work. The natural represents pure Nature, which has not been adulterated by human passions. A great deal of man's misfortune is due to the fact that, although he lives in Nature, he does not comply with her laws. Instead, man tries to govern his life by his own rules. Human and natural laws are at loggerheads and Nature, sooner or later, destroys the creations of man, unless he learns to live in harmony with her.

A responsible and mature view recognizes that two basic forces exist in the Universe: the creative and Divine, the soul-killing and the corrupt. God and Satan (Satan is merely a name which symbolizes the manifestation of the dark powers of death, dissolution and destruction) are in a state of eternal war and the ultimate outcome is unknown to us. Unfortunately, the world of *homo sapiens* is too close to that of Satan's and too far from God's. This is so obvious that great philosophers and thinkers have even said that "upon contemplating the world, they cannot believe that it is God's work, but rather Satan's." Light and darkness struggle for the kingdom of the Universe. We are still living in the dark ages of materialism, bestiality and unleashed passions.

Observe how simple it is to destroy something and how tremendously difficult it is to create it. In human reality, chaos and disorder are present with much greater effect than the power of an ordered structure.

Mankind simulates love and that is why love, for man, is confusing, sensual, deceptive and soul-killing. In its present condition, love cannot fulfill man's once-upon-a-time desire for a deep and true union with the loved one. Men and women separately are only halves of a whole; an incomplete reality of one total truth. It is this integral structure which lovers unconsciously try to achieve. Reality, however, reveals the fantasy of illusory desire. There are exceptions though to this general condition, just as there are men who live to be 120, or people who have never been ill in their lives, and amazingly enough, men and women who are saints, magicians and immortal beings.

It is quite possible to form the spiritually-centered couple through education, but this education cannot be taken lightly or viewed as a game. The inner training of the ancient temples of initiation in Egypt, Greece and other places did just that.

Only those who use their intelligence properly can aspire to a knowledge of Divine Love. Those who are guided by base and selfish motives cannot imagine the existence of a higher love. They are content with the simple mating habits of animals. To achieve higher love, an unprogrammed and objective intelligence which comes from conscious awareness is necessary. This awareness can be reached in a school for initiation, but not through the programmed intelligence of rote memory.

Divine Love is not an abstract or ethereal subject based on Platonic concepts, nor an idea which excludes or limits the sexual aspect. On the contrary, Divine Love means attaining an integral love which covers every facet of love not normally taken into account. Divine Love aims for a love that not only satisfies the body, but also the soul, the mind and the spirit as well. All people who operate from a purely instinctual point of view are excluded from the possibility of attaining true love because the key to love is through transcendence of the baser side of Nature.

Corrupt love leads invariably to psychological and spiritual self-destruction. The dissolution is neither violent nor spectacular, but rather one produced gradually with the passing of time, which submits the individual to the raw force of Nature. The subject, in effect, is gradually absorbed by Nature's stronger principles, little by little, almost unwittingly, losing his higher faculties, while his bestial side is strengthened. A man who might possess exquisite qualities becomes a boor and a caricature of what he once was. A woman, delicate, lovely and refined, gradually becomes hard and vulgar. These changes are not necessarily the result of ageing, but of the rupture of natural principles caused by a loss of "interior innocence." The loss of innocence not only causes a loss of looks, but also causes a face to become dirty and contaminated in appearance, as if it were a silent witness of great interior sin. There are beings who reach old age with a clear forehead and eyes, and who, despite the years, manage to keep a sort of internal purity. They are the ones who have complied with the laws of Nature, or who have at least not violated them in the extreme.

In order to achieve the aims set forth in this work, the principles of Hermetic wisdom will be used, which will require the repetition of many words and ideas in order to bring the reader to an integral understanding of this Teaching.

PART ONE

THE ELEMENTS OF CORRUPT LOVE

If the great majority of the human race practices corrupt forms of love, it is not by choice, but is a result of the ignorance and limitations of its human-animal condition. Man chooses the corrupt due to a lack of awareness and an inability to love God within himself. He can therefore do nothing else.

Generally speaking, the biological and psychological make up of the human being leads him to take the line of least resistance, which often results in mediocrity and a waste of his higher possibilities. People do not deliberately choose not to know about love, but they do not make the effort required to grasp its dynamics. This tendency is especially evident when people repeatedly fail in love and marriage. Despite these failures, they do not seek the reason for the relationship's failure, but simply attribute it to not having found the right person. The fruitless search for the "right person" may last for all one's life. At no point do people stop to think that the reasons for failures in their relationships lie in their own inability and ignorance of the nature of love. Erich Fromm states in The Art of Loving that love cannot be something which is improvised and practiced haphazardly, but must be studied with the same enthusiasm and care used to approach a knowledge of any art. As it happens, very few people have understood this and still believe that "love is easy."

This book presents the Hermetic secrets of love, the profound and esoteric side of love that the world does not know about, and authentic love, how it is manifested, how it should be practiced and kept distinct from false love. This knowledge, which has been kept secret from remotest antiquity, is still veiled in mystery for reasons given in previous volumes of this series. Because of the depth of this Teaching, one should not expect instant understanding, but anyone who approaches the study of this knowledge with sincerity, honesty, intelligence, objectivity and humility, will find the true path to happiness and fulfillment.

One cannot see light without first knowing what darkness is, therefore the first part of this book will be devoted to explaining what false love is. Only after examining corrupt amorous behavior in the human being, will the essence of genuine love and its deepest mysteries, be revealed.

WHY DO PEOPLE

GET MARRIED?

Primarily, people seek "union with others." According to Erich Fromm, this union is one of the true objectives of love. In some people, this urge to unite can be mistakenly acted out in sadistic or masochistic behavior.

The instinct to reproduce can also lead a person to marriage as an acceptable way of having both children and sexual gratification. The etymology of the word "matrimony" comes from the Latin *"MATER"* and *"MUNIA,"* meaning respectively, "mother" and "duties," a reflection of the responsibility of children who come as a result of marriage. In ancient legal texts, Pope Gregory IX wrote that "the child for the mother is onerous before birth, painful at birth and burdensome after birth."

The most commonly acknowledged reason for marrying is love. The prospects and expectations for a man and a woman, however, are quite different. She seeks the security of a home and all that this implies; economic well-being, protection, romantic tenderness and the opportunity to become a mother. A man, for his part, looks for sexual gratification, a home that supports him and cares for him and a mother-caretaker for his children. Marriage has become the fundamental unit of society and the structure which permits the reproduction of the human species.

Millions of marriages throughout the world comply with the accepted aims of the procreation of children and mutual love and protection. However, the aspect of marriage which most often fails is the most important aspect: love.

Marriage has become utilitarian; based on economic upkeep for the wife, administration of the home for the husband and education for the children. A similar attitude applies to the sexual side of marriage; a utilitarian approach or manipulation of the spouse for one's own physical pleasure. This situation is emotionally dangerous and is a form of psychological bondage.

In true love, there is a higher purpose in the union, one transcending self-interest. True love, little known to the human species, is a form of *Divine Love*. This love is the opposite of the darker and selfish love known as *Corrupt Love*, which is the expression of a "corruption of the natural" and a deviation from Nature.

The painful reality is that people don't have the slightest idea of what love really is and don't know how to love the opposite sex, the world nor themselves. This work will reveal the true and profound bases of love. The intent is different from that of Erich Fromm's, whose Art of Loving has a psychoanalytical and philosophical approach, which although brilliant, has only been partly understood. The aim of this book is to show the Hermetic aspect of love, the deep, but mostly unknown laws which involve the mechanics and physics of Nature. These laws apply not only to love, but to all phenomena of life and are expressed not in numbers, but in truths which are self-evident only to those who reach a higher state of consciousness. These teachings are for those who act from a spiritual direction and not from their animal nature. According to Hermes Trismegistus, the "Master of

Masters," spirituality is not religious bigotry or easy mysticism, but an elevated state of consciousness, in which "the spirit manifests itself through one's own brain."

This definition of spirituality requires clarification. When a person reaches an elevated state of consciousness, he attains an "integral intelligence," a precious possession which can lead to true love. Cerebral intelligence is highly limited, as it keeps a person bound to rigid programming, which denies experience if it is not part of the original programming. Cerebral intelligence, however great it may be, lacks the necessary power to achieve happiness in love, human fulfillment, a higher state of consciousness, full communication with others and inner peace.

The aim of this work is to teach the "Hermetic ABC's" of the science of love. Any person who understands this art well and applies it accordingly, will reach a state of love and spiritual happiness of unimaginable intensity, force and quality. This happiness will be stable and imperishable. However, no one can expect to gain this "nectar of the Gods" by the rote performance of certain acts or through technical fulfillment of certain mandates. However correct one's behavior, it is useless if not motivated by an essential understanding of the Hermetic laws which govern love. Love cannot be "unconscious love," but must be "wise love." To many people, this statement might seem contradictory, as it is traditionally believed that love is a force which flows as spontaneously as a mountain stream. This notion is perhaps the greatest error of all, for love does not exist as a gift or as a natural faculty, but is instead a technique, a science which one must master if one is to be successful. Without guidance and training, the most probable result in the attempt to love will be frustration and failure.

Fruitfulness in love is not measured by the production of children, but by the level of communication, tenderness, friendship and happiness of body and soul. The true and rarely achieved aim of the human couple, is a union of souls which leads both spouses to the highest desires of both. The union of body and emotion only, is a shadow and parody of true marriage. Ownership, the possessive approach of the marital contract, and its mutual obligations, are only an artificial attempt to bind two people. The less love there is between two beings, the more rules, obligations, vows and conventions are needed to keep them together. The Hermetic approach advocates union through true love, not through social or personal convention, nor through the fleeting mirage of ardent passion. When the human being understands and practices union through genuine love, humanity will have found the right path to human perfection.

CORRUPT LOVE IS

IGNORANCE

There are many ways man allows himself to be guided by his instincts. Man is not taught the need to care for his emotions and imagination in the same way bodily cleanliness is taught, nor has he been told that he needs to take lessons in love. Normally, passionate and amorous feelings are allowed to flow and fuse between a loving couple, who give themselves to the delight of the experience of their sensations. The results of these experiences however, are often far from satisfactory, as today's high rate of divorce and separation shows. Official statistics do not take into account couples who are unhappy, ill-suited, or who are kept together through convenience, habit, religious obligation, or to spare their children a separation.

People do not know what true love is and because of this, will hardly be able to attain their expectations of happiness. Love is one of the basic needs of a human being and individuals try to fulfill themselves through this impulse. In practice, however, love can be one of the greatest sources of frustration for an individual, creating an inhibition which generates unhappiness, aggression and loneliness. Those who have effectively managed to achieve genuine love are really in the minority.

When one analyzes the state of love today, the

inability of individuals to love stands out. They fail through ignorance and together with their partners, bring to their union a heavy load of prejudices and misconceptions. People do not know what love is and in this respect have only capricious and self-centered concepts of love. Depending on the persistence of their illusions, a couple will be disappointed in a relatively short time, because fantasies of love are not often the same for both partners. When personal fantasies coincide, it is harder to break up a relationship. The process is slower and more painful and, in many instances, leads to tremendous emotional and psychological trauma. We all know the various forms the drama of love takes: divorce, separation, quarrels, abandonment, physical abuse, perhaps suicides and in most cases, a lifetime of bitterness, unhappiness and frustration.

It is not easy for a person to let go of his illusions about love and to adapt a realistic approach to the situation, for fantasies of love are only a small part of each individual's dreams and these in turn are only part of the fantastic dream world of the human race. Giving up these illusions does not mean giving up hopes and desires, but only the fantastic dreams that are motivated by the sum total of a person's hidden desires and fears. If a person for instance, ingests a dose of hallucinogenic drugs, he can have erotic dreams which obey unconscious erotic fantasies. Such visions are capricious and bear no relation to logic or reality. The interesting point of this example is that the origin of these fantasies does not originate from the drug itself, but in the fact that it acts as a device which unleashes the contents of the unconscious.

There are many devices with similar, but gentler effects, which have nothing to do with drugs or stimulants, but which react according to their type or given psychological predispositions to set off the individual's world of fantasy. According to the frequency and potency of the chosen stimulant and its use, a person becomes an occasional, frequent or continual dreamer. Such an individual is hardly ready for a satisfactory experience of love, unless it is at the expense of great moral and psychological suffering. Just as a child suffers in order to become an adult, the lover suffering from the disease of fantasy must undergo a painful process if he is to be cured. At times, it is difficult to persuade people that building castles in the air may lead to unhappiness and pain. There are people who would give up anything except the secret pleasure of constantly imagining pleasant situations, with themselves as the heroes. Unfortunately, these people lead an inert existence, without significant or stimulating events, except those they dream up. One could say that such people have given up real existence in favor of an imaginary one; instead of doing and living, they prefer to dream. They suffer from a form of cowardice and impotence which leads them constantly to avoid the risks of life, for the "dream" risks nothing.

A woman looking for her "Prince Charming" will be greatly disappointed because she lacks any real concept of love. A realistic view of love is the first step to avoiding the trap of a corrupt love. Often, people have the idea that being realistic means sacrificing something and giving up what they desire. The truth is that just the opposite is more likely: that a person relinquishes realistic expectations just to satisfy harmful romantic ideas. This behavior can be seen in all walks of life: a student who lives in a world of fantasy with delusions of grandeur will find it hard to become a professional, for instance. Only those who have realistic expectations can succeed and even this will not ensure total success in love.

A definition of love, what it is and what it is not, can

help a person, depending on motivation and degree of understanding, to overcome fantasies and become realistic about it. Most often, what an individual knows of love is limited to a knowledge of anatomical differences, without knowing truly how men and women differ. This knowledge is indispensable for anyone wishing to define himself and his partner and to act consciously. Only conscious love is worthwhile; the other type leads to the bottomless well of nothingness.

"Masculine" and "feminine" do not simply represent difference in gender. They are universal principles. The masculine sex is in ratio to the universal male principle and the feminine to the female force. A man radiates the active principle of God, and a woman the passive or conceiving force of Nature. Neither is superior to the other; they are merely different. One should understand how different they are so that there may be understanding and communication between them.

A man may frequently underestimate a woman due to her apparent physical weakness and apparent lack of intellectual brilliance. This negative concept disappears, nevertheless, when he realizes that her intelligence is as effective as his, although it is directed another way. It is of a more practical quality than an abstract one. In a sense, one may say that a man is more intelligent than a woman in abstract fields, whereas she is far better prepared to face practical situations. She rarely invents things but she is better prepared than a man to use the inventions in a specific way. Men must once and for all, destroy the myth of their supremacy over women, thus forcing them in turn to relinquish their feigned attitudes of defenselessness and weakness, which they have adopted from ancient times to wield power over men and thus balance out their physical strength.

One of the first requirements in the formation of a real couple is to establish an equal relationship, otherwise one will always exploit the other, as the weaker will take advantage of the stronger. Equality, in this case, refers mainly to the maturity of the Ego and the intellectual level of the person. It is hard to believe, however, that a woman really wishes to compete equally with a man, in view of the fact that, out of convenience, she is used to transferring her responsibility to him. Through deeper analysis one can conclude that a woman has two perfectly clear possibilities in her life: either she becomes the protege of a man, thus prematurely ending her possibilities of evolution, or else she places herself on the same level by undertaking similar responsibilities. In the first instance, the couple will be unbalanced, for most of the "matrimonial space" will be occupied by the man. This occurs in a case we will study later, where a woman adopts extreme attitudes and allows the man to maintain her, assuming this is how it should be, on account of her attitude of a "fragile Eve." In reality, she will tyrannize the man implacably, to satisfy her thirst for power and dominion. This type of behavior can be open or hidden, for in this field the man cannot compete with the woman in astuteness.

In order to go into greater depth in the Hermetic study of the human couple, the laws of magnetic polarity which govern the relationship between the sexes must be discussed. First of all, neither men nor women are entirely masculine and feminine, for men possess only 3/4 masculine energy and 1/4 feminine energy. Women have 3/4 feminine and 1/4 masculine energy. This one-quarter part of the opposite sex in each, is what causes the majority of clashes in a couple and what impedes a harmonious relationship. This percentage represents a norm, but the percentages can be different, either from birth through genetic problems, or from childhood or adolescence as a result of phenomena outlined in this book. When the principle which rules each sex is diminished to below normal, the one-quarter percentage of the opposite sex traits increases and becomes exaggerated, giving rise to homosexuality and lesbianism. This change in ratio also accounts for the shy, diffident and effeminate man, and the domineering, manly woman. It must be understood that a man has a brain with a feminine polarity and a woman with a masculine one. The importance of this fact will be evident as this work unfolds. For now, the focus is on the percentage of the opposite sex which we all possess, a percentage which should be gradually eliminated so that a couple may attain harmonious perfection. A man should become 100% male and a woman entirely female.

How did this portion of the opposite sex traits, which we all have, originate? Where did it come from? Hermetic tradition informs us that before Adam and Eve appeared in the world, man was androgynous, possessing both sexes and that the masculine organ of one inseminated the other and vice-versa, so that both gave birth. Sexual differentiation arose when some who were stronger than others and who feared the pains of childbirth, tied down the weaker ones in order to possess them and not be fertilized by them. With this, one organ became atrophied and the differentiation arose. The energy of the atrophied organ persisted, which is preserved however, in the form of that percentage of opposite sex traits which exists in the individual's psyche.

To understand what love is and how the human couple should behave, it is necessary to understand how this portion of the opposite sex manifests itself in people. What are feminine characteristics and attitudes in men and masculine ones in women? It should not seem strange that many of the characteristics which are masculine in women become feminine in men. The condition of gender does not lie in the quality itself, but in its application.

The following is a brief list of the characteristics which stem from the opposite sex traits in each person. In addition, there are many other traits which are difficult to describe, for there is no adequate language to define them.

Masculine Characteristics in Women:

Aggression	Lust for power
Bad temper	Matriarchal behavior
Bitterness	Morbidity
Capriciousness	Narcissism
Coarse language	Possessiveness
Destructive impulses	Pride
Disloyalty	Prudery
Emotional frigidity	Sadism
Envy	Selfishness
Hate	Self-pity
Hypocrisy	Sexual frigidity
Hysteria	Sharpness
Irresponsibility	Talkativeness
Jealousy	Vanity
Laziness	

Feminine Characteristics in Men:

Avarice	Lack of will power
Bad temper	Laziness
Boasting	Love of comfort
Cowardice	Macho behavior
Disloyalty	Masochism
Emotional & intellectual rigidity	Narcissism
Exhibitionism	Passion
Explosive character	Physical & verbal aggression
Fanaticism	Pride
Fantasy	Prudery

Hate   Selfishness
Hypocrisy   Sensuality
Hysteria   Subjectivity
Irresponsibility   Talkativeness
Jealousy   Vanity
Lack of self-control   Weakness of character

Feminine Qualities in Women:
Balanced libido   Loyalty
Clear, controlled imagination   Naturalness
Equilibrium   Objectivity
Frankness   Prudence
Generosity   Realism
Gentleness   Responsibility
Friendship   Security
Harmony   Self-control
Humbleness   Sweetness
Love   Understanding

Masculine Qualities in Men:
Activity   Lack of prejudice
Capacity for understanding   Logical reasoning
Controlled strength   Mental & psychological
                                  stability
Courage   Modesty
Emotional & intellectual flexibility   Moral rectitude
Equilibrium   Non-chauvinistic behavior
Frankness   Responsibility
Harmony   Security
Humbleness   Self-control
Intelligence   Spirituality

In order to understand how these opposite sex trait characteristics work in men and women, two examples will be given. It is necessary to understand that what makes a woman feel jealous, aggressive, bitter or hysterical is the tremendous insecurity she feels about her lack of definition as a female. Feeling weak in her femininity, she seeks an exaggerated compensation for her lack of self-esteem, which unfortunately manifests itself in domineering, bossy attitudes more suited to the opposite sex. In a man's case, he also feels his virile qualities are weak and to compensate for this, he adopts attitudes which are marked by escapism (lack of manliness), infantilism (insufficient virility), passivity (lack of controlled aggression) and exhibitionism (the hyper-compensation of the homosexual or asexual man).

This list of masculine and feminine qualities gives rise to a double phenomenon: the presence in each individual of a given quantity of the energy of the opposite sex, which is to be found in a latent form, and the psychological behavior which this force brings about. In this very simple phenomenon lies the secret of the unconscious behavior of the human libido. For this reason, we usually only know the physical sex of a person, without being able to determine the psychological sex. Many men are psychologically female and a large number of women are psychologically male. When the psychic component of the opposite sex is too strong, the individual easily slips into homosexuality.

Several elements contribute to and strengthen the development of opposite gender sexuality in early childhood or infancy. This occurs, for example, when a male child is educated by his mother as a girl, or dressed in feminine clothes, or when his feminine-like behavior is stimulated or when he is over-protected. Thus, the foundation is laid for a change in gender orientation, due to this outside stimulation of the feminine side of the male. The same happens in the case of a woman, particularly when her father openly proclaims his dissatisfaction with his daughter's sex and brings her up as if she were a boy.

The masculine and feminine sexes are universally represented by the symbols which indicate gender: the egg and the sperm. These two symbols correspond to two basic attitudes of the human being: aggression (sperm) and flight (egg). An attacker attempts to make his victim embrace a different way of being. One who flees attempts to outwit the aggressor by absorbing him, as the egg does with the sperm. This is why aggression and flight are primary behavioral norms of an extraordinary force, for they correspond to equivalent forms of cosmic energy.

"Male" and "female" are only terms that express gender and the fact that a male individual is psychologically female only indicates a variance of the universal principle of gender and cannot be used to prove the goodness or badness of an individual. Pure gender is not found in the human race as a spontaneous or natural vital manifestation, that is, the individual is not born thus, but only attains it by means of Hermetic study. To express it in other words, a man is not born one hundred percent male, neither is a woman born completely female; there only appear beings with less than 100% of same gender traits.

The variance in gender traits does not rule out the presence of normal qualities in a human being. On the other hand it is one of the main obstacles to fulfillment in love for the human couple. Full satisfaction is only attained when two individuals who are one hundred percent defined, unite. Many love quarrels of couples have come from the contact between inadequate polarities, between the feminine part of a man and the feminine part in a woman, or between the masculine part of a woman and the masculine part in a man. This inappropriate communication provokes a true emotional "short circuit."

FIGURE 1

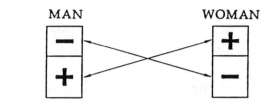

CONTACT THAT IS UNBALANCED AND CAUSES
REPULSION BETWEEN THE TWO POLES

FIGURE 2

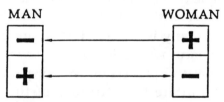

MAGNETICALLY WELL BALANCED POLES (ATTRACTIVE)
BUT PERVERTED IN THE PURITY OF THE GENDER PRINCIPLE

FIGURE 3

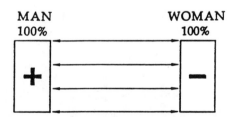

PERFECT RELATIONSHIP OF THE COUPLE BETWEEN
AN INTEGRALLY MASCULINE MAN AND
A COMPLETELY FEMININE WOMAN

The secret of the attraction between men and women also lies in the proceding figures. The reasons are clear why a woman with a highly developed masculine side always feels attracted to the same type of man, one who is effeminate, shy, weak and insecure. Because she is highly masculine, her preferences will be directed toward feminine men (in the psychological sense). In reverse, an effeminate man will often be attracted to a manly woman. A highly feminine woman will feel attracted to mentally and psychologically masculine men.

Observation of human behavior in our own time shows that man's scale of values has been totally upset and that relationships are not exempt from this confusion. A good example of this can be found in the images certain film stars project of their virility. The projected image of masculinity actually is obscured by a number of highly feminine traits incorporated in the image, which contribute to the confusion and perversion of their passive admirers who blindly imitate the attitudes of their idols and sometimes model their behavior after them. A male viewer can be led to believe that macho behavior is the best token of his virility and a woman can be led to believe that jealousy, hysterical outbursts of feeling and passion are outstanding displays of femininity.

CORRUPT LOVE IS

USING MARRIAGE AS AN ANCHOR AND A GOAL

A human being is a creature of habit who faithfully obeys the norms of behavior that society approves and rejects. Marriage, as a social institution, has an extremely strong symbolic image. In primary fantasies, it seems to become a sort of magical garden in which the individual can satisfy his dearest wishes, receive the backing of social respect and be filled with pride as he displays his own fertility to the world through the procreation of a new living being. A woman feels fulfilled when she marries. She obtains what everybody expects her to obtain; a man, and she is "legally" accepted by all the world. A man will proudly show off the woman in whom he is to deposit his sperm. As a sign of respect and admiration, she must be eternally faithful to him, give him children, suckle them, bring them up, educate them, and if this were not enough, keep house for him and feed him.

A woman hopes for a "good worker" to maintain her. A man hopes for a "good machine for making love and giving birth to children" and sometimes, a second mother, too. When all this has been fulfilled, society smiles complacently and the couple tries to show their friends and relations the lovely children born of their sexual pairing and how happy they are. Thus it would appear that everything is in its right place and that the cycle of Nature has been completely fulfilled through its manifestation in animal and human couples, who parade their cubs or children in perfect formation.

It is a fact that marriage can provide prestige and respectability, along with an aura of seriousness and maturity. This is why so many people come to marriage as if it were a goal and live totally disoriented as far as their true situation in love is concerned. They do not realize that marital union is only a tool for the full realization of something which should have existed quite plainly before the wedding, that is, love. Many young women will feel mistakenly happy merely at having managed to get married, without considering that, far from having reached a goal, they have only just begun their journey. The wedding is no more than the starting point in the search for happiness and fulfillment in love.

One of the basic problems within the reasons for marrying is tremendous hypocrisy. Even when failure is obvious, neither party will acknowledge it and they will invariably try to salvage the relationship artificially. "What the neighbors will say" and concern for one's own image are reasons for the hypocrisy because self-esteem suffers a hard knock when it has to publicly acknowledge failure. There are a great number of totally aborted marriages whose participants refuse to acknowledge failure to other people or to themselves. With "professional" hypocrisy, they strive to play out the farce that "everything's O.K.," a game which functions at both an internal and external level. The couple communicates with each other on an internal level according to their usual habit, but when in front of other people, they immediately change to the external, thus hiding the true nature of their relationship. If they are quarrelling over something, they rapidly wipe out their anger, exhibiting the best of smiles and as soon as the outsiders withdraw, they once more gnash their teeth at each other. It is evident that there is a type of behavior which is directed toward artificially maintaining and asserting the relationship. The attempt to appear happy at any price keeps a couple forcibly together, engendering internal dissatisfaction and very serious problems, which by their very nature are cumulative and may result in a tremendous psychic explosion.

When love is lacking, the couple seeks its own "adhesive cement" which enables the relationship to remain intact no matter what. For many, marriage is precisely the adhesive which will give them this forced and artificial stability. This is what allows marriage partners who intimately detest each other, to stay united to death, even though they experience daily the most profound unhappiness.

The more insecure and immature the partners involved in a couple are, the more rigid will be the rules which they impose upon themselves to regulate their behavior. Mutual commandments must be complied with blindly, so that the marriage can survive, because if they are not respected, the whole edifice will crumble. This is why the couple, as well as observing traditional commandments, develops its own commandments in order to build a life made up of emotional, social, professional and intellectual aims with rules which cover all aspects of each individual's life. Expressions that should be spontaneous and natural, become rigid and inflexible and generally frustrate the inner impulses of both spouses. The responsibility of having children plays a very important part in the problem, as "union by obligation" is substituted for "union through love." Precisely when love is not sufficient to unite two people, is it necessary to resort to external force to achieve this aim.

For a great majority of people, the anchor of marriage provides a solidity in life which is lacking in the individual alone. In general people drift like ships, without a course, a destiny or any higher purpose. The stronger the obligation of marriage is for them, the more firmly are they incorporated into the social structure. Children further strengthen the mutual obligations, creating chains of remarkable force and duration. Frequently, a new couple anxiously awaits the arrival of children, and if the children at first fill their parents with joy, they soon tire or exasperate them. Nevertheless, the obligation which they bring with them persists.

A sort of conspiracy of silence causes a couple to conceal how discontented they feel about their children. Couples who are parents, take great care that future parents do not realize the real situation and keep the golden illusion of parenthood intact. Nature, with great zeal and care, takes pains to maintain the species by means of an adequate number of births. It will be argued that human beings need children to fulfill themselves. This is especially true in the case of a woman who longs for the experience of maternity as she envisions it, profusely glorified by artists, poets, intellectuals and the Church. In fact, the belief is that women are born solely to have children and take care of the home. As a result of this conviction, important aspects of their education are neglected and they are taught to first look after babies, cook, keep house and do needlework. No one teaches them or the man in their lives how to love. No one explains that marriage and maternity, at least in their conventional aspect, are but a small part of what a couple can accomplish together.

CORRUPT LOVE IS

WITHHOLDING ONESELF

In love, there is another long-standing pattern based on a materialistic outlook, which causes men and women not to "give themselves" deeply in love relationships, while demanding at the same time unconditional giving from the other person. For women, this approach echoes the era when they were considered "chattels," a custom which still prevails in certain primitive cultures, and in hidden ways in more developed ones. This can lead a woman to an awareness of her own economic value, which is invariably proportional to her physical attributes as a female. The man, who is the main player in this game, knows that he has to pay a high price for this woman, whether it is to keep her forever or to satisfy all her whims. When a woman is portrayed as an object, it stems from the fact that she is in some way an object of commercial value. On one hand, she is aware of her value, and on the other, a man knows that he has to pay a price to obtain and keep her, thus giving rise to a commercial transaction. This situation is another factor which encourages and maintains "love without love."

Because the price of a woman or a man is not calculated in units of fixed value such as money, there may be a wide difference between the value which a person sets upon him or herself and the value that the other party sets. There are certain women who value themselves very highly and as a result demand that the man give them something of equivalent value. If the exchange is not equal, the woman feels used, deceived and defrauded, believing the man has taken advantage of her. This is why those women who over-estimate themselves generally marry men with large fortunes or men of great fame and renown. When mating has been motivated by financial and material reward, a partner must keep up the level of his financial reward for a woman to likewise maintain the continuity of her giving. When the economic side deteriorates, the giving side is also interrupted.

There are two distinct types of giving: that of the body (physically), and that of the mind and spirit (psychologically). Giving one's body is put to the test whenever there is a physical relationship, but psychological giving only occurs when a man and a woman are convinced that the transaction is fair for both parties. Often women passively allow men to possess them without true psychic participation. By giving only her body, a woman becomes an "object-woman" through her own will and she must be paid a high price for it. This price may be paid in the form of money and other goods or in the form of emotional bondage and other undesirable demands, such as blind admiration, obedience, psychic slavery and so on.

As a result of such a situation, a man does not give himself either, but resorts to the simplest, most expedient way of buying the woman. Neither party makes a true gift of themselves, but carries out a transaction in which one thing is exchanged for another. The customary practice is the giving of a woman's body in exchange for maintenance or economic compensation. The object-woman gives her body; the man, his wallet. If there is equal value in the prices set, then everybody is satisfied, but love does not come into it at all.

Under these circumstances, a woman never thinks of the need to give herself psychologically to her man. If she believed there was a reason to give herself this way, she would be trained and counseled accordingly. As it is, she devotes her efforts to cultivating her body as if it were goods to be bartered. Women lacking in physical attractiveness are obliged to develop their higher faculties and cultivate character and intelligence. They have the possibilities to succeed in many areas of life such as in the successful practice of a profession or art. More intelligent women who are less attractive physically, compensate for their lack of physical appeal with other qualities esteemed and rewarded by society, although there are definitely exceptions to this rule.

In this area, a man is more fortunate because he does not need to be physically attractive. His good economic position suffices for his appeal. Of course, neither will a man give himself to his woman in this type of relationship, for he is quite aware of a constant need to buy her which makes any profound giving of himself unnecessary. When a man buys a woman, he pays for sexual gratification, children, clean clothes, food and cleanliness in the home. The woman pays for her upkeep, protection, food for her children, and sometimes, for the upkeep of her parents and relatives, and if she is attractive or desirable enough, for luxuries and whims. Thus this custom forms a sort of infernal circle: a woman must be more beautiful every day, or at least keep herself physically attractive, otherwise her value will drop considerably and will not be enough to pay for what she had previously acquired. A man in turn must earn more and more money to satisfy the ever-growing demands of his wife, who will need more and more money to preserve her beauty. This is really a situation which only Satan could have invented. Ironically, this situation favors the female sex to some degree because society has seen fit to protect her with a series of laws so that the man cannot abandon her with the passing of time when her beauty fades. This is why marriage is a legal joint-stock partnership. It is quite understandable that if genuine love existed, there would be no need for these legal dispositions, because a man would never leave his wife unprotected.

A beautiful woman does not need to give in order to receive something valuable; she needs only to lend her body. Therefore, the more beautiful she is, the greater will be her awareness of her own power. Such a woman looks at herself in a mirror and smiles contentedly, deriving satisfaction from her awareness of her own power over men, and she must keep this feeling constantly alive in order to be happy. Psychological analysis would show that the money-minded woman does not experience life, but lives through men; she therefore feels desperate and finished when her beauty begins to fade and she fears being abandoned. Only the truly intelligent woman is able to free herself from reliance on her "market place" value in a relationship and gain autonomy for her own life. This is really the only true feminine liberation. It is not enough to demand equal rights with men, but it is also necessary to assume the same obligations. It is only logical and natural that each member of the couple should contribute to the welfare and common happiness of the family. This contribution should always be made based on love and not on the expression of purely material values.

There are other reasons why a woman will withhold herself in a relationship. The reasons are related to various complexes which will be discussed in later chapters. One pertinent complex, however, is that of the "virgin queen." In this complex, a woman considers herself to be a beautiful doll which all men should adore and respect. The act of sex itself is humiliating for this woman. It implies that she must "descend from the throne" to place herself on the same level as the "hairy beast" who invades her body. This type of woman can only maintain a normal relationship with a man who, either openly or secretly, thinks of her precisely as a "queen on her throne." When anyone thinks of her as an equal, she does not respond, because she feels humiliated.

For a man, there is also a common form of refusing to give himself to a woman. It entails male chauvinistic behavior, which aims to dominate the woman constantly, as a way to feel secure as a male. Upon analyzing the problem of not giving oneself in a relationship, one discovers many motives apart from the materialistic approach. Some are based on selfishness, laziness or diverse complexes and frustrations, however, there are also well-founded motives for these, as the following pages will show.

The corrupt element, which is absorbent or vampire-like in nature, motivates a majority of people to look for something from their partner in love, rather than give him or her love. The most demanding individuals, in terms of love, are often those who give the least. A demanding person assumes that the other person has a similar nature and keeps ahead of the game by making constant and exaggerated demands for emotional giving. The person who does not give needs to be given to, but formulates his demands in a possessive and obsessive way, because no amount of giving will make up for the lack he feels. This is an extremely primitive form of dominance, for it reflects quite clearly the behavior of certain animal species.

CORRUPT LOVE IS

NARCISSISM AND JEALOUSY

Jealousy is an extreme form of selfish possession in which one person, who is expected to give his or her love exclusively to the other with no deviation from the established norms of conduct. Jealousy ranges from the feelings experienced by the deceived lover to the restlessness felt by a man who senses that the woman he loves is receiving too much attention from another man. There is a wide range of jealous behavior which fluctuates between what is considered normal and what is pathological. The source of jealousy can always be found in a central motive however; fear that the loved one or a supposed loved one might prefer a third party. The occasions for jealousy can be numerous and may exist only in the imagination of the jealous person, who misinterprets and enlarges upon the various attitudes of the object of his passion.

The jealous man is a total exclusivist, who imagines the loved one to be an object without liberty or a life of her own. To safeguard this object, he would like to put it into a mental prison, built out of a set of rules, mandates and prohibitions, which he believes will help him wield his psychological tyranny. The jealous person is emotionally unbalanced. Through his attitude, he only projects his own lack of love, for he does not really love the individual he claims to be in love with; all he seeks is a psychological servant upon whom to batten himself to, thus getting a sense of false security by controlling the behavior, feelings and actions of the other. The jealous man is an empty and insecure one who needs to fill his inner world with the emotional life of the other being. From the point of view of love, he is generally perverse due to the fact that his affections, instead of flowing towards the other person, the world or people, are centered upon himself. Strangely enough, the jealous man is not really a perfect narcissist, who believes that his partner, people and the world at large exist only to serve him. This attitude, or type of character, is the manifestation of a deeper problem within narcissism, an infantile conduct which represents a fixation in the first stages of the child's development. The fixation originates when the infant observes that the sole reality is that of his own body, for he cannot feel an Ego independent of another. He is united to the world but cannot act in it. The world only serves as food for his needs. There is also a later stage of narcissism called secondary narcissism, which occurs when the child develops the capacity to love, or rather when he loses it. There is only one reality for the person thus affected; that of his own thoughts and needs. He does not perceive the world as existing objectively, but as molded in accord with his own internal processes.

A narcissist does not know how to love, not even himself, for true self-love is, as Fromm has said, quite the opposite of egoism. Egoism is born of an insatiable affection that the individual feels for himself and which originates in a lack of true love for his own person. Egoism is a failed attempt to compensate for the lack of love for oneself.

The partner of the jealous narcissist only represents the ideal servant, whose bondage will not only be physical, but also sexual, emotional and imaginative. It is almost impossible for a true couple to exist with this subconscious attitude, which leads only to a corrupt relationship. In all fairness, it has been said that jealousy is the death of love, for neither inquisitor, nor victim, loves. The latter may perhaps have begun by loving, but the exorbitant demands of the partner will inevitably take its toll, leaving the victim exhausted and devoid of any feelings of affection.

An interesting phenomenon related to jealousy is its destructiveness. A jealous individual never thinks of creating something new to amend the situation as a non-jealous lover would do, but in his heart there is only room for revenge, hate, suicide or murder. None of these attitudes are those of a person who truly loves another. When there is love, there is only a desire to save the loved one from problems or anguish. Some may argue that with suicide, for example, the intention is to leave the way clear, yet this is not really the inner motivation of a jealous person's act. The act is not an unselfish gesture, but, on the contrary, is intended to heap more trouble on the head of the supposed loved one; a revenge from beyond the grave. This is the real motive for a suicide of passion.

From the point of view of the person contemplating suicide, there are multiple advantages to this act:

1) The partner is punished through the guilt caused by the suicide. This sentence is a life-long curse, for there is no way of wiping it out.

2) The perpetrator frees himself from all blame by his posture as an innocent victim, a sort of sacrificial lamb.

3) He avoids the total breakdown of his self-esteem brought about by the deceit, whether real or imaginary, which caused the jealousy. A suicide for

no specific reason would be a difficult stigma to wash away, but suicide "for love" takes on a particularly interesting nature.

4) The perpetrator's self-esteem is raised by the refusal to give rein to his aggression, which is turned against himself and brings about his self-destruction.

By this act, the rival is eliminated, the faithless one is punished, the problem is waylaid and responsibility, which is pushed onto the partner, is shirked.

Jealousy is not exclusively a product of selfishness nor an infantile or weak personality, but is a syndrome composed of several negative elements which together provoke the problem. These elements form a subtle poison which gradually causes a breakdown in communication, love, equilibrium and union. The jealous person is a mentally deranged person who leads an apparently normal existence, but the slightest incident may set him off, leading him to commit aberrations that display his surprising degree of alienation. Whoever marries a person suffering from this derangement runs the risk of not realizing the potential magnitude of this perturbation, which may be slight or simply monstrous. When a relationship begins and self-esteem is strong, the individual represses his jealousy in order not to project a bad image of himself. Later on, when he feels in control of the other person, the mask drops and his true feelings come to light.

Jealousy goes beyond the scope of the couple itself and is projected into other aspects of the individual's life, which will be spent in constant fear of other types of rivals, which in turn will arouse his most inflamed jealousy. The social and professional life of the jealous individual also suffers, for he generally feels unfairly left out by those who could potentially replace him in his current position or block his path to a better one. Envy is the inseparable companion of jealousy, because whoever feels jealous of a real or imaginary rival, does so by passionately envying what the rival may have achieved or may manage to achieve.

Perhaps the most important element in the syndrome of jealousy is the libido. The libido has a far greater influence on our lives than may be imagined at first glance. Speaking in Hermetic terms, the libido symbolizes the strength and force of life; it represents generation. Sex and the power of generation are two different things. Electricity has gender, but not sex; the atom has gender, but it has no sex. The human couple, on the other hand, has both gender and sex. The libido, or generating power, can be represented as a circle of energy (360 degrees) in which the sexual organs perhaps only take up 30 degrees. The generating power is the creative energy of life in the individual, a force which goes beyond voluntary control and which resists any attempt to be controlled. This energy works by the impulse of its own directing force, which has been implanted in the form of a program, similar to the personality. This conditioning is what establishes the degree of naturalness or perversity in the libido of the individual. Even though sex is only a small part of the libido, it is the most easily observable part. It is found at the center of feeling. For this reason, any perception of a stimulus is sexual.

The interrelationship of the libido and sex gives rise to a third element, the "erotic factor," which is normally manifested in the form of sexual excitement. Under normal circumstances, this energy is bound by the limits of the individual's sexual conditioning. It flows through the generative organs which also receive natural stimuli from the imagination and feelings. Under certain unnatural or abnormal circumstances, a short-circuit occurs between sex and emotion so that sexual energy gets lost in its path and flows through the emotions. There is a remarkable vibratory difference between the sex, the emotions and the imagination. Putting this difference in terms of radio-communication, we would have to refer to different wavelengths or frequencies. The slowest frequency would be the imaginative one and the fastest, the sexual one; the emotional one existing somewhere in between. The emotional factor cannot be fed with sexual energy, which is something like a high-octane super-fuel. This is precisely what happens in an attack of jealousy, however. The sexual super-fuel feeds the emotions, thus provoking a calamity; the person affected is inflamed genitally, but in a perverse way, through an abnormal flow of energy. He is sexually excited, but only through the heart, which is the brain of the emotional apparatus.

This is a form of unconscious depravity, similar to mental rumination, in which positive and negative ideas are imagined in endless alternating patterns. The mind goes over the same subject again and again, a process which creates certain "pleasant" feelings. Since all feelings are sexual in their stimulus, it is not difficult to establish the relationship between mental rumination and sex, or between jealousy and sex. The jealous man is really an habitual "mental masturbator," who uses his emotions and imagination to give himself pleasure in a devious way. Psychologically, the jealous person is often masochistic, for he frequently imagines certain erotic situations between his partner and his rival; fictitious situations which simultaneously give him pain and excitement. He feels pain at being deceived and excitement at contemplating the erotic scenes he visualizes.

It can be said that jealousy, as well as being a mental disturbance, serious enough in itself, is also a form of sexual perversion. The person thus corrupted, will constantly seek certain situations which will let him enjoy these experiences in his own way. Curiously, if the person has been married several times, he will always have the "bad luck" of marrying an "unfaithful" person, unless his spouse's deviations are greater than his own, and she is led by a masochistic impulse to submit herself completely to his desires. In this situation, he will admit to having found his ideal woman, or rather, in objective terms, "the ideal instrument."

There is a very special form of jealousy, which must be mentioned briefly. It is projected jealousy, in which the individual assigns his own inability to be faithful to his partner's character. In an unconscious way, he perceives her as unfaithful or disloyal, but what he is actually doing is taking his own situation and projecting it onto his partner. Another interesting case is the person who, when he suspects his wife of having an affair, finds himself becoming interested in the other man. The other individual will not be the rival. Instead, the wife becomes the rival, coming between him and the other individual. The original man feels a type of homosexual attraction toward the other. The jealousy which tortures him as he imagines sexual scenes leads him, subconsciously, to assume the role of the woman by putting himself in her place.

In this way, jealousy is one of the most common and most harmful forms of corrupt love which prevents the individual from attaining genuine love. Throughout this book, all the points which define corrupt love will be discussed. The points encroach upon each other, although they are different manifestations of corrupt love.

The corrupt element, which is a single concept, manifests itself in diverse and varied forms of behavior that together make up the human ways of unnatural love. Once the sum total of these points is deeply explored or examined, one can clearly understand what corrupt love is.

CORRUPT LOVE IS

THE AMOROUS HUMAN AUTOMATON

In a union of the "amorous automaton" type, an individual finds a new means of fulfillment and a different expression for his narcissism. With jealousy, a person seeks exclusive domination and possession of his partner, whereas the exclusive passion of the "amorous automaton" is totally unbridled self-love. Jealousy is not excluded from the picture, but is no longer the dominant factor.

The key to this type of behavior lies in the narcissist's irrepressible anxiety for an expression of some kind of self-adoration, which he achieves by transforming his loved one into a simple projection of himself. The narcissist projects himself on her with such force, passion and desire, that he becomes psychologically split. He takes possession of his partner, identifying himself with her; not to love her, but to idolize himself through her. She is no longer a person, but a simple intermediary between his will and his craving for self-adoration. This type of union can only flourish with the total alienation of the "victim"; the victim has to give up any ideas, emotions or impulses of her own to make room for only the Ego of the narcissist, becoming thus his passive Alter Ego. When this occurs, an "amorous automaton" comes into being as an instrument in which the narcissist sets up his "psychic dwelling." The narcissist's aim is to be able to love the greater, more important, more desirable and more lovely living being: himself.

Meanwhile, the automaton exists as an instrument lacking any life of her own apart from her biological functions, for her only role is that of constantly sacrificing her own impulses to give her "master" pleasure. Science fiction often deals with sexual or amorous relationships between robots and human beings. This has often been judged as sinful or evil. But what is worse? To elevate a robot to the rank of a human being or to abase a human to the level of a robot? This is precisely what happens when an amorous automaton is created.

It may be argued that this phenomenon could only arise in very exceptional circumstances, but the sharp and dispassionate observation of a lively and intelligent eye suffices to realize the awesome frequency of this phenomenon. Of course, as psychological manipulation takes place at a subconscious level, the whole process is decked out in a thousand different florid ways with the aim of giving an illusion of great and ardent love. In this type of union, one can observe how the passive subject (the automaton) grows dangerously devitalized, becoming debilitated, languid, depressed and diminished, while the manipulator (the narcissist) waxes euphoric, strong and lustrous.

This type of marriage may be surprisingly stable and long-lasting, for conflicts only arise when the couple is at loggerheads; however, this is not the case here. The marriage may seem to be a model one, to be aspired to and imitated from every point of view. The narcissist may appear to others as a charming, extraordinarily solicitous individual; one who worries about his wife while he is really a cold, hard tyrant inside. If the automaton one day undergoes a crisis of realizing the true nature of her condition and manages to liberate herself, people will probably call her a "bad woman" for not having known how to respond well to her husband.

As an aside, the assignment of the masculine sex to the narcissist and the feminine sex to the automaton in this discussion, is meant only as an example, for this amorous twist is as frequent in women as it is in men.

One might think that a relationship between a narcissist and an automaton would be lacking in amorous tenderness. Nothing is further removed from reality, for it is even possible that they spend more time caressing each other than other couples. However, when the narcissist says, "I love you," he really means, "I love myself through your person." Any effusive expression of love reverses itself and does not remain with the partner, but merely "bounces" back to return to its starting point. And what happens to the other party? The same thing that occurs with all alienation when the subject is "outside of himself." He has no idea of what is really happening.

The case described is an example of a process which has reached its peak, but there are in-between situations in which the narcissistic impulse is not displayed openly or situations in which the potential automaton refuses to play the game. There are also cases of real "love at first sight" because the person, when he gazes into the eyes of someone of the opposite sex, sees his own reflection there and this attracts and fascinates him. This is similar to the well-known psychological transference between therapist and patient. In this case, the transference is spontaneously generated to some extent and the individual contemplates himself through the eyes of the other person.

Why does a narcissist need a person of the opposite sex to be able to love himself when he could do the same in a simpler way alone? The narcissist lives so intensely absorbed in self-contemplation that he is unable to observe anything that does not pertain to his own image. Moreover, he grows tired of the game, but cannot change his focus.

CORRUPT LOVE IS

VAMPIRISM

Absorbing other forms of life and benefiting from them for one's own nourishment is an everyday occurrence. Food is a coarse form of conveying energy to the body, but there are other more subtle forms such as breathing, for example. Among the lesser known processes is the magnetic nourishment of the individual which takes place by absorbing solar energy, cosmic rays and terrestrial magnetism. Magnetic influence also occurs in cases of healing done by the "laying on of hands" (magnetic transmitters), but little is known about the magnetic contacts or exchanges which take place between human beings. People possess a magnetic force which Mesmer has called "animal magnetism"; an energy which the human being constantly projects and absorbs. The experience of magnetic contact is familiar to any sensitive and observant person. It occurs upon establishing communication with a specific individual or simply by being in their physical presence. So it is that there are people who give us a shudder of revulsion without our being able to explain why. The reason is simple. Their magnetic irradiation contains elements of a vibratory tone antipathetic to our character. Just as there are pleasant or unpleasant smells, there are also repulsive or attractive forms of magnetism. To prove this, there is an experiment which is quite easy to carry out: when we blow through half-open lips we emit warm and cold breath simultaneously. The warm breath is attractive and the cold repulsive. If we blow cold breath onto a cat, we can immediately observe its reaction to these forces.

Human beings in their normal relationships exchange magnetism through physical and psychological contact. They have no need to touch each other, for magnetic irradiation goes beyond the boundaries of the physical body. Each individual's magnetism is "tinted" or saturated with positive or negative vibrations. A pessimistic and negative person always projects a negative, destructive force. A human being also saturates objects of personal use with his magnetism, as well as the places he lives in or frequents. Simply by going into someone's home one can immediately perceive a welcoming or hostile atmosphere, regardless of the arrangement or decoration of the house.

In a couple's relationship, a large quantity of magnetism is exchanged; it is both given and received. There are, however, certain cases where this equilibrium is upset, resulting in a type of vampire-like absorption in the relationship. One of the parties, guided by an obscure animal instinct, takes as its sole interest and motive, the sucking of the vital energies of the other person. The "vampire" grows in strength and energy while his victim gradually declines and grows weak, anemic and feeble. Vampirism has always been associated with the drinking of another's blood, but really, what people don't realize, is that the vital essence of this precious fluid is the magnetism accumulated in the iron which the blood contains and which is projected through the spleen. In time, the unwitting vampire feels a growing and urgent need to absorb the energy of his counterpart. He becomes totally dehumanized, because he is not motivated by love and, impelled by his passion, he does not flinch at inflicting ill-treatment and humiliation on his involuntary victim. The vampiric process is only possible when the exploiter dominates his partner tyrannically. Many cases of macho or matriarchal dominance have their origin in this instinctive, selfish and absolutely "anti-amorous" need to vitalize themselves. In a sense, no difference exists between eating a chicken and devouring a person. The chicken is physically ingested while the person is psychologically consumed. One cannot assume that this vampire-like parasite knows what is happening; on the contrary, he seldom realizes it. There is a primitive and unconscious impulse in him which leads him to act like a vampire. The most obvious thing is the victim's behavior. He or she becomes a lifeless entity devoid of any personality, for this is lost in order to feed the master.

Unfortunately, many couples have a relationship which is parasitic. The vampire sincerely believes that he "intensely loves" his partner, because when he is separated from her, he feels real sadness and a void which he finds difficult to fill. These symptoms are very similar to having an empty stomach and this is the true origin of many cases in which an individual states that he "cannot live alone." The vampire cannot bear the lack of magnetic food which he is used to absorbing daily, but he does not see the situation in this way and attributes his anxiety to psychic causes. There are many marriages in which one party does not really participate in the social or emotional life of the couple, but merely acts as a sounding board or echo of his or her partner. In any conversation which takes place in a social gathering, the vampire usually has the most to say, while the other party does not dare to express an opinion. If the vampire is a female, her partner will be shy, cowardly and incapable of making his opinion clear as a man. If on the contrary, the vampire is male, his partner will resemble a frightened child who does not dare contradict him for any reason. She will do only as he tells her, without any means of rebelling against him.

Careful reflection on these cases of vampirism will reveal the pathetic position of the victim, who is really like a milking-cow, because when the cow no longer gives milk, she is sacrificed by her master. Children also are subjected to the negative influence of the parasite and can become totally dependent beings, growing into negative, pessimistic and not very intelligent people. When a mother has the parasitic qualities and the children are male, homosexuality could be a logical outcome due to the loss of masculine magnetism so profusely absorbed by the domineering mother. Generally there is a vampiric force behind any highly domineering woman. The same is true in the case of a male chauvinist.

The only way for the victim to get free of the vampire is through an effort of the will aimed at emotional and psychological independence, until a suitable degree of personal autonomy is achieved. This process shuts off the currents of the tyrant's influence and he will be obliged to stop his feeding.

In addition, some people believe that older people absorb the magnetic energies of younger ones. This, however, is only true in cases where the older person is negative in relation to the younger one; when the development of the older person's spiritual awareness (the active element in an individual) is low and when he simultaneously lacks a positive frame of mind, displaying negative behavior appropriate to a "professional loser." On the other hand, when an older individual is highly positive, the chronological difference is balanced by a higher contribution of active energy. Of course, there are older people who, upon marrying someone younger, show themselves to be remarkably rejuvenated. This is different from the case of negative older people who are genuinely depleted mentally, emotionally and spiritually.

In the sexual aspect of corrupt love, there is a different type of vampirism, that of passive homosexuals who are easily rejuvenated by frequently absorbing the hormonal vitality of male semen. One has to understand that this statement applies to homosexual activity in its strict sense, and not to heterosexual relations. A woman cannot be rejuvenated by simply receiving semen, because in sexual relations between the sexes one gives to the same extent as one receives. This is not the case in a homosexual relationship, in which equal polarities face each other.

A love relationship of the vampire type has not the slightest trace of genuine love in it, but only parasitic magnetic hunger.

CORRUPT LOVE IS

MAGNETIC DRUNKENESS

Magnetic drunkeness, although far less harmful and deadly than psychic vampirism, turns a person into a blind being whose intelligence is extinguished, rendering him or her incapable of thinking clearly or of making the correct decisions. Ironically, this situation is usually observed as "ideal love" and is placed high on the scale of romanticism. Many people are so disoriented about love that they idealize and accept as real, relationships in which no true love exists. Thus, Cupid has always been revered as a charming, amusing character whose arrows, fired at random, inflame hearts with love. In many instances, the individual shot by Cupid is often instantaneously transfixed and fascinated, as if he had been struck by lightning. An analogous example of this magnetic force is a small bird mesmerized by a snake. The bird is unable to escape, however hard it may try. It is as if it were hypnotized by the snake, which, for some reason, possesses a certain magnetic power.

For a person to be struck by Cupid, a chain of circumstances must occur; the individual must have his psychic defenses open and there can be no shell to protect him from the magnetizing influence. Hermeticists believe that the magnetic field surrounding the planet Earth is a sort of universal receptacle in which everything is kept and that this field surrounds us everywhere, flowing and circulating to and from our physical bodies. This magnetism is neutral in its natural state, as far as its good or bad features are concerned, but the magnetism we project from our bodies is saturated with our personal vibrations. It is projected through our glances, hands, words and genital organs. To say that a person has "sex appeal," is a highly accurate term because it refers to those who possess great personal magnetism. Under certain psychic conditions, we receive a magnetic impact from a person to whom we are physically attracted. As a result, this energy "spears us through" like an arrow.

Who is this mythical Cupid? He is universal magnetism personified in a specific individual to whom we feel attracted. This individual radiates Cupid's force at the moment of the encounter. If the first contact is followed by deeper and more frequent contacts, most likely both lovers will become so magnetized to each other that they will fall into a state of drunkenness, similar to that induced by alcohol. This magnetic type of drunkenness produces a state of euphoria well known to those who have undergone the experience. It does not, however, mean there is love, for it is a mere electrical phenomenon. The couple thus intoxicated will feel as if they are floating on air with the door of their sensorial perceptions open. They will think that the world is more beautiful than before and that their worries are over. In short, magnetic attraction is a state very similar to an electrical phenomenon. It is not strange that the superior intellectual functions and critical faculties are totally asleep while this state lasts. When a person does not know what love is, it is understandable that he will interpret this experience as the highest, strongest and most positive form of love. He will close his eyes and ears to anyone who might try to contradict him or show him the reality of his situation. Only in this way can one understand the inflamed passion produced between two people united by Cupid. It is easy to see why such a relationship can suddenly end just as unexpectedly as it began, for feelings count for nothing and neither do instincts nor ideas. This is not an amorous problem, but an electromagnetic one.

While magnetic euphoria lasts, and it may last for days or years, a couple swears a thousand oaths of the most passionate, tender and ardent love, just as drunks in a bar swear the warmest oaths of friendship. When Cupid's influence wears off and the void takes over, the lovers, now disoriented, are unable to understand what happened and blame or reproach each other in a useless attempt to explain the situation. Their batteries, which were formerly united in a parallel circuit, have run down. This explanation is far too real to be accepted by illusion seekers who live under the sway of their longing to "romanticize" everything. Therefore, the existence of a motive, when unknown, is often invented and the one which is most appropriate to save pride and self-love is used. In the case where love runs out, it is said that "love just died," because one's partner changed dramatically. It is hard to admit to a simpler reality; that there is no love for the plain reason that it was never there in the first place.

Initially, something made the couple vibrate. Whether it was true or a lie, an illusion or reality, they tasted the fruit of their relationship and the result was "passion," (a word which seems to have been invented just to describe what happens when an individual is flooded by a magnetic force which sweeps him into a feeling or action.) He becomes passive and turns into an instrument of external energy. Passion is passivity; passion is to be possessed or taken over by something bigger than one's own forces. Love does not enter into the picture, because only passive affections have been generated, feelings and instincts of a compulsive nature. The origin of these feelings is not under the control of the Ego. This way of falling in love, like many others, has not the slightest resemblance to real love.

CORRUPT LOVE IS

HETEROSUGGESTION:
THE INFLUENCE OF COLLECTIVE BELIEF

Cultural influences wield an irresistible power over the individual. Custom, tradition, morals, public opinion, religious commandments of the faith professed by the individual - in sum, the conduct which society approves and all that is fashionable - obliges the individual to view outside goals as desirable. The individual will struggle to attain the goals he considers positive and civilized, and will zealously reject those which do not fit into the cultural pattern of the human race. A "matrimonial pattern" is subconsciously being formed with the passing of time. The pattern differs according to different cultures. In the West, a man marries only one woman and it is an offense to marry several at once, while in some parts of the East it is quite legitimate for a man to have several wives, as long as he can reasonably support them. What is acceptable in one culture, is unacceptable in another. The approach to marriage, therefore, does not obey natural law. It does not correspond to "mandates" or "acts" of universal intelligence, which are observed through Nature in the germination of plants, the growth of trees or the changing of the seasons. Man does not respect universal harmony and he does not participate in the cosmic order of Nature, but perverts the laws, usually creating his own arbitrary ones in irrational and chaotic ways. Religious precepts are inherently correct when they speak of the need for "respecting God's Will."

Unfortunately, they only demand fulfillment of the commandments of dogmatic faith, as they address only the human heart and forget about human intelligence.

Human beings have turned away from the natural path which should be followed, from the path of consciously evolving as humans whose aim is to attain higher and higher levels of humanness. Man's passion for comfort, luxury and his consumer appetite, have led him to an intrinsic degradation of his truly human qualities and in exchange, he has exalted his purely animal qualities.

This drama is reflected in the arena of love relationships. The matrimonial pattern designed for the couple by humanity itself has a vulgar and superficial aspect, tainted with materialism and ignorance. The norms the individual is obliged to follow are part of the instinctive passional element of *homo sapiens*. Man no longer heeds the natural pattern, so perfectly designed by God, which governs all of Nature. Man prefers to consider himself as the "conqueror of Nature" and prefers to impose his arbitrary vision over the immutable, harmonious and perfect structure of the natural world.

There is a basic pattern in the human couple which varies with cultural differences. Fashionable opinion also functions in this way. Opinion motivates a person's conduct in love. People invariably fall into the hands of what is called "collective suggestion." This influence on human beings is called "heterosuggestion." Heterosuggestion leads the individual to have all kinds of erroneous and absurd expectations of marriage. Because the generations follow one another, traditions are created which are automatically accepted without critical thought, just because "things have always been done that way," or because parents, grandparents and great-grandparents behaved that way.

A classic example of a pattern stemming from heterosuggestion is the secondary role assigned to women in the cultural pattern of human couples. The woman's implied function in life is to bear children, bring them up and educate them. Heterosuggestion relegates her to the role of a "wet nurse" and keeps her from responsibilities which demand a particular intelligence and insight. A man who marries cannot help thinking that he has "acquired" a bearer of and a nurse for his children, who must permanently, by order of society, stay in the home environment and bring up the children, clean the house and look after him, playing the part of the ideal servant. If a woman turns away from this norm and does not wish, for example, to have children, everybody sees her as strange. Perhaps people think she is disobeying the biblical mandate to "be fruitful and multiply."

Where their liberty and honor are concerned, women have also been the losers. Thus an unfaithful woman is considered, either openly or secretly, to be a prostitute. This is not the case with men, for in the same situation, a man to a certain extent, demonstrates his manliness and virility according to male custom. Not so long ago, it was common for important men to beget countless illegitimate children; a source of enormous virile pride and a "secret" which they took great pains not to hide. The act was neither disapproved of nor criticized by anyone, but on the contrary, the author of the "deed" became someone worthy of even greater admiration. What would have happened, on the other hand, if a woman had children by a man who was not her legitimate husband?

What accounts for this difference in standards and why should different yardsticks be applied? It is simply because a woman has always been considered man's property, as an object which may be bought or sold. It has

always been this way and still is. Even wanting to believe
otherwise, people come to marriage emotionally,
intellectually and instinctively programmed. A person gets
married because "one should get married," has children
because "one should have them" and sets up the marital
relationship exactly as society indicates.

From the time of marriage onward, an individual's
whole future will be programmed. Even the last journey to
the burial ground will be carried out according to existing
traditions and customs. It is even possible to anticipate
accurately what the funeral rites will be, what the behavior
of the bereaved will be, what the opinions of friends and
relatives will be. One of the most significant messages of
heterosuggestion deposited in the human brain concerns the
idea that a person will find love and happiness in marriage.
Cause and effect are inverted and confused in an attempt to
have love and happiness through marriage. The opposite is
correct: one should only marry if love already exists, along
with a reasonable certainty of happiness.

Heterosuggestion tells us that a woman should be
pretty and desirable in order to be shown off and that a man
should be sufficiently important for a woman to be proud of
him. Heterosuggestion tells us that passion is a sign of love
and that jealousy shows how much one loves. It makes us
confuse sex with love and it forces us to long for what
should be utterly undesirable or irrelevant and it makes us
forget the path we should take. Fundamentally, as part of
the human race, individuals enjoy giving themselves to the
passions of the group, fusing with them and losing their
sense of individual definition. What accumulates in the
group psyche, however, is not virtue and intelligence, but
rather, stupidity and mediocrity.

We do not realize to what extent we build our own

love life on material taken from bad novels or popular TV series as well as from the examples our parents, relatives and acquaintances have given us. We do not realize how much we lack judgement, authentic opinion or higher knowledge in love. We do not stop to think that we are mostly unable to write our own script and instead stick to imitating the worst examples. Due to this, all kinds of strange, hidden motives make up the usual pattern of human existence: drama, self-pity, affectation, sado-masochistic behavior, macho and matriarchal type-casting.

Most of us think that in love, it is enough to imitate birds, flowers and insects and that it is only necessary to "let oneself go" on the wings of an hormonal stimulus to attain a desired state of happiness. People have apparently placed love on a scale that is the opposite of responsibility, learning, technique, intelligence and will-power. Rather than relating love to a higher act of man, people think of love as spontaneous generation. In the cultural pattern of humanity, there are no descriptions of what love actually is and so, most human couples practice a parody of what a sublime relationship should be.

If it were enough to simply point out and explain the bases of true love, this problem would not be perceived as serious. However, this goes against human nature, for man as a species has never understood intelligent explanations when they differ from habitual cultural norms. Enlightened knowledge is reserved exclusively for the few individuals in possession of a higher consciousness which accompanies spiritual development and evolution.

Programmed cerebral intelligence can only understand what it has been programmed to understand, which in the end is only the small world of the visible. The invisible inner world of the individual is not accessible to one's companions and often, to a great extent, not even to oneself. A person is almost totally unaware of his true inner world, having only a vision altered by his psychological mechanisms of adaptation and defense. A "higher state of consciousness" is a psychological condition in which the individual penetrates into his own interior space and manages to communicate with the inner world of his fellows. This experience is of a spiritual and non-technical nature, achieved by higher development and not through techniques of mental control. Spiritual development refers to the expansion of the spiritual essence or "divine spark." The process could be termed mystical, in the sense that the individual really discovers God by discovering himself.

A person's concept of God does not matter, nor whether he believes or not in His existence. True spiritual development is something which goes far beyond belief; in fact, belief is the antithesis of spirituality and is at the root of all kinds of superstition. True spirituality can never exist without a genuine understanding of all the invisible processes of Nature and the unknown laws which govern the creation and evolution of the human being. Spirituality is true wisdom and not devotion which has its limits.

Are we straying from the subject of love completely? Not at all, for true love is something which involves the whole individual and not just his emotions or hormones. It is not possible to grasp love without first gaining control over one's inner world through spiritual evolution. Spiritual evolution and love are two concepts which go hand in hand; they are inseparable. Without spirituality, one can only have an imitation of love, a sad comedy whose inevitable end is disillusionment in the face of nothingness.

There is a need for a philosophy of love. One must understand its true meaning, as an integral knowledge of life and of the individual, who must be guided by his own spiritual evolution. When Jesus said "love one another," he was not preaching the need for turning the other cheek or giving good for evil, but rather he was giving an exoteric verbal expression of profound, esoteric integral knowledge. "Love one another" is equivalent to an arithmetic exercise in relation to a complete knowledge of mathematics. It could not be otherwise, for it is impossible to understand how only practicing Christian love could lead to spiritual perfection, developed intelligence, culture, scientific progress and greater awareness. Furthermore it is unlikely that even science, under normal conditions, contributes to the spiritual progress of the person. On the contrary, it often alienates him and dispossesses him of his human qualities. The problem is not with science itself, but the way human beings handle it, because a higher type of control is necessary for the evolutionary development of the human being.

This book is not simply a list of recommended ways to gain happiness in love. It presents and establishes the integral science of love as the knowledge which not only leads the individual to full happiness in love, but also to spiritual advancement and evolution.

CORRUPT LOVE IS

THE OEDIPUS AND ELECTRA COMPLEXES

The intention here is neither to explain nor refute already known precepts of the Oedipus Complex and its feminine equivalent, the Electra Complex. We will discuss very generally the classic way these complexes of "being in love with the parent of the opposite sex" are acquired.

The beginning stages of the Oedipus Complex occur when a small child wants his mother for himself alone and his father, appearing as a rival, stands as an obstacle. The child is jealous of his father and subconsciously wants him to leave his mother so he can have her to himself. He would like his father to leave, disappear or cease to exist. The situation can be summarized as follows for each of the complexes:

The Son:
> He loves his mother and wants her for himself; this causes jealousy toward his father; the child wants to eliminate his father, but at the same time he suffers from pangs of guilt regarding his feelings toward his father.

The Daughter:
> She wants her father for herself, which causes jealousy of her mother; she wants to eliminate her mother; she feels guilty and remorseful for this wish.

These complexes persist even into adulthood, because they represent a fixation in the subconscious which knows neither past nor future, only the present. Their effects are extremely painful, for they can destroy a person's life. They can cause a man to be effeminate and a woman to be virile. they bring about shyness, failure, impotence, frigidity, inner aggressiveness, feelings of inferiority, guilt, an inability to carry on life's struggles and sexual perversion.

With this brief explanation, which can be found in more detail in specialized texts, one can understand the tremendous effect of these complexes on a marriage. The Oedipus Complex carries with it a great weight because very few people are free of its influence. Its effects are often disguised in a way that make it difficult to discern its true causes. Whenever there is a distancing of what might be called the "natural emotional relationship" between father and child, it is possible to suspect some type of oedipal disorder. It should not be assumed, for example, that a child in love with his mother will need to show any extraordinary affection toward her. The child can develop a profound aversion to the mother as a defense to protect himself against the possibility of an incestuous relationship.

People very often come to marriage seeking a substitute for the mother or father. In the terminology of *Transactional Analysis*, "from his child's Ego, the individual seeks the mother-Ego of the woman," or "the father-Ego of the man." A man wants a woman to play a role similar to his mother; he wants her to adopt him, protect him, look after him and "emotionally suckle" him. A woman unconsciously seeks protection from a man that is equivalent to the protection of her father. This is not always harmful, but in practice, it is a factor that substantially hinders the relationship between the couple.

Three very serious problems occur which prevent a healthy relationship:

1. *A Desire to Perpetuate Childhood Situations*

The Oedipus Complex represents a state of being in love with one's mother, which brings about the psychological need to perpetuate a state of union or fusion with her. A state of psychological dependence develops which helps the individual feel calm, supported and protected. The feeling of "being in love with the mother" does not refer to love as a pure feeling, but rather as a dependence on her, for in principle both had once made up one body, a fact which can never be forgotten. In this case, the expression "being in love with mother" means "needing the mother," because she originally provided the child's total needs. This relationship is a purely selfish one. Many children, in the normal course of their development, manage to achieve complete psychological independence from their mothers. Unfortunately there are a great number who never manage to do this and continue to live out their psychic bond with the maternal cloister until the day they die. These persons are the ones who feel a greater need at a mature age to keep up the level of the maternal relationship they had in childhood. To achieve this, they internalize the maternal image and turn it into a sort of psychological womb in which they seek refuge. However, when a man meets a woman with whom he will have a relationship, it is possible that the maternal image will become exteriorized and be projected onto her so that he has a sort of "mother-lover" of flesh and blood. The individual confuses mother and wife in his unconscious, running the risk of having the same type of relationship with his partner as he once had with his mother: that of provider and ideal servant. He will try to use his partner for his vital needs and will never truly love her.

The problems will be even greater if the person had been spoiled by his mother in childhood. This increases his narcissism as she made him feel he was a perfect being. One often goes from narcissism to the fantasy of omnipotence and all these ingredients form a perfect infernal brew, a sure passport to matrimonial unhappiness. The "spoiled" husband, just as when he was a child, will demand immediate satisfaction of his needs in the most complete and effective way possible. Should he not get immediate satisfaction, he will fly into a temper or insult, harass and reject his partner. The same behavior is unleashed in the case of a woman who is in love with her father.

The exorbitant demands made by an individual affected by this problem and that person's inability to give of himself make the achievement of matrimonial happiness an unlikely event.

2. *The Feeling of Guilt*

The Oedipus Complex always generates strong feelings of guilt because the individual unconsciously feels that he has an incestuous relationship with his mother. The Super Ego, the moral conscience, represses those libidinous tendencies directed toward the mother. It considers the tendencies morally unacceptable. This creates great inner tension, because anything which is repressed tends to reappear cyclically and will need to be repressed continually, causing psychological rigidity and a great waste of energy. It is quite possible that the person will project his own guilt onto his partner and therefore feel she is unworthy of his love, a situation which logically has only subjective value. The most likely event is that the affected individual will alternate between periods of euphoria and depression in his emotional relationship. It is also quite possible that he will unconsciously seek pain and suffering as a way of expiating his own guilt.

3. *An Unbalanced Relationship*

When one of the spouses has an oedipal problem, it causes inequality in the couple's relationship; there will be no relationship of equals, because one of the parties will play the part of child, while the other, that of father or mother.

Hermetic wisdom holds that a healthy relationship is only possible for a couple when there is balance between the father and mother aspects. In practice, that means a man can only perceive his partner as a mother if he himself can act as a father. In turn, a woman can only feel a man to be a father if she can act as a mother. In this case, their relationship would not be a selfish one, but an expression of the well-known saying that a woman should be a friend, daughter, wife, lover, partner and mother, while a man should be a husband, son, lover, friend, companion and father. The father aspect should be thought of as the amount of masculine energy which acts in the couple and the mother aspect as feminine energy. There are couples whose sum total of feminine energy is 80% or more, and there are couples who have 70% or 90% active masculine energy. Both types are unbalanced. A balance of 50% masculine energy and 50% feminine energy in a relationship greatly contributes to success in love. In order to achieve this harmonious ratio, both men and women must overcome their egoism in order to avoid the disease of "absorption," a sure springboard to failure and disillusionment. A person who tries to absorb or dominate his mate is not usually aware of his behavior. Whether he is aware or not, the results are always the same, unless the assimilated party suffers from masochistic disorders and passively allows the dominating behavior to continue.

One must understand the decidedly negative impact of the Oedipus Complex in relationships. Of course, understanding alone is not enough to avoid these obstacles. If the negative factors, which lie hidden, are brought out into the light of conscious awareness, a couple can learn what the weak points of their relationship are and which elements impede true communication and they can then experience the birth of genuine love. Certainly, no one should feel distressed about oedipal tendencies, but should simply be aware of the phenomenon in order to learn how to change their attitude. Behavior can be modified when people understand that there are happier and more successful ways of confronting different situations in life.

This is precisely what happens in the case of an Oedipus Complex: a person's attitude of maternal dependence places him in an inferior condition for success in love and life. If the individual fully understands this and realizes that he is wasting life's opportunities, it will not be too hard for him to change his attitude. At least, it will be no more difficult than it would be for an adolescent to leave his parents' home to become independent.

It is essential to realize that the Oedipus Complex is a conditioned psychological response which can only be changed or eliminated to the extent that the automatic or mechanical reflex is broken; change is only possible with an adequate awareness of how the phenomenon works. The affected person must learn to describe his inner experiences as faithfully as possible and interpret them in the most impartial way. A basic study of what the Oedipus Complex is and how it works is necessary if we are to obtain the indispensable elements for correct judgement. Bear in mind that love does not happen spontaneously, but pertains only to those who struggle and train themselves to master its technique. True happiness does not grow like a wild flower, but is the product of an adequate knowledge of self-discipline and spirituality.

CORRUPT LOVE IS

THE DIANA COMPLEX

The Diana complex consists of exaggerated masculine development in a woman, which thus makes a healthy relationship with a man almost impossible. Only a highly effeminate and weak-willed man would make a good companion for Diana, at the cost of putting up with constant tyranny. Masculine men systematically refuse to have anything to do with masculine women. The woman with this problem faces a difficult ordeal, because she has become a kind of amorphous creature that is neither male nor female, but rather, is a sort of undefined being. Psychologically, this is true even though she may appear to be completely normal, physically. Once again, childhood reveals the origin of this disturbance, which stems from the following causes:

1. A Reverse Sense of Castration

There comes a moment in the normal sexual development of a male child when he discovers the importance of the penis as a symbol of virility. After this stage, he normally acquires a deep fear of being deprived of his penis. This is known as castration anxiety and is sometimes brought about by jokes or threats from parents or others.

For a female child, there comes a moment when she

also discovers her anatomical differences. Her differences from boys make her feel as if her penis "didn't grow" or was castrated. In this situation, as in all conflicts that arise during the development of the personality, the person either adapts or fails. If the little girl does not adapt, a feeling of contempt for her own sex may arise, a belief that it is inferior. At the same time, she will envy the male and think he is superior to her. This could lead her to want to compensate for her supposed inferiority by becoming a man in some way. Because she cannot effect a physical change, she undergoes a psychological transformation and adopts masculine behavior, becoming authoritarian, aggressive, discontented and insatiable. This complex could be the basis for the behavior of certain women who are eternally discontent, who are dissatisfied with everything although they have everything, because unconsciously they seek the impossible; to have a penis.

2. An Effeminate Father Who Has an Oedipus Complex

The Oedipus Complex may lead a man to lose his virility and become excessively effeminate. When a girl's father suffers from this problem, it will seriously harm her definition of her own sexuality. The effeminate father believes he hates women while he really fears them, for he feels in some way inferior to them, because he lacks masculine virility. Unconsciously, he conveys this supposed aversion to his daughter and does his utmost to stop her from becoming a true female. He will try to make her more masculine, stimulating masculine traits and praising male activities, such as those in which she competes with men. The result of this behavior will be an obvious masculinization, as well as strong anxiety neurosis over the opposition of two tendencies: a profound and instinctive desire for femininity versus an aversion to femininity because of the family background.

3. *A Despotic Father Who Humiliates His Daughter*

Several psychological problems cause a father to punish and humiliate his daughter, encouraging masculine development through his aversion to femininity. Because he constantly frustrates and debases his daughter, she comes to hate her father, a feeling which she will extend to all men in the following ways:

a) She will refuse to submit or give herself to men, for she despises them. She rejects femininity and becomes masculine, competing aggressively with her opposite. She will probably be frigid. If she marries and has a male child, she will do her utmost to bring him up in a feminine way.

b) She will not reject femininity, but will refuse to submit to men and lean towards a lesbian orientation.

It is clear that a woman suffering from the Diana Complex will be unable to have a healthy relationship, for the most she can aspire to is a type of symbiotic relationship, which she will have to form with an effeminate man. She will thus be complemented contrary to her own sexual identity. This type of relationship is clearly an expression of corrupt love.

A woman suffering from this problem should not adopt a defeatist attitude, and even if her parents bear a lot of the blame, change lies within her hands. Knowing who is to blame for her dilemma does not offer the solution. If the woman does not consider herself responsible, she may adopt a passive self-indulgent attitude. In this case, as in all neurotic conflicts, there are only two possible attitudes: avoid the problem or face up to it. Avoidance is not a healthy attitude even if it temporarily relieves anxiety, because it leads to a disintegration of the individual in a form of psychological suicide. It would be quite easy for a "Diana" to become an embittered, frustrated, aggressive and disillusioned woman without hope for any liberation. Giving up in advance is the line of least resistance and is the path of those who lack self-respect. The healthy and constructive attitude is to understand the problem and to become aware of it through patient and scrupulous observation of herself. The observation of her inner world cannot be carried out directly, but should be done indirectly, by analyzing her own acts, words and emotional states and later assigning their possible cause to her inner world.

From the moment a person knows the cause of his failure in love, instead of resorting to the easy way out of blaming his partner, and attributing negative behavior to or misunderstanding his mate, he should feel the need to prepare adequately for love. Naturally, it is easier to focus on the other person. Self-love and vanity are the enemies of truth and will conspire to make a person unable to criticize and observe himself. Most often, in love, each of the spouses has a basic problem which hinders a healthy relationship. When problems or behavior typical of corrupt love come out into the open, the couple no longer acts blindly. Each person will have to stop "expecting the other to change," to be happy. Occasionally, only one of the partners has the more serious problem, however, some people have small, unimportant problems which are aggravated simply by their contact with other people who are "sick in the soul." When the conflict lies in only one of the partners, it becomes evident as soon as the members of a couple separate and begin new relationships with different partners. The person with problems fails again, while the other achieves a satisfactory relationship.

Anyone who has understood the basic idea that love is a science which goes beyond the everyday concepts of love, will not be content with a relationship that is only satisfactory, but will want to have the best type of relationship which leads to the fulfillment of supreme love.

CORRUPT LOVE IS

SYMBIOSIS

Symbiotic love is a form of union in which the couple fuse into each other, in a negative and destructive manner. In this type of contact, individuals need certain vital elements from each other, just as two organisms become dependent on one another for their existence, each possessing elements that the other considers necessary for its survival.

The formative elements of true love are lacking in a symbiotic relationship. Each party, in an unsuccessful attempt at love, loses his or her individuality, liberty, dignity and integrity. Symbiosis in love has its origin in the relationship between the fetus and its mother. The subconscious pattern from this organic union, this mutual need, persists into adulthood, fueling a symbiotic appetite. When an individual loves according to a symbiotic pattern, he displays his need for his mother and longs for that ideal situation in which all his needs were immediately provided for.

In the psychic sphere, the format of a symbiotic union changes in expression from a physical union of bodies, to a psychological union. The possibility of true love is destroyed by this state, for true love can only appear between two independent beings, each of whom must keep their liberty and individuality. Love needs poles; it cannot occur in unity but only in duality. True love is the free flow of energy between two poles, not their union. Symbiosis and love are two different things.

There are many types of symbiosis and all, without exception, impede or destroy true love. However, many symbiotic unions resemble fairy tales from the movies because of the spectacular nature of their development. Both lovers are totally submerged in one other; they live only to love each other and think and feel only in terms of the other. They appear to have attained the most desirable type of love, but what they are actually doing is clinging desperately to a means of salvation for their own lives. They each absorb the nourishing elements of the other as a way of neutralizing their own unhappiness, in an attempt to gather up and reunite the scattered remnants of a weakened Ego. There is nothing which resembles love in these situations: they more likely resemble despair or cannibalism.

Basically, there are three types of symbiosis: active, passive and compensatory symbiosis. Active symbiosis corresponds to the need to dominate the other person and is a manifestation of sadism. The sadist seeks to overcome his loneliness and to "inflate" his own Ego by turning the other person into a part of himself.

Passive symbiosis is the need to submit oneself and incorporate oneself with another person, seeking guidance, security and protection. Passive symbiosis is related to the masochistic impulse. It also reflects a lazy attitude, for it allows the individual to passively avoid making decisions, avoid taking risks, avoid taking responsibility or facing up to any kind of problem.

In order to understand how far a symbiotic type of

union can go, one must refer to the relationship between a master and a slave. Apparently the slave loses his liberty, but deeper analysis clearly shows that the master is just as dependent on his slave as the slave is on him. The master's role can be identified as sadism and the slave's as masochism. Whether a person follows the impulse of either domination or submission, it is of no importance, since both options lead to "dishonorable slavery."

Compensatory symbiosis is the type of union established when opposite personal characteristics are bound together, establishing a compensation and an equilibrium. This occurs with the union of a shy man and a brave woman; an untidy woman with a highly organized man; pride with humbleness; sloth with activity; ignorance with culture; seriousness with frivolity. In other instances, an association is formed which could be highly advantageous to one of the parties and excessively harmful to the other. In certain instances the couple increases their capacity for action at the expense of their individual liberty. Compensatory symbiosis does not mean creating a union of partners who contribute their own resources freely, but rather a union similar to the blind man and the deaf mute who stay bound together through their defects and not through their good qualities.

Now we come to the crux of the problem of love as well as an understanding of the eternal controversy between love and symbiosis. To love invariably means to give and this is only possible when there is a certain degree of inner development. To love is to give the exuberance of life itself. Symbiosis in love is the desperate search to fill the inner void, the attaching of oneself to the psychic and emotional life of another person and greedy devouring of those vital elements which one's own soul lacks. Symbiosis is marked by frustration, envy, pettiness and eventually, resentment and hate. Love is the splendor of life in action, the creative and expansive force given generously. Symbiosis is the pathetic drama of two beings or two Egos who are sick and deficient and who know nothing of generosity, inner nobility and spiritual richness. To love is also to give to humanity.

Only by defining the conditions which are not love can we really come to know what true love is.

CORRUPT LOVE IS

THE DAYDREAM PHANTOM

Daydreaming is such a common and seemingly harmless habit that no one stops to analyze what actually occurs in this state that dominates much of a person's life. All kinds of fantasies and castles in the air are born due to this activity. When a person daydreams, he constantly examines his material and psychic states and vents his fears, hidden desires and frustrations. For many people, the act of daydreaming allows them to avoid facing specific problems and to replace them with fantasies. In the grandiose character of daydreaming where everything is possible, there is no limit to the enormity, complexity or improbability of the fabricated fantasies. Everything is possible in the world of daydreams. Nothing is beyond the reach of the dreamer; no abyss nor barrier too difficult to overcome. In addition, there are advantages: no effort is required on the dreamer's part and no risks need be taken however outlandish the adventures he dreams up.

Daydreaming, however, does not have its origin in simple mental entertainment. Its roots lie much deeper, back to the time when a child intensely grasps the contrast between what he does and what he should do to comply with his parents' and teachers' demands. He notices a great difference between what he is and what society would like him to be. As the child becomes aware of his failings and weaknesses, he feels the need to fashion within himself a series of ideal requirements, some of which come from the demands of parents, teachers and others. Perhaps most of these spring from feelings of envy and admiration for others. There are personalities he would like to emulate to achieve the same fame, honor or prestige.

A whole galaxy of well-known personalities offers a veritable marketplace of illusions; famous sportsmen, film stars, historical figures, heroes from TV series, young idols from the world of pop music, wise men, famous millionaires, presidents, statesmen, adventurers, intellectuals, philosophers. Any individuals who are outstanding or likely to be admired for their real or imagined qualities become models for the child, who will use their material to carry out that odd activity which will have such transcendental influences on his own life; that of dreaming about himself, the world, and other people. This absorbing occupation that will last throughout his lifetime, is what determines the events of a person's life. It is the pattern that unwittingly molds the individual's behavior.

The process of dreaming of oneself is a highly creative activity in which the "ideal" being is shaped. The ideal is a mixture of many models, a kind of Frankenstein creature, a being which, as in the classic tale, can just as easily destroy its creator. The "daydream phantom" is a being created from the person's fantasies and dreams. The dreamer is the father of the creation and the creation will hence feed off the father for his entire life. Even though its creation begins in childhood, its values still have influence in maturity, without any change in its essence. The original ideal only incorporates new models to add to those already there, however, the original elements are still the most important. Often the adult rediscovers his infantile fantasies in his dreams. The "daydream phantom" is equivalent to the "idealized image" of orthodox psychology, but there is an important difference in the two concepts. In psychology, the idealized image is an inner phenomenon which exists only in the individual's mind. For the Hermetic philosopher, the daydream phantom has validity in the world of energy, for it is an energetic being, born of thought. Its effectiveness must be acknowledged in the world of energy, for in this domain the daydream phantom loses its phantasmagoric qualities and becomes a material creation. The idealized image is only a subjective entity for psychology. For the Hermeticist, the daydream phantom has an internal and external existence which is both subjective and concrete.

The Ego of a young person is naturally very weak and the child is powerless to resist the tremendous influence of the social models he admires. Even adults are rarely able to resist them and idly imitate these examples.

The daydream phantom comprises everything the individual would like to attain. The individual takes his models from the "marketplace of illusions" offered by the world. With these materials, he builds his daydream phantom, which, as it takes on bits and pieces of admirable heroes and figures, becomes, at least in an illusory form, a sort of super-hero of science fiction; a character which could not exist in concrete reality. The whole process of dreaming of oneself as a superman is neither conscious nor deliberate, but stems from the unconscious and compulsive nature of the dream state. In fact, a person does no more than seek fantastic compensation allowing him to escape harsh, frustrating reality. This description makes daydreaming seem to not be too serious a problem, but instead a way of making life more pleasant and bearable. However, the wisdom of a thousand years of Hermetic teachings defines the daydream phantom as a highly destructive force. Its action is not obvious, but hidden, like an invisible enemy which amuses itself by playing with the ambitions, desires, emotions, fears and inner wishes of individuals.

What obscure cosmic mysteries allow such a sly, malignant enemy to dwell in our inner world and prowl in the planes of consciousness surrounding us? The daydream phantom lives at the expense of the individual from whom it sucks the best energies, under the guise of offering him the vision of a great number of dream choices, each more attractive than the other. The daydream phantom is not a mere rhetorical figure of speech. Its perversity lies in its very function of encouraging illusions.

The most horrifying part of this game begins when a person loses his own identity and believes he is his idealized image or daydream phantom, when the dreamer subjectively becomes the dream. From this moment on, the person enters a vicious circle of euphoria and depression. He feels euphoria at the fictitious enjoyment of his personality of super-hero and depression at the trauma of discovering in the light of harsh reality that his behavior does not correspond to the high standards he presumes to fulfill. The proof of his lack generates anxiety upon feeling far inferior to what he believed himself to be, and guilt for having failed.

Anyone might think that at the first disappointment with oneself, a person would understand that he is not the dream character and would immediately stop considering himself a hero. However, things work out differently in practice, and the person, far from mending his ways, tries with ever increasing anxiety to identify himself with his daydream phantom. This will allow him, at least temporarily, to free himself from disappointment and the anxiety of inferiority. The circle has closed in on him, and the victim is trapped in the snare of his own inner weakness.

The most dreadful aspect of this process is the fact that goals, which no human being could ever achieve, are created. This process inevitably leads a person to chase illusions all his life. The daydream phantom will be his compulsory companion and will push him with an irresistible force to meet the requirements suited to the models from which he has built up his daydream phantom. Caught in this trap, many figures - Napoleon, Julius Caesar, Solomon, Casanova, Superman and James Bond - will all be internalized, demanding that the person carry out the same great feats. This urge to strive for the perfection of idealized heroes creates an intense flux of anguish. The higher the concept of the idealized image or daydream phantom, the greater the tyrannical inner demands and the lower the possibility of fulfillment. People's goals are copied from the lives of famous characters, from the dream images built from advertisers', poets' and writers' dreams.

What has all this to do with love? This time the answer comes from the psychoanalyst Theodor Reik, one of the few men of science who have written about love in a truly specific way. Reik believes that love always stems from an inner discontent with oneself, a discontent which is generated when one finds out that he is not what he thought he was and that he cannot fulfill what he demands of himself. Realizing this, the individual seeks love as a last hope, as an event that will permit him to realize in a magical way what he desires internally. In a brilliant and perceptive statement, Reik says that "love is a permutation of idealized images." By this he means that the lover transfers the essence of a daydream phantom onto his beloved and vice versa and manages to transform the phantasmagorical into a flesh and blood being. Now the individual who was once enslaved to a phantom is a prisoner under the yoke of a "real being." As Reik says, "we come to the comparison between the ideal and the chosen being; the image was a phantom, while the loved object is real and living. However, the loved object is also a phantom, something like the hook on which to hang illusions. The real person is only the material for the creation of a fantastic figure, just as a sculptor models a statue from shapeless stone."

Reik continues, "I shall never know why I love her so much,"... "you love her because she satisfies your secret Ego." Reik considers love as a substitute for the desire to reach the ideal Ego or idealized image. Love by these standards is weak, false and inevitably condemned to failure. The individual, just as he had deceived himself with his daydream phantom now deceives his loved one with his own image. Soon the moment will come when he will feel that his beloved does not respond to the concept which he held. The fact of the matter is that he is beginning to reclaim his daydream phantom for himself once more. He first projects it and makes it incarnate, investing his beloved with an ideal, almost magical image, full of virtues and free of any faults. Then when he recovers his daydream phantom and incarnates it once more in himself, as if by magic, the beloved suddenly becomes a vulgar, empty woman devoid of all charm. The lover thinks that she, for some unknown reason, has undergone a great change, but the truth is that she has always been the same. Only the spell of the daydream phantom invested her with an irresistible charm.

Why does a person at a certain point recover the daydream phantom he had made incarnate in his beloved? The cause is the gradual disillusionment he feels at finding that the woman does not correspond to the dream image he had forged. One can agree with Reik that this concept of love belongs to the undeveloped type of man and is a false love practiced by many people.

This book, in its progress, will shed light on the characteristics of authentic love. Only those couples who manage to moderate the type and intensity of the inner demands of the daydream phantom have an opportunity to realize true and authentic love. With time and work, they can dispel to a certain extent, the demands of this idealized image and come to understand that these demands, compared to concrete realities, are fantastic and exaggerated.

CORRUPT LOVE IS

SADO-MASOCHISM

It is very possible that no one is a complete stranger to the manifestations of sadism and masochism, because these conditions are not limited to the spectacular and exaggerated characteristics found in literature. Neither whipping nor torture show the true nature of sado-masochism, for they only express extreme cases of perversion of the libido. In practice, sadistic and masochistic behaviors occur in such subtle and hidden ways that a person often is not aware that he or she has these behavioral traits. Sadism has been defined as enjoying the suffering of others and masochism as the pleasure received from one's own suffering. It is hard for the Super Ego to allow a person to consider himself a masochist and a person must rationalize and justify his conduct to make it morally acceptable to himself. In any case, this is only a small part of a disguised complex which rises to the surface of the person's consciousness. The most important development of this problem is at the subconscious level and that is why a person remains unaware of the true extent of his behavior. He simply experiences the negative results of the complex in everyday life and does not know what the cause of his experiences are.

The failure of many marriages can be found in the behavior of a husband who chases his wife to dominate her sadistically, something that he enjoys. He submits her to a wide variety of humiliations, contempt, insults and punishment, although he hides the motive for his behavior and attributes it to imagined faults, disloyalty or other offensive behavior on the part of his wife. Of course, she despairs and comes to believe that she really is guilty of the acts of which she has been accused. One need not have a very vivid imagination to picture the large number of unpleasant situations this perverse relationship creates, giving rise to a vicious circle of accusations, guilt, humiliation, repentance and impotence.

Masochism has a much wider significance than might be thought, for it involves a particular attitude and outlook on life. Masochism is not only a sexual aberration, but is also a type of behavior which includes relishing in suffering and accepting with pleasure all kinds of humiliations and mistreatment. The desire to suffer is undoubtedly at the root of this problem. Without realizing it, an individual is guided by this irrational impulse and seeks ill-fated relationships which generate the type of emotional food he needs, chiefly suffering. The affected individual will always look for a way to sabotage his own projects, which will mean that "bad luck" seems to dog him constantly.

In his outlook on love, the afflicted person will adopt an inner attitude of failure and suffering, which in reality means he will carry within him the seed of his own destruction. It does not matter how qualified the masochist's companion is; he will always find the most elaborate reasons for suffering. He will not cooperate to help his own matrimonial success and will seek failure on purpose, all of which will submerge him in an uninterrupted and "exciting" state of bitterness and frustration. Self-pity will guarantee that he keeps the fires of this torture burning so that he can fulfill the bitter destiny which he has marked out for himself, to suffer. Outside observers are surprised to find that the pain of this person is not occasional; the pain is not a result of chance or natural circumstances, but is a deliberately pursued goal, one sought with persistence and tenacity. Just as a craftsman works eight or ten hours a day weaving carpets, so the masochist devotes the greater part of his energy, of his emotional and instinctual vitality, inflicting pain and suffering on himself, satisfying the dark appetite of his libido.

It is clear that this person will constantly fail in love and that he will achieve only apparent success if he finds a sadistic partner who will feed and fulfill the fantasies of his libido. In his heart of hearts, the masochist will always be unhappy for he will unconsciously perceive the feebleness and falsehood of his emotional muddle. He will often notice the artificial and unreal quality of his life, as if he were leading an alien existence, not his own.

To understand the extent of the problem which affects the masochist, one must bear in mind that the person's libido is perverted and that he or she is a victim of a vice that is hard to erase. There is a subconscious force in him which drives him to shun success and normal pleasure and to search for punishment from destiny and from life and its circumstances. Placing himself in such circumstances is a prolongation of the chastisements inflicted upon him in childhood by his parents. The person's Super Ego, or subconscious censure, condemns him to various punishments. These are desired and expected by the individual, who has not the slightest awareness of his attraction to suffering. This is the essence of a "psychological quality of bad luck," a device which predisposes the person to the most varied misfortunes.

Although it is not clear how a person manages to derive sexual pleasure from pain and suffering, it is plain that he does. The masochist often unwittingly feels an erotic force which burns in his interior in the face of distressing situations. It is not therefore a casual fact or matter of circumstance that a large number of people are fond of television or literary dramas which revolve around unlucky and distressing themes with humiliating situations, unrequieted love and betrayal, fed by envy and a desire for vengeance. Through these tales the libido of the viewers is aroused. The negative or morbid emotions of pain and suffering can lead to a type of psychological masturbation which turns a person into an addict of this type of pleasure.

There is also a social type of masochism which can dominate the life of social groups and whole nations. With time, the masochistic impulse may become so incorporated into the collective unconscious that it becomes an innate characteristic which will automatically take root in the individual during the process of growth and development. The human being has not yet stopped to consider the danger which alienates him from his subconscious through the threat of masochism. The union of pleasure and pain in one single mechanism is a phenomenon which often remains unnoticed, as do most of the forces in the subconscious.

This book will not describe the several types of masochism or sadism, or explain them in depth, because it is only concerned with what affects love. Masochism is a tremendous hindrance to happiness in love because the individual subconsciously pursues precisely the opposite.

Although the psychological cure of masochism is not a simple thing, the person, if he really wishes to, may gradually change this behavior, when he understands how much harm he is really doing to himself and when he sees how much happiness is within his reach, but which escapes him through his own mistaken attitude. The psychological problems are only crutches which allow the affected person to walk upright, but he must understand that even when his illness is not imaginary, he uses crutches out of his own free will and not of any real need. His attitude bows to a desire to avoid mature confrontation with certain problems. Even though a person may well know what his real problems are, he instinctively seeks out distressing situations. Each person chooses the cross upon which he wants to be nailed in this life. "Consent" is needed for this choice, or the desire of the subconscious, which is the real hidden judge of our lives. Just as an individual chooses the cross he has to bear in life, he may also descend from it whenever he wishes to do so in his heart of hearts. The deep desire has the effect of a "magical mandate" over the person's unconscious and the profound, powerful decision made in his heart is the same as the faith Jesus spoke of when he said, "if your faith be like a mustard seed, you will move mountains."

The inner decision to change is really the true magical formula for shaking off psychological disorders of all kinds. There is no worse patient than the one who does not wish to recover. Pointing out erroneous attitudes about love can help the individual to find the path of true happiness. He needs only to understand that the apparent advantage he gets from his problem is worthless compared to the wide range of possibilities which are beyond his reach as a result of mistaken and negative conduct.

The balance in an individual's life will reflect his psychological equilibrium. The individual can judge his progress and fulfillment on a scale of gain or loss, and can assess his situation accordingly.

CORRUPT LOVE IS

THE COMPULSIVE SEARCH FOR SEXUAL PLEASURE

There exists a remarkable ignorance about love and sex, for sexual attraction is often confused with amorous interest. The more aroused their passion is, the more a couple will believe that they are in love. In time, the concept of what love is becomes distorted, killing all romanticism and reducing a relationship to a utilitarian physical approach. The range of possibilities for love is reduced to a physical function which excludes all communication at a higher level. This view of love is as limited as describing a human being as a simple biped able to walk upright, feed and defend itself.

Sex simply is not love, even when it forms part of love. A man's stomach is not the whole man, but only a part of him. However, the point is not to show that sex and love are two very different things, but to comment on the interesting phenomenon of the compulsiveness of a certain type of sexual hunger and the harm this may bring.

If one accepts the idea that physical intercourse mainly gives relief from biological pressures, and the resulting pleasure is the consequence of the relief of these inner pressures, one could call the impulse "biological sexual appetite." A person's sexual drive is not limited to this area though, and is of a far greater force and craving.

This force, which goes beyond the biological side of sex, is the "psychological sexual appetite." As long as a person satisfies only his biological sexual need, even with an active psychic participation, he will have no problems because sex will be clearly differentiated from love. However, when he is driven compulsively by his "psychological sexual appetite," he is unable to control, or even predict, what will happen in his life and it will be difficult, if not impossible, for him to attain true love. The reason is simple: psychological sexuality is not a natural appetite in a human being, but a cultural creation belonging to the sexual pattern of the human race. Psychological sex is the mystification of sex; the deformation of the purest and most powerful force in a human being. Eventually, this book will explain what love and sex really are. For now, the focus of discussion is sexual compulsiveness.

Movies, advertising, fashion and consumer ethics thrust constant messages at the individual's unconscious, creating needs of all kinds. The use of sex in advertising is a part of the process. The advertising world promotes products using the image of highly sensual women in provocative poses, showing off pants which generously display feminine curves, or touting lipsticks, eye shadows, clothes, shoes and cosmetics. These ads present a sort of "super-woman," who is extraordinarily attractive through the magic of advertising. The whole feminine sex immediately takes advantage of this tendency by using products which heighten their appeal to men. Thus certain types of stockings, special skirts, lipsticks and cosmetics have become synonymous with eroticism. Not only are male hormones manipulated to be conditioned by certain stimuli, but this whole display raises sexual desires, creating false sexual appetites. This appetite is based on psychological, not physical, factors. As an example, this false appetite takes hold of a person who, when he has little money, feeds himself only to satisfy natural hunger, but who, when he has more money, feeds himself emotionally through exotic dishes. With these exotic dishes, he satisfies his self-esteem and psychological cravings through the stomach. The individual's eating habits may unwittingly undergo a degeneration. When gluttony is mentioned, few people realize that this means the artificial creation of a psychological hunger which exceeds natural limits.

This same type of artificial hunger occurs with the "psychological sexual appetite." The erotic union does not only satisfy the biological sexual appetite, but also the compulsive need for intercourse for its own sake over and above natural urges. Nature's action is distorted, and the individual becomes a pursuer of "sexual illusions," avid for physical pleasure. He does not stop to realize that his reaction is only the instrument for an artificial appetite. The serious problem is that this appetite is fatally destined never to be truly satisfied by the normal act, because the desire for satisfaction does not come from a sexual need but from a psychological need.

This is the unacknowledged cause of many types of depravity, for a person desperately seeks to satisfy in any way possible the powerful needs which consume him. Advertising, by using sexual symbols to sell products, fails humanity in its basic attempt, because it sells both a product and sex in the same package. Using sex to sell products creates an unbalanced "psychological appetite," which promotes and exalts compulsiveness about the sexual act. The driving force behind sexual attacks and rape cases is often this type of erotic mental impulse from which the individual cannot detach himself.

Psychological compulsion for sex causes serious problems for a married couple because at times both parties believe they are closely united and feel great love when they are really only giving rein to a compulsive energy. Any relationship based on compulsion is doomed to failure for fatigue, tedium or inner discontent will soon prevail. Many types of impotence and frigidity arise from the frustration of comparing the sexual expectations of the compulsive appetite with the true satisfaction derived from intercourse. The individual who expected symbolically to receive one hundred percent pleasure, urged on by his imagination, finds an erotic level of satisfaction which goes no further than thirty percent. He experiences frustration and thinks that something has gone seriously wrong, for he feels that he has lost pleasure, while in fact he had never found it. He has been prevented from finding pleasure by the compulsive nature of his expectations, because genuine pleasure goes beyond the barrier of the compulsive. Consequently, a person may subconsciously feel that "it was not worth it." A woman may become frigid and a man impotent. With these two types of appetites, different styles of sexual approaches and climaxes arise. The natural way gives rise to an ardent relationship, calm in the sense that it is lasting, without anxiety or hardship of any kind. The compulsive way always brings about a distressing relationship with an urgent need to reach orgasm as soon as possible. The former satisfies, while the latter stirs the fires of passion and disillusionment.

What is most interesting about psychological sexuality is that it produces disorientation in the individual, which he interprets as a token of genuine love. He may waste years of his life before he realizes that "this was not love." In the meantime two lives are spoiled, important opportunities are lost and sometimes children are conceived who will be doomed to imitate the false love of their parents' partnership.

Love is not "letting things flow"; it is not "letting oneself go" or being led into a situation; love can never be passive but, on the contrary, its very nature is vitality and voluntary activity. The forces which create and nourish love should come from the person himself and not from popular images of love. Love cannot be based on passive imitation, but on voluntary creation. Unfortunately, there are many people who wander through the world in pursuit of the mirage of dream images. Once they find their dream image and come to know the person more intimately, they no longer desire that person, but believe they have made a mistake and transfer their sweet, but destructive hallucination to the image of another who is a substitute for the previous mirage. The cycle is often repeated indefinitely.

Something similar happens to a woman. While a man may desire a "superwoman," from infancy, a woman is drawn to the image of an ideal "Prince Charming." The material of her dreams of love will be taken from novels, from movies, TV or magazines. The search for "Prince Charming" may cause a woman not only to waste her whole life, but even to come to prostitution as she gives herself to one and another in the pursuit of her dream ideal. When she feels attracted to a man, she will swear that she has found her ideal, but when she becomes quickly disillusioned, she believes that she has made a mistake and decides to take up the search once more. Before long a substitute appears to fascinate her again, for a short while. In her old age, or near the end of her life, she may come to understand that she has only been pursuing a phantom, and that this futile search has deprived her of a companion of flesh and blood. She has also unwittingly become a victim of compulsive sexuality. Nobody came along to warn her of the danger which lay in wait for her, for few people know the nature and extent of these problems. In fact, people confuse the means with the end, setting sexual satisfaction as a goal rather than realizing it is only one of the ways of achieving happiness in love.

CORRUPT LOVE IS

MACHO AND MATRIARCHAL BEHAVIOR

The biggest obstacle to love and a source of great difficulty, is weakness or immaturity of the Ego. When a person lacks a strong, mature, rational and well-integrated Ego, he will resort to all types of emotional tricks to defend a self-image which seems threatened by the game of love. Just as a weak person becomes a powerful bully to hide his own weakness, lovers also take on certain psychological poses to keep their self-esteem at an adequate level.

This book does not deal in theories, but aims to present evidence of concrete, tangible reality that anyone can test through their own or others' relationships. The aim of this work is not to make the reader a master of the theory of love, but a lover capable of truly finding happiness and fulfillment through the practice of love. This practice must be supported by a science of love and must first be understood from its theoretical angle. This knowledge differs greatly in its depth from conventional wisdom or orthodox knowledge, for its practice is a technique which acts first upon the observer and then upon the outer world.

Men and women are the instruments through which love is created and the science of love must act upon them first of all in an integral way. One cannot work exclusively with feeling or intellect, for the human instrument from which love is born is composed of many parts, none of which can be left out if one wishes to have true love. The problem of love touches and questions the whole structure of society and puts in doubt the truly human condition of *homo sapiens*, denying the possibility that true love can exist between two rational animals, and maintains that only when each person in a couple reaches a truly human and intelligent condition, can the couple have access to genuine love. If a couple does not create genuine love, they will mate as animals do and their physical union will be empty and mechanical. The union will produce new animal "cubs" who are destined to repeat their parents' pattern.

Macho and matriarchal behavior are two very ancient elements in the behavior of the human being in love and like all expressions of corrupt love invariably block the existence of true love. With the psychological games of macho behavior, the individual is lost in a jungle of hidden messages and cross-messages until he is so far lost in the tanglewood that he can no longer see the light. This is the story of many couples: they unite under the luminous, promising mirage of a sun which would illuminate them forever in an ever-increasing love, and yet end up in the sterile monotony of a relationship which is merely habitual. The relationship is bogged down by the issues of child rearing, economic security, tedium, hard work and anxiety.

"Macho" is a popular term referring to a masculine attitude characterized by all of the following: male pride and vanity, a male sense of superiority over females, a belief that a woman should obey a man and be dependent on him, a conviction that a woman should not have the same rights as a man, the application of different standards to judge the moral actions of men and women, the belief that a woman should be a sexual object destined for male pleasure, a belief that she should adore and revere the man, and a tendency to undervalue her and consider her an inferior being.

Macho behavior reflects a psychological distortion which affects very weak men who, when they see their own lack of virile qualities, make up for the lack by adopting an exaggeratedly masculine attitude in a caricature of the male image. This behavior is the same as putting on a man's mask and does nothing to change the innate weakness of the male chauvinist.

Behind every male chauvinist there hides a being with a pronounced feminine side. Macho behavior is not synonymous with virility; in fact, it is quite the opposite. Because people are integral units of energy, a lack in one area is compensated by its opposite. The male chauvinist is basically a feminine individual who subconsciously intuits this fact and goes to the other extreme, trying to play the part of the super-male. Ironically, he does not realize that his behavior only shows his true colors. In fact, macho behavior reveals a "feminine man" and matriarchal behavior reveals a "masculine woman."

In women, matriarchal behavior is known by other labels: "Diana Complex," "phallic woman" or "Amazon." Matriarchal behavior applies to the following types of female behavior: contempt for a man, the need to compete with him, a desire to manipulate him and dominate him, a lust for power in marriage, a general desire to control and command a man until he becomes a psychological or physical servant, a wish to be adored by him as a queen, subconscious envy, an instinctive impulse to castrate him, a hidden desire to possess a penis, authoritarian behavior, domineering, hypersensitivity or intransigent attitudes and resentment towards the opposite sex.

Similar to the macho male, matriarchal behavior

occurs in women who have not managed to develop their femininity, women with very weak femininity reinforced by masculine energy. Bear in mind that both men and women are bisexual in the sense that they have 25 percent of the energy of the opposite sex. This percentage may vary according to the individual and in certain cases may reach pathological extremes.

The real issue in this chapter is the distortion of how the male chauvinist and matriarchal woman perceive and erroneously classify themselves and their partners. They cannot communicate with their partners and fall into a type of "phantom communication" between what one believes one's partner to be and what one believes oneself to be. Unless the real essence of the other is discovered, communication will be nil and any attempt at love will be impossible.

There are couples in which the male is a chauvinist and the woman a victim, or in which the male is the instrument of a matriarchal woman. There are also impossible marriages in which both parties are affected by the same problem and practice a sort of love which resembles guerrilla warfare and ends with one or both parties physically, emotionally and mentally mistreated.

The drama of our times lies in the fact that we live in a time in which pseudo-men and pseudo-women proliferate. The men are weakly defined and the women are manly. The sad thing is that society itself through the media, orchestrates and applauds this conduct by advertising and glorifying through movies, TV and the written and spoken words, both overtly and subliminally. It is easy to recognize hysterical heroines and effeminate heroes. The media has fashioned weird and whimsical concepts of what a feminine woman and a masculine man are and these models are imitated and adopted for people's own use. The "passionate" woman and the "violent" man are prototypes which many wish to imitate. It is not understood that exaggerated passion is synonymous with alienation, and violence, with a lack of intelligence and good reasoning. Adding the concept of "sin" to sex has to a large extent contributed to this situation, because when the libido is artificially repressed through various prohibitions, the lower instincts are aggravated and what is morbid is disguised as purity. Many women are masculine because the world, through a distorted moral message, tells them that "sex is sinful and dirty," a belief which makes them renounce their own femininity. Certain men become effeminate for the same reason.

A highly curious and interesting phenomenon also occurs in this age in the world of relationships: women complain that men are "chauvinistic," and are not fit for a happy relationship. Men in turn say that women are "not very feminine" and are "highly domineering." These complaints are only theoretical because most of the time it is the chauvinistic men and the matriarchal women who are successful in the game of love. Those who do not share this orientation are looked down upon and considered weak.

Humanity must understand the magnitude of this conflict, which has led people almost inadvertently to a quasi-sexual inversion. The time will soon come when macho and matriarchal behavior develop as primary elements in human beings and this behavior, inbred in the individual, will be inherited in the collective unconscious.

CORRUPT LOVE IS

SOCIAL SUBSTITUTES FOR LOVE

Society's duty is to organize itself in order to take care of the safety and welfare of its members. From the couple stems the family which is the touchstone of society. For society to survive, it must preserve the union of the couple because if this is not maintained, the foundations of society will crumble. This basic premise helps to understand certain phenomena which make up the hidden web of what society knows as love. In order to preserve the family, society realized long ago that union through love was a frail structure, because the little known and hypothetical element of love was not sufficient to maintain the union of the male and the female as a couple. There was the danger posed by promiscuity, which might have lead to disease, death or under-development of the human offspring, the latter being indispensable for the survival of the species.

Thus certain devices were designed to protect the couple, which would keep both parties together and prevent their separation. Basically, this meant creating a sort of "adhesive" which would keep the couple united even when there was no longer love, by foreseeing the event that love would weaken and finally fade away. With this provision, the offspring would be ensured sufficient protection and an adequate food supply.

As a result of looking after its own good, society found the most appropriate methods of creating obedient consumers, without which it could not exist. Consumers are needed for education, justice, entertainment and the different products society offers. Society needs well trained members who obediently accept political and religious leaders, that is, consumers who keep "the social machine running." As a result, the social custom of marriage came into being and was later perfected in a legal contract. The real aim of marriage is to oblige the couple to stay together as long as possible, not to publicly regulate their physical union. Religion, however, usually goes further than the law and preaches the indissolubility of the matrimonial bond. This makes the act of separation difficult and almost impossible. While this is certainly advantageous to social organization, there are other elements which, although highly positive, are incomplete and which therefore sometimes lead humanity to more subtle and profound problems than those which they were intended to solve.

What happens with societal restrictions of matrimony is that a substitute for love is sought to bind men and women with the same or greater intensity as love itself. The trouble is that this solution has fallen heir to the problem of the majority of all substitutes, that is, when a substitute is kept in use for a long time, people tend to forget the original purpose and sometimes obtain results opposite to what was originally intended. Thus the obligation of matrimony often becomes a bondage that is hard to bear because the most important element, love, is missing. Love cannot exist by mandate or through an acquired duty. Unfortunately, many marriages become precisely an experience of love by mandate. In this case, society is the mandating entity which decrees that a couple should love each other just because they are married. The natural process is inverted. The designs of Nature are twisted since a couple's union should only be set up and maintained through the members' own wishes, without need of contractual obligation. Love should come through marriage and not be the slave of marriage. The true bond which unites a couple should be love, and not a legal obligation. One should not fall into the trap of worn out, repetitious patterns, whose original significance has been lost, while not knowing what they mean. Marriage cannot be a goal, only a complement of love. It should occur as a logical consequence of love, and not be the device which obliges it.

The concern in this chapter is not marriage, but the way love is devalued when it is used as an agent that binds and when its original purpose is lost. True love unites couples; social mandates bind them but do not unite them through love. The life of the couple bound by social mandate is quite different from the life of the couple who have come together spontaneously and naturally through the exercise of true love. Social union is alienating; true love is liberating. When a couple has true love and marries freely and not compulsively, the union loses its obligatory quality and becomes spontaneous. True love is free and is not subject to any type of pressure or obligation, only the voluntary and natural consequences of the act of loving.

Society unites couples in its own interests, putting aside love and relegating the individual's interests to second place. It cannot be said that people get married because they want to, because the individual's behavior is irresistibly conditioned by social patterns. The individual is born, educated, lives and dies within an integrally programmed social structure, whose influence he cannot resist unless he acquires the wisdom that Hermeticism offers, which will allow him to master his own brain and free himself of the alienating forces which harm him.

The legal obligation of marriage is only one of many elements designed to strengthen and uphold the bond of love. Public opinion, that hidden judge which approves or penalizes people's actions, is another of the long and often punishing, arms of society. Public opinion is a hidden monster which rewards or punishes, but never shows its face and which lacks a central intelligence to direct and control its acts. This entity punishes, by means of shame and dishonor, those couples who unite through love and do not legalize their relationship. We shall never know why what the majority thinks constitutes what is legitimate, or why the majority should determine the legality, justice or correctness of things. The opinion of the majority is mediocre because wisdom never belongs to the masses, but on the contrary, is the privilege of a few superior examples of the species.

Many couples do not love each other but seek marriage as the best way to win general approval and consent, and to enjoy the "social well-being" which is considered to be the greatest reward that society offers to the obedient consumer.

Many other elements encourage the marital bond. The sexual impulse and union is perhaps the strongest biological need and by satisfying this appetite, strong inner tensions are released. Because society does not approve of concubinage, however, people have to marry to avoid social ostracism. Religion and morals take great pains to publicize "how sinful" extramarital sexual activity is, indirectly thrusting the burden of its mandate onto the individual. From childhood people acquire a pejorative concept of sex, because there is a silent and inadequate conspiracy designed to repress sexual impulses. They are taught how sinful sex can be, not as a point of moral education, but with the purpose of repressing their libidos. It is even explained that

God punished man for his great sexual sin by expelling him from Paradise and that woman bore the guilt for tempting man. It is added that all this was the devil's work. It is no surprise that there are so many unhappy people, sickened and frustrated by their serious repressions and by the terrible guilt complexes arising from their inevitable "sexual slips," or their inability to stay celibate. People experience inevitable natural episodes, which are the logical result of cumulative biological pressures. Dikes have been built to dam up the force of the libido and block its natural flow. As a result, the individual either drowns in his own impulses or else obeys social designs submissively. Libertinism would be a far worse state for man, because it is a disruptive force in the social order which, despite all its faults, serves a purpose for humanity.

The only in-depth solution would be for man to gradually learn to sublimate his libido, through the science of love, in the fulfillment of true love. Otherwise, he has only three options: repress his libido, marry, or become a libertine. None of these options is positive, for they represent failed attempts to solve a problem which has only one solution: true love.

There are many people who marry just to live out the romantic adventure of a wedding and to feel themselves wrapped in an aura of respectability and coming of age, which the current matrimonial situation offers. To be married, to have a home, to procreate offspring and to form a family, all seem to the individual to be the final proof of social approval. There are very few people who do not fall under the sway of the cultural pattern of marriage which is almost inevitably complemented by the pattern of parenthood.

CORRUPT LOVE IS

THE WRONG REASONS FOR HAVING CHILDREN

Having children is a logical consequence of marriage. No one is surprised at their birth, but if children do not arrive, there is a feeling of sadness in the family. It has always been assumed that the aim of love is to reproduce and those who are unable, feel profoundly unhappy. It is the common belief that a woman is designed chiefly to be a mother and no other reason can be given for her existence. The species needs to reproduce itself and to achieve this goal, the individual must once more comply with the mandates of society and Nature. This seems to describe a reasonable and logical situation in light of the natural criteria of survival of the species of *homo sapiens*. The aim here is not to defend, study nor analyze the survival of man, but to penetrate deeply into the mystery of love. To do this, we must analyze what love is not, what the masses confuse love with, and what purports to be love but is only a parody of love.

Children are often described as "the fruit of love." Those who are able to see this differently will realize that children are rarely "the fruit of love," but are often the product of chance, boredom, frustration, failure, inner dissatisfaction, social conformity or selfishness. The following, is a list of the common or main reasons couples have children. Surprisingly, none of these is related to love.

1. A Woman's Curiosity

A woman may want to have the experience of maternity to know what this experience means and to "fulfill herself as a woman." The new mother often finds that she has not fulfilled herself and that maternity has brought her no benefit or transcendental experience. She sometimes discovers very late in the game that she has fallen victim to the "maternity myth," the glorification of a natural process which has nothing exclusive or special about it, as all animal species are able to do so in a more natural and perfect way than the human being. Procreating offspring is what all animals do.

The image of the mother has always been surrounded by a halo of sanctity, goodness, immeasurable love and total devotion, which is certainly true in most cases, as far as her children are concerned. The image has been created of the mother as a pure, divine being. A woman will unavoidably feel that she must comply with the process of maternity in order to identify herself with the "divine maternal image" and achieve social recognition. This is why being a mother is an experience longed for with deep desire. To what degree is childbirth a product of the maternal instinct or of a social pattern? Finding the answer to this question would be of great benefit to us. However, the aim here is to point out the general absence of love in this vital process in the life of the human couple.

2. Failure and Frustration

When people feel that their lives are a failure and that it would be very hard to improve them, they feel the need to have children, hoping to achieve through them the success that they have been unable to find for themselves. Very poor mothers pray daily for their children to find fortune and, should this happen, they feel fulfilled. A similar thing occurs in the case of the "daydream phantom," as a mother, without realizing it, transfers her own "daydream phantom" onto her child in the hope that he will achieve all that she would have liked to achieve.

3. *Boredom and Tedium*

Children of tedium certainly abound. Many couples, through boredom with their everyday lives, decide to have children who will in some way fill their time. The birth rate appears highest in rural areas where activity is scarce and there are fewer possibilities of entertainment.

4. *The Sexual Instinct*

The sexual urge impels an individual to have intercourse with a certain regularity, independent of his desire to have children or not. Whether the person intends to reproduce or not, many children are in effect born of this mating. They are not the product of a voluntary act, but rather of chance.

5. *Ensuring the Permanence of a Husband*

One frequent motive for having a child at a certain moment is the concern a woman feels to ensure the fidelity, affection and protection of her husband because it has always been believed that children unite a couple. The law gives special protection to the mother in cases of conjugal abandonment. There are some women who, by taking advantage of their status as mothers, try to gain through their children a selfishly disproportionate dominion of their partners. It appears that some women use their children as true "hostages."

In practice, rarely is only one of the outlined motives the sole reason for procreation. These motivations are combined to act together and produce the expected result.

In the past, other elements came into play regarding

the need to procreate, and these needs were mainly economic. Those workers who earned their living from craftsmanship, working on the land or managing cattle found that it was easier to make money with the help of children working with them as free manpower to help increase the family fortunes.

Looking closely at this whole problem is not a very pleasant exercise because we come to the conclusion that children are born out of dissatisfaction, frustration and personal lacking, and only rarely from vital, emotional and intellectual fulfillment. This is one of the main causes of decadence in a humanity ruled only by consumer urges, drowning itself in the trap of its built-in programming.

Inevitably, not only does love not figure at all in the process of having children, but neither has the human being ever had any notion of procreative responsibility. Men not only beget offspring without love, but the children are the product of a purely instinctive act, with no participation from the individual's intellectual and spiritual parts. Men procreate like animals and not like humans. They come together physically as animals do without knowing or exercising a mental or spiritual technique which would let them procreate higher beings. Thus man reproduces himself by an "act of animals" and not by an "act of man." It is curious and disconcerting to think that a human creature could be the product of an "animal act." Not even the naive farmer acts in this way with the seeds he sows. He prepares the soil, awaits the right time of year before sowing and then sows according to rules which ensure a good result. Here we have preparation, knowledge, dedication and technique all ruling a process. Human reproduction often occurs without any kind of preparation; the male simply feels a need, and acts. The sexual act in animals is actually more perfect compared to humans since from the remotest times, it has been governed by Nature and her rules. An animal does not improvise, but carries forward the most expedient technique engraved in his instinct.

Man's problem lies in the fact that he is neither animal nor human. He no longer possesses the wisdom of Nature, nor the knowledge of higher man. This is why he improvises and does not even manage to attain the higher levels of consciousness. Current humanity is the result of improvisation in its rites of birth. Apparently it is enough to place the sperm in the egg to create a real human being. Doesn't this create only a world of "misfits," of beings artificially created, without souls, spirits or wills of their own, instead of true human beings?

It is legitimate to fulfill the wish to have children, but it is a serious error to manufacture love situations around the goal of procreating them. The aim should always be love, and only when this has been fulfilled may the individual decide whether or not he wishes to reproduce himself. This situation is often reversed in practice as some people seek to achieve love through marriage and children.

There are some questions of crucial importance. Can a human being transcend or immortalize himself only through physical children? Is carnal descent the only possibility for human procreation? Do other ways exist? In reality, the physical aspect is the most primitive form of reproduction and there are other higher possibilities, although people do not see them. We refer to the possibility of having "spiritual children," an option reserved for beings of a superior intelligence and consciousness. A spiritual child may also be physical, with the difference that he will be a complete being, a child of both body and spirit. Common people are only "children of the body," for their parents have brought them thus into the world. When we speak of "spiritual children," we mainly refer to the fruit of the mental and spiritual energies of a higher man. The pupils of a good teacher are to a certain extent his "spiritual children." A spiritual child may be either a person or a work, but the result is always the same: the father creates a being that will transcend time and space, contrary to the physical child whose existence will be limited to a brief earthly span. To illustrate this point, we have the example of Leonardo da Vinci, Michelangelo and Benvenuto Cellini, celebrities who belonged to Hermetic schools in which spiritual procreation was taught. Da Vinci's works, for example, were spiritual offspring through which he attained immortality, by projecting himself in his creations. He gave birth to beings with an immortal existence in the world of pure energy.

The material transformation caused by death only has an effect in the material world, but not in the field of pure energy. Hermetic tradition maintains that there is a primordial energy of which everything is born, a unique force which is the essence of all. This energy may be called "spirit" and it is the gift which God granted us when he gave us the divine spark. A man is spiritual when he has developed this power within himself. Spiritual men may have spiritual children. Those who have not reached this level cannot do so, but must be aware that the possibility exists and that the door is open to those who have the inner desire to extend and surpass their present level of development.

To raise oneself spiritually is to achieve, by means of certain techniques and psychological and mental processes, a development and growth of the essence, which like a seed may grow and bear fruit. The subject of spiritual procreation covers far deeper secrets than those suitable in a work of public scope, for this art is the secret of immortality itself. It is the means by which the Hermeticist may produce an "avatar" and consciously reincarnate, thus keeping his consciousness after death, independent of the destroyed material body.

CORRUPT LOVE IS

ARTIFICIAL OBLIGATIONS

When a couple realizes how fragile their union is, they fear losing the expectation of happiness their relationship represents. They try in any way possible to imprison each other in an invisible prison of promises, oaths, rules, obligations and prohibitions. This procedure tends to seek a nexus of union (which certainly cannot exist) through material obligations, for the nexus would be too fragile if love were free to follow the natural regulation of the free will of each party.

Gradually, each of the lovers feels that his or her counterpart belongs more to him each day even when this "belonging" takes the form of "the convict and the keeper" rather than "the loved one and the lover." In fact, each of the spouses generally moves within the limits of the invisible prison which they have mutually constructed. No matter how strong the desire to do something from the inner depths is, it cannot be done if it is expressly included in the list of matrimonial prohibitions. If the rules are violated, one usually speaks of "treason," as one of the parties did what the other has forbidden. This offense of "treason" takes on an even greater force if one of the parties should be so "vile and unworthy" as to fall in love with another person. This represents the highest possible degree of felony and is to be punished with the stigma of evil or dishonor. The one who is naive enough to submit blindly to his emotional impulses will feel wretched and contemptible. Through tacit social agreement, the "traitor" becomes a sort of pariah. The deceived party, on the other hand, derives a certain benefit from the role of victim which makes him or her seem free of blame.

Most probably, however, both parties are responsible and their greatest error is to replace union through love with union through obligation. When a couple discovers that the love they believed in is non-existent, they are compelled to artificially manufacture it, imitating the supposed behavior of a loving couple. They begin to act as if the purest, most ideal love existed between them. They think, feel, procreate and love as if fiction were reality. To give greater weight to this comedy, they must live with each other, communicate and proceed in the way a truly loving couple would act. As no one really knows what true love is, the deceit is hard to dispel. The couple imitates love, adopting the image of love as a disguise.

In a similar way, there are people who, in an attempt to be pure, imitate the ways of those who are supposed to be saints. There is no difference between the imitators of Christ and the imitators of love. Regrettably, imitations always lack a comprehensive notion of why and how something should be done. Imitation lacks an intelligence of its own, for it is only a mirror image. Therefore, people live out an image of love which makes them believe that they possess the original product. They behave as if they had in fact attained true love, building up their lives around this supposition. They structure their lives together the way they believe a loving couple should act by blindly imitating the very qualities that they believe could breed success in a relationship.

These qualities are: 1) being faithful, 2) respecting each other, 3) being happy, 4) caressing each other, 5) communicating perfectly with each other, 6) fusing into one sole being, 7) sharing mutual knowledge and comprehension, 8) procreating, 9) having a common destiny, and 10) establishing habit and custom in their relationship.

There is no objection to the practice of these points, except for the fact that they are an imitation and not a creation of one's own. Blind emulation is not the best means of leading a human being to higher fulfillment. Intelligent reflection, not conditioning, should guide an individual's acts, especially the person who wishes to be free and not subject to the inflexible mandate of the norms of social conduct. Prefabricated marriage, according to an exact copy of the social mold, cannot be a dynamic self-generating structure, only a lifeless skeleton which serves to support the illusions and expectations of the spouses. Mindless imitation is generally the prelude to mental blindness, because it is easier to imitate blindly than to make the effort to plan, analyze and act intelligently.

Marriage has unfortunately developed into the machinery of love and this explains one of the reasons behind the wretchedness humanity has fallen into, for true love cannot be mechanically programmed nor can it be the result of simple enthusiasm, romanticism or emotion. Love can only be born of an integral mature relationship between two beings who have also undergone the development and evolution of their own Egos. The exercise of true love is an act of integral manifestation of the consciousness of intelligent, mature beings. Love is never the instinctive relationship of sick or psychologically underdeveloped people. To these individuals, love can only represent the search for some means of salvation which would seem to be the door to an ideal situation.

A couple who only imitate love in their union handle the ten points of love in this way:

1. *Being Faithful*

Being faithful usually refers to physical exclusivity, each party granting the exclusive sexual use of his body to the other. Meanwhile, latent dissatisfaction unleashes imaginative and emotional adultery. The structure of pseudo-love is mainly based on all those things which are physically controllable or visible, without taking into account the inner being. What value can corporal fidelity have if there is no psychological loyalty? Is it acceptable to be faithful in body and adulterous in thought and desire? In the couple's social pattern what matters is physical exclusivity. Social gatherings at which men and women meet are often only a pretext for practicing psychological adultery without suspicion, and apparently nobody is harmed by this.

2. *Mutually Respecting Each Other*

In practice, this translates into: "I must not displease my partner nor go against his wishes." This approach would seem reasonable but it in fact may become a death trap. This premise is expected to refer to mature, intelligent people, to psychologically healthy individuals. But what happens if someone has linked his destiny with a person suffering from psychic disorders or serious disturbances? In this case, a person will fall into a sort of human bondage, which will oblige him to satisfy the most absurd whims of his partner. If his partner thinks that to prove his love he must go down on his knees half an hour each day, he will have to do it for fear of being seen as not showing his interest and affection. There are a wide range of demands from the perfectly logical and natural to the perverse and unbalanced. Can either partner determine what is balanced behavior and what is not? Both partners should be able to make this determination, but to do this they should both have perfectly healthy psyches. This would be the exception, rather than the rule. Keep in mind that when a partner demands something, he does so because he considers it to be fair. He will feel deceived or betrayed if he is not granted what he asks for. Meanwhile, the other partner is caught in the terrible dilemma of "betraying himself" or "betraying his partner." In fact, if he gives in to the irrational demands, he will do it with the inner conviction that he is being forced to do something absurd, twisted or unfair, but if he does not do it, he will be subject to blame. This infernal dynamic in real life is the stifling environment in which most couples' relationships are challenged. The dilemma is posed in the following way: "If I don't do what he (or she) wants, he will stop loving me and I will be letting my love down; if I give in to him, I will lose my self-respect." In this way, strong resentment or even hate is built up in proportion to the number of times the individual has to give in to his partner in matters in which his judgment was totally opposed to his partner's wishes. This situation varies depending on which member of the couple is the healthier, more rational, intelligent or unselfish one.

It is possible for a person to feel that his partner is forcing him to do something against his principles, but it may really be that the principles he upholds are capricious or misguided, in which case the one who makes the demands is the one who is legitimately right. Thus, traumas may occur in the conjugal relationship through the fault of either party. The one who puts out irrational, exorbitant demands will be just as traumatized when he is rejected as the one who is unjustly blamed for making legitimate and reasonable requests. Unfortunately, the one who behaves irrationally acquires a conviction that he is being betrayed and is unloved. Believing this, he will shirk responsibility and try to unload his responsibilities on to his innocent partner, and he will lose any chance to correct his unhealthy and misguided behavior.

3. Being Happy

When a couple starts a life together, they begin the game of happiness. The rules of this game dictate that they must keep the ideal of conjugal happiness at any price. What never existed will be replaced by an act of enjoyment and satisfaction, modeled after society's conventions. The right number of social gatherings, movies and TV, sex and consumer goods, the upkeep of an economic status or of situations which continue to bolster self-esteem and personal prestige, make the couple feel they are happy. Disorientation in their values and a lack of maturity make them confuse the external with the internal. Missing an inner element of happiness, the individual tends to live out pleasurable and stimulating material situations which to a certain extent help to fill the void of his inner world.

The individual anticipates the terrible emptiness which grips him and, subconsciously, knows that he cannot be happy. He then seeks the path of sensory intoxication, mistakenly believing that to be happy is to "have a good time." However, in the compulsive search for the happiness which always eludes him, he experiences the ambivalence of feeling happy at times, while knowing in his heart of hearts that he is profoundly unhappy. In the game of the search for happiness along the misguided paths of pleasure, comfort, the vanity of social standing and the procreation of children, the couple loses all chances for true happiness based on genuine love. In their confusion and intellectual abandonment, they mix happiness with pleasure, and love by adopting the amorous cliche. The juxtaposition of social and economic positions, the increase in consumer power, the pursuit of security in material wealth become false goals which powerfully alienate the individual's intellectual, emotional and instinctive life, dragging him down to the dehumanized condition of the obedient consumer.

Under these conditions, the seed of love cannot blossom and the couple, after many years, will have to acknowledge that happiness really escaped them. However, the "illusion" of happiness is kept for life and the individual constantly expects events which will lead him to it like one who believes that he can obtain something through a miracle. This will not happen, for when a person obtains what he thought would bring happiness and finds that it does not, he wants something else.

4. Caressing Each Other

The "obligation" of giving each other caresses is caused by the misinformed belief that this type of attention indicates the magnitude of love. By silent agreement, each establishes and regulates the type, quality and frequency of the petting stimuli which he will give his lover. Often, this is set up mechanically without any inner force, but simply as a repetitive ritual act that one knows one should do, but whose origin and purpose have been forgotten. This ritual of caresses, far from satisfying any legitimate inner desires, leaves an aura of dissatisfaction caused by all acts in which the inner being does not participate. The individual acquires a split personality: one that carries out the sexual act mechanically and the one that draws into the corners of himself. Inner participation becomes nil, for the person's motivation is guided by pseudo-love and is caught up in the inner tangle of his fantasies, desires, fears, anxieties and frustrations. Ritual caressing is no different from sex with a machine or a robot with mechanically perfect sexual organs, or even improved ones, but without soul or content. With this example, we can imagine the difference between really making love or simply bringing on an orgasm. The clumsy routine of ritual caresses must soon lead to boredom and dissatisfaction. If the couple does not learn to make love with true inner participation and if they cannot discover the need for a permanent creative renewal in their relations, they will not even be practicing animal coitus, but the coupling of empty machines.

5. Perfect Communication

The myth that good communication exists between partners, despite occasional quarrels, becomes a sly trap that separates the couple. Beyond occasional discord or quarrels, there is the conviction that communication is perfectly maintained in some mysterious way. The truth is that each communicates with his own unconscious, which he uses as the voice of his fantasies. When he speaks to his lover, he is really talking to himself. At the same time, his partner is not listening but only hears a person speaking and when she responds, she is only addressing her own unconscious. As a result, they live out the fantasy that they communicate perfectly and that they are always in agreement at heart, always together and completely united. Certainly, this phantom communication only functions to the same extent as their own capacity for self-deceit. Often the capacity for self-deception in this respect suddenly disappears after several years of marriage and the couple realize for the first time that there is really no communication whatsoever, that they speak totally different languages and that they have really always been out of touch. This is a highly painful discovery and each partner tries anxiously to blame the other for what has happened.

There can only be real communication in the same measure as there is absolute sincerity in both lovers. This frankness can only be reached by removing hypocrisy.

Hypocrisy means not showing oneself as one is, enabling one to keep up a high level of self-esteem. As long as people keep their masks on, communication becomes highly unlikely, even when messages circulate regularly. For sincerity to exist, there must be a complete absence of fear. Lying is caused by fear of something; in this particular instance, the anticipation of a possible violent or negative reaction on the part of the other person. Only when there is the security of a mature, intelligent and rational attitude, can one have the peace of mind to bare one's soul completely and build the foundations for proper communication.

6. *Fusing into One Sole Being*

The idea of a common identity, the fusion into one sole being, is taken to be proof of the indissoluble union of the couple. It is thought that this ideal sharing of a common identity represents the couple's greatest achievement. Sustained by this notion, the couple will try to think in the same way, feel alike, have the same opinions, keep to the same values and generally behave alike. However, the result is almost always quite different from the goal they desire, for such behavior leads to a loss of identity. The price paid for this coveted fusion is too high: fusion means the death of one's chances of self-fulfillment. In fact, this amalgam cannot represent any sort of productive marriage, only a sterile partnership. Instead of developing the potential of each party so that each may fulfill himself as a conscious, intelligent being, mutual weaknesses, limitations and faults are stored up and these imperfections make the experience of fusion a heavy burden to bear.

When two clashing forces are mutually stimulated by giving too great a part of each to the other, they become too much alike and are no longer a stimulus for they become one single energy. This is the description of the

negative effects of fusion in the process of love. Polarization
at one extreme of two opposite forces is the most certain
means of ending amorous and sexual attraction. In addition,
it is essential to keep up the opposite polarity of these
forces; they must come together harmoniously and not
violently or destructively. If these opposing forces are
equalized in order to suppress any opposition, life energy is
extinguished. This is the problem with many dead
marriages (energetically speaking). The couple, to keep up
a false harmony, destroy their vital dynamic and
automatically repeat hollow formulas whose only purpose
is to keep up the illusion of perfect union. Preserving
individual polarity is not only the secret of love but also of
life, which is born and maintained by the opposition of
contrary forces.

It is not enough just to preserve individual polarity
in love, for a great many other factors are also needed.
Imagine, for example, what would happen to a
psychologically sick or alienated couple who try to keep this
individual polarity; the results would be destructive. For
there is more than one kind of individuality; there is an
obscure and selfish type of individuality and a higher type
of individuality.

7. *Mutual Knowledge and Understanding*
If we do not know the other person in our lives, we
cannot understand that person. If we do not know
ourselves, we will not be able to channel relationships in an
intelligent way for we will not know what we really want
from inside ourselves. In marriages of long standing one
partner can be totally unaware of the other person to the
extent of not knowing his or her desires, thoughts, needs,
qualities or faults. Often, the true personality of a husband
or wife is totally unknown. When one observes them, one
discovers that they only know each other very superficially,

on an elementary or incomplete level, even after having lived together for a long time.

Living out this fiction, there often arises a situation in which the husband believes he has made his wife happy and that he is a model husband. However, he may be surprised to discover how unhappy and frustrated his wife has been for many years. The competitive nature of our society, along with the responsibility and care of children, leaves one very little spare time to concern oneself with an adequate knowledge of one's spouse. A husband can become convinced that if his wife has material security, she must be happy and content. There is no serious concern on his part for knowing the inner world of his wife with the aim of making her happy and ensuring his own happiness. The individual's egoism is so strong that he makes an object of his partner and ascribes to her his own inner world, where naturally, within the rules of his game, "it is impossible for her not to be happy," or "she has everything necessary to be happy." The person is blind, believing that his partner is a mere appendix of himself and lacks an inner world of her own. He cannot imagine that she could have different opinions, that she might have a different scale of values or that her emotional and intellectual needs could differ from his. There is no genuine awareness that each individual has the right to his own opinions and to stick to the criteria dictated by his inner world and to avoid becoming an instrument of others.

It is essential to reflect on the meaning of the partner's inner life and not to slip into the automatic belief that simply living together brings adequate knowledge and understanding of the other. This belief may lead the individual to convince himself that he has in fact found true love.

8. Procreation

Children are one of the most important elements which help to keep up the illusion of love, for their very presence seems to show how fruitful and happy the parents' relationship must be. They represent a material confirmation that love really exists. This subject has been raised before. Here it is necessary to underline the fact that one must not project the illusion of love onto the children in order to see them as living proof of the couple's success. Often, the offspring fill and structure the couple's time in a way that makes it difficult for them to find the necessary time and space to analyze their relationship. Children are also the elements which artificially prevent any impulse toward separation; their parents stay together through obligation, not through love.

9. A Common Destiny

A common destiny means a joint goal rather than an individual path to be followed. A common destiny refers to the purposes which the couple have set for themselves to realize their desires and ambitions. In their minds, they create the story of a life they wish to lead and simply try to comply with these wishes. The concern here is the plot of marriage, that is, the story couples tell themselves to convince themselves that all is well. It does not matter if fights and arguments arise; the couple is convinced that, with certain exceptions, its problems are basically due to "changes in the other person." However, because they hope their relationship will improve and they are afraid to lose a certain way of life, they are powerfully motivated to keep up their marital status. The notion of belonging together as a couple to the same vital life pattern, is one of the veils, which often obscures the magnitude of a rift or alienation in the relationship, or even the fact that a relationship does not exist. Carrying out the numerous jobs necessary to keep the home running, with all the joint effort that this implies, causes each to identify closely with the other, giving them the assurance that they really love each other even when certain things fail. When one of the parties blames the other for lack of love, the person never stops to think about what he or she is giving or to realize that the problem could perhaps be a joint one and not individual in its origin.

10. Habit and Custom

In truth, most couples have quarrels and it is common for one or both parties to think that they are unhappy and must separate. But habit and the custom of life together are so strong that even when life goes bad or lacks feeling and affection, the individual prefers to carry on, for that joint life is the center of gravity psychologically, a refuge which protects him from a hostile outside world. A person may tolerate frequent chastisement from their spouse and prefer to put up with it, rather than face the obligation of seeking a new, uncertain destiny.

Possibly habit is the strongest barrier the individual must overcome to appreciate the difference between "love" and "union" between a couple. Guided by habit and custom, people who have separated, hating each other, may still yearn for each other to the point of returning to start all over again. Others will put up with any situation, however bad it may be, as long as they stay together. Apart from this, the message of religion maintains that marriage is indissoluble and the couple must stay together until death.

Finally, love flows through different channels, into promises, agreements and contracts, and its birth or death does not depend on pressures alien to the individual's interests. Love is neither born nor cultivated by "spontaneous generation," but requires the will and concern of both a man and a woman. Love is a mixture of attraction, empathy, harmony, sentiment, reason, concern and communication between inner worlds. It is reserve, modesty, respect, admiration and giving. It is also mutual recognition of two mature Egos who seek to penetrate each other.

CORRUPT LOVE IS

LONELINESS AND ANXIETY

Love should never be sought as a remedy for problems. When love is controlled by selfish interests and aims, when it is artificially created under the pretext of solving conflicts, its very essence is distorted because its fundamental condition is extinguished. One of the basic tenets of this work is that "love is not always love," that most forms of love in human society have no bearing on what love really is. What, then, is love? This will be analyzed in further detail in later pages, and for the moment, the subject still concerns what love is not.

Love cannot be an improvisation, a saving grace, a habit, or a hook on which to hang illusions. Love, if it is to be true love, must be above all these things; it should flow at a higher level than these concerns. If an individual is able to solve problems through love, or to satisfy his personal needs as a natural result of a relationship, then that is splendid. One must however, establish some order of priority in motivation and one must understand that one cannot seek love to solve problems. On the contrary, if love appears, even when one has problems, its very existence will help to dispel them. Genuine love should be unselfish, if not, it will only become a means of manipulating the other person to derive pleasure for oneself. The individual, in this case, only adopts the appearance of being in love, using this attitude to further his own interests without any respect for his partner.

Often when a man or a woman seeks a partner, they are not motivated by love, but by the hope of finding a person with whom love can be developed. However, the individual does not envision a relationship from the point of view of what love means, but of the personal advantages to be gained from love. Sexual gratification, protection from solitude and anxiety and economic security are all some of the most common motives in both men and women. In other instances, people may seek love for love's sake, wanting to satisfy the fantasy of a romantic love with no practical purpose, no idea of what is to come after the initial stage of the romantic relationship. They only think that they will live a fantasy of love without any specific definition.

The main point is that love cannot be compulsive, nor the result of neurotic conflicts or unleashed impulses. The compulsive expression of love is not found in Nature. Such expression is a fiction and the individual plays his part under penalty of painful repercussions. The person forced to act by his compulsion will resort to deceiving himself and to believing that he really knows and enjoys the part he must play. The strength of his alienation is such that he totally forgets that his behavior is compulsive and convinces himself that it is really voluntary.

The weight of loneliness is something which strongly pushes a person to participate in a false relationship, because he believes that the relationship will relieve his loneliness. This belief makes the individual give himself to his new object of affection with such passion so as to convince his partner that he is deeply in love, when in fact, he is only looking for a way to quiet his feelings of anxiety.

Several elements are involved in the problem of love and loneliness: an inferiority complex, a weak Ego and the anxiety these cause. The sense of not belonging to someone, of being cut off from humanity, makes a person seek love as a way of both giving and belonging, freeing him from his isolation. There are two different types of solitude, a natural one and a neurotic one. The experience of normal solitude makes a balanced and psychologically healthy person want to share his experiences with other people. Neurotic solitude is a result of narcissism, shyness, an inferiority complex or traumatic experiences in childhood. In neurotic solitude, the person himself establishes the solitude. He cuts himself off from people, shutting himself away from the world, letting himself be considered as alien and strange, dissociated, cut off from his own emotional reality. When this person forms part of a couple, he manages to achieve some sort of connection with the outer world through his mate and feels he has conquered his terrible solitude.

Such a union is neither generated by nor sustained by love, but by neurotic need. Love does not offer a real solution to the problem of the lone neurotic; only a cover-up. The individual has not solved his existential position by living through another person. He is more or less in the same position as seriously ill people connected to machines which keep them alive in some way. Such a relationship is born of corrupt love, a love that is not genuine, a form of pseudo-companionship whose imbalance is expressed through manipulation and selfishness.

This situation occurs in individuals hounded by the anxiety of loneliness, and in all persons whose psyches are unhealthy and unbalanced. Unconsciously, like a parasite, they cling to a healthy creature to feed on its vital life force and emotions. These people really love no one but themselves and, like parasites, contribute nothing. They only know how to make demands. There are two classic types of lonely neurotics: those who have been very spoiled by one or both parents, and feel abandoned as a result of no longer receiving such indulgence, and those who did not receive adequate affection and protection in childhood and felt the anxiety of loneliness from then on. Neither of these types will ever be able to really love; they will only use other people as instruments of connection with the outer world. They will be convinced that their interest in their partner is true love, but the healthy partner really suffers great harm because in his honesty, naivete or simplicity, he does not realize he is being used. If he does eventually realize it, he will most likely try to protect and help his partner even more, motivated by the tenderness he feels toward that person. Sometimes, this sacrifice is of such magnitude that the healthy individual gives up his own integrity and offers himself unconditionally to the needs of the other person. Finding a solution for loneliness is not the focus here, but is rather the need to warn against setting up a relationship as a way to search for contact with the external world.

What happens when two equally lonely and empty people connect? This situation is not so different from the one described above, except that in this relationship, it will be harder to keep up the fiction of love. Now there are two people demanding love, companionship and fulfillment while neither of them is in a position to give these things. The relationship is similar to two hungry people, both without any food, or two business partners, both without any capital. Since neither of the partners is in a position to satisfy the other, they will perhaps drift to the simple path of sexual gluttony. Although it brings temporary satisfaction, it inevitably causes boredom and a sense of not being truly cared for by the other partner as soon as the moment of pleasure is over. Both will alternately feel hope and disillusionment. They will feel hope when they believe that things can go very well and disillusionment when they see that things really do not get better at all.

This situation may be prolonged indefinitely or become a constant factor in the life of the couple. Persons suffering from the trauma of loneliness will make excessive demands for affection from their partners, continuously requiring demonstrations that the other person is really there for them. The demands can be so harrowing and distressing that the person experiencing them feels persecuted. A couple with this problem might look for other outlets, such as an active social life which can disguise the sadness of loneliness. But artificial solutions are not satisfactory. They are external reinforcements for inner problems and ensure that the main conflict persists indefinitely. If an individual has not managed to feel comfortable with himself, he will not find comfort in other people. Inner desolation cannot be dispelled with external company; a solution to the problem comes with maturity and proper development of the Ego.

CORRUPT LOVE IS

MAKING WOMAN A SEX OBJECT

From remotest antiquity, woman has been considered by man as an instrument of pleasure. Primitive cultures alike have assigned the value of "sex object" to women. Some aboriginal societies, using their own scale of values, estimate the worth of their young women in a fixed amount of cattle or grain. In modern cities, this transaction is far more elaborate, hypocritical and concealed; yet it is no secret that the richest men usually get the "best" females available, those considered to be the most desirable by aesthetic-social standards. Men who lack a good economic status must be content with women who are not so high on the scale of aesthetic and erotic standards, unless they are privileged enough to find a woman of superior substance who puts love before money. The primitive tribesman has to work for twenty or thirty years to pay the family of the bride for the wife he has acquired. Civilized man has to work all his life to keep his wife, who does not work in general, contrary to the primitive woman.

A man is also viewed as the object of a business transaction because if a woman cannot achieve buying power through him, she will accept suitable substitutes such as impeccable lineage, titles, fame and prestige. No one today is surprised when a woman sells herself to the highest bidder.

Perhaps a man is born with male chauvinist tendencies which make him look upon women as inferior beings unworthy of taking an equal place beside him. With such extremes, many wonder what purpose the feminine sex serves. Thus, in a man's unconscious view, a woman is first and foremost a "pleasure doll" acquired with the aim of satisfying his sexual appetites. A woman transformed into "goods" is robbed of her highest feminine and human qualities. It is even more serious when a woman accepts this situation, because even protesting vigorously, she complacently falls into the game of making love a commercial transaction. Although she protests against a man's chauvinism, she may despise non-chauvinistic males, considering them weak. This attitude reinforces male chauvinism.

Women have looked to secure economic situations rather than the dignity of love in a relationship of equals. Feminist movements are not concerned with love; they attempt only to achieve equality for the sexes in their individual legal rights, to abolish laws which diminish a woman's comparative status in a man's world. In the game of love, women recognize only too well their condition as merchandise. They are especially concerned with legally capturing the male, for advancing old age and the deterioration of physical beauty, lowers their value and might cause a man to leave them later on. They do not want to be left with nobody to belong to and without a financial benefactor. In our era, the focus is on a mistaken love of the body, in which a relationship goes no further than the physical sphere. A woman gives her body to a man and he in turn rewards her with economic status. The more valuable the merchandise, that is, the more beautiful a woman's body, the more profit she will derive in the game of love and economics. This is another form of corrupt love which hinders the development of genuinely human qualities.

When a woman who is made an object marries, she will feel that when she gives her body, she should have an equivalent reward. The higher her opinion of herself, the higher will be the standards of her financial demands. The whole problem has brought her to a very difficult situation, because the feminine sex has become divided into two basic groups: those having physical beauty and those who lack it. Beautiful women have no problem at all; they only need a little intelligence to know how to manage for themselves. They do not need to make an effort in childhood to develop their intellectual possibilities, for they have felt sure of their future since childhood. What is this future? Giving themselves to the right men so that they can reward them accordingly. From the moment they marry, they are no longer intelligent members of the female sex, but objects belonging to their owners, whom they must respect and obey. There are all kinds of owners, from the very good, to the highly corrupt. As self-defense against the discovery that her husband and owner is corrupt, a woman's only recourse is to deny him the use of her body, or break up the marriage in exchange for an adequate economic compensation. If her husband turns out to be good, she will not need to defend herself, but she will inevitably suffer the loss of her own identity.

Because of this mistaken approach to love, beautiful women are often far less intelligent than the less attractive ones. In fact, they compensate for their lack of intellect with an attractive and erotic body. Of course there are special women who are beautiful and intelligent, with great human qualities. Those who lack physical appeal have to do their best to develop their intellectual or artistic potential to attain the only really lasting type of appeal, that is, inner beauty, which is a combination of intelligence, common sense, charm, knowledge and human qualities. However, in this money-minded world, the inner qualities of such women can only be appreciated by exceptional males who are truly intelligent themselves. From this point of view, a woman who is not beautiful has more possibilities of finding a superior man in the spiritual, intellectual and human sense, than a beautiful woman. Unfortunately, because such males are scarce she may feel the weight of solitude far more than a beautiful woman. A woman lacking physical appeal does not become a sex object admired by males for external qualities only. Human values have worked this way since ancient times. People have not yet developed the social scale of values with elements of a higher spiritual or human elevation. Only the material factors of power and wealth are highly valued.

The beautiful woman who usually has no profession, is obliged to belong to a man who will keep her. The one who is not beautiful does not normally have this problem, believing that the realities of love and the marriage market have pushed her to have a profession, a well-paid job or her own source of income.

When a beautiful woman marries, her mate may feel that this beauty was not born for heavy work and should be protected and shielded from all types of difficulties and problems, that her way should be smoothed in every aspect. He does not however, smooth her way in a friendly, fraternal, free or generous manner, the way one individual helps another, but with the certainty that he is protecting his private property.

The laws which punish adultery have different standards for men and women, for a woman is punished far more severely. Obviously, the legislation governing marriage relationships is meant to protect "private property." Although this is not the stated spirit of the law, the practical result is the same. Only within a setting of equality between men and women, as far as their rights and abilities are concerned, is it possible for a couple to maintain adequate communication. In a relationship where one of the parties is considered inferior to the other, responsibilities and ideals will not be shared. There will be only a protector and a protegee, beings who will be permanently alienated on different levels, giving rise to an association of mutual convenience or a bond between the "user" and the "used."

Rather than entertaining their competitive aspirations, women would do well to fight for equality and try to define just what a genuine relationship should be between a man and a woman. Women should set as a goal, before winning an easy economic situation, having children or social prestige and recognition, the achievement of true love. Women should fight to vindicate love; fight for a movement that would purify love of its alien elements and reinstate it to its rightful role in forming an ideal complementary relationship of man and woman in an eternal romance governed by mutual collaboration. If a woman wishes a man to respect her as an equal, she should make herself respected, not through the state's legal authority, but through her moral strength that is born of a genuine development and maturity of her Ego.

Two mutually aware and intelligent beings, who have similar standards of development and who unite themselves through love and respect in a marriage, reach the highest possibilities of self-fulfillment, as each partner lives out a developed inner life. This is a concise definition of what marriage should be when it is born of love and not of prejudice, convenience or social obligation. However, to achieve this union, a man should have some relief from the pressures of his career, from the compulsive need to produce more in order to consume more. He must be able to turn his attention to his inner world, the only source of his real happiness or unhappiness.

One cannot assume love will be an act of spontaneous generation, as is the case with animals, flowers and insects. Only through a conscious study of a genuine science of love can the human couple be united by natural means, instead of by compulsive elements which lead to poor imitations of the happiness of love. A human being must understand the vital role of bonding with another and be conscious of the enormous influence the couple plays in the role of destruction or higher evolution of the species.

We have shown that just as children are rarely the result of love, in the same way, humanity, being the common child of the human couple, is also not the result of love. If this humanity is rapacious, beastial, egotistical, materialistic and a lover of destruction and war, it is because of the denial of the science of love that integrates the human couple in the truly amorous spiritual and human relationship.

CORRUPT LOVE IS

FALSE ROMANTICISM

The dictionary, in its unemotional approach, defines romanticism as "sentimentalism, predominance of fantasy and absence of the practical spirit." However, when this term is applied to the practice of love, the term refers to a state of mind or a special mode of feeling: the sentimental and amorous experiences of the couple, an exaltation of chivalry, generosity, altruism and idealism. The romantic person vibrates intensely to the music of love; he is particularly tender, sensitive and affectionate. He especially appreciates the combination of human and natural elements which make up an essentially pleasurable situation that is unique or "ideally pure." These characteristics not only apply to love, but are the formative elements of a romantic nature or behavior. The romantic individual is a lover of beauty and all that exalts the human condition towards the experiences of goodness, fraternity and harmony.

This ensemble of qualities can be called romanticism, a condition which tends to disappear under the pressures of a materialistic life, progressively desensitizing the individual's capacity to perceive beauty and harmony. Healthy romanticism is a form of behavior which women usually wish for in a man, but which men often reject out of an attitude of false manliness. There should always be a certain amount of romanticism in the couple, to act as a sublimating element on the libido, which will then flow toward higher channels. Unfortunately however, there is a type of "blind romanticism" which is one of the main causes of failure in love.

Cervantes, in his immortal <u>Don Quixote</u>, tried to show people the effects of blind romanticism. He copied the notion of romanticism prevalent at that time, from the rules of chivalric orders which were no doubt, once effective for their members, but useless for mere imitators. Doing good, acting out imaginary undertakings, wielding one's lance in a lady's service, protecting and saving the oppressed, all made up the essence of chivalric behavior. Despite the passing of time, there is not much difference between Don Quixote fighting the windmills and those who pursue the fantasy of a purely idealistic love, existing above and beyond all logic, limitations or material obstacles.

To believe that love comes easily and that any transformation, sentimental or intellectual, is possible thanks to love, is simply "Quixotic." With false romanticism, just as with the "daydream phantom" mentioned earlier, the lover turns his partner into a vehicle in which he incarnates his dreams and personal fantasies. In order to understand this, analyze what happens, for example, when a woman feels attracted to a man for the first time. This attraction always has a larger or smaller dose of "voluntary falling in love." The woman thinks that the man has a certain affinity or likeness to the image of the ideal man which she has forged in her subconscious. Perhaps the individual in question does not correspond at all to the ideal, but as he is nearby and appears for some reason to be an easy "catch" and she unconsciously manipulates herself to see him as an attractive and very special person indeed. Even though, this individual may be mediocre, unintelligent and very limited, by the magic of self-deception, he will appear as splendid as

"Prince Charming." The end of this very common story is predictable, because it is hard work to sustain an illusion which will constantly be in conflict with objective reality. Inevitably, she will think that her man has changed completely, for the worse naturally, unless she is brave enough to admit that she had deceived herself and that, in fact, he is just as he had always been. Although it is often assumed that much is learned from this lesson, people who have gone through this experience, will time and again repeat it always in the hope that the new love is the true one. Only the proof of a sad and lonely old age will convince the romantic dreamer that she, in the case of women, had permanently deceived herself and that her deceptions had led her to despise those men who courted her and who had possessed real qualities which did not, however, match up to the standard of her personal fantasies.

This phenomenon may affect women more than men, for women are the incorrigibly romantic mistresses of self-deception in love. Their open sentimentalism may lead them straight to this type of "silly romanticism" and to a fictitious or unreal existence in love, thus missing the chance of genuine and true love. Fantasy and dreams usurp reality and individuals affected will go from dream to dream, from fantasy to fantasy, guided by whatever appearances suit them, despising and ignoring the real essential content of people and situations. Frequently, a woman falls madly in love with an unworthy person, but she is the only one who does not realize this, considering him to be extraordinary and highly desirable. She is also a specialist in the art of "adopting" males with serious weaknesses or mental and physiological failings. Guided by her maternal instinct, she tries to protect the weak individual just as she would one of her own children. Some people's behavior in love is often inexplicable because the web of their personal dreams and fantasies is so thick that it becomes impervious to rational thinking.

The wish is not to advocate coldness or insensitivity in love, but only to criticize an extreme type of behavior which insidiously destroys the chance of attaining true happiness. It is neither the "cool heads" nor the "hot heads" who are successful in love, but the "clear heads." Love cannot be improvised, neither can it spring forth as an act of magic in the fertile terrain of personal fantasies. It has its origin in conscious planning and in the higher practice of the science of love.

It is obvious that, for most people, the mapping out a plan for love seems difficult and contrary to its very essence. It seems as though the planning of love were like programming a computer. The object of the science of love is to attempt just the reverse, to de-program love from the dynamics which lead to failure. Many people think that love is born just because two people are apparently "made for each other" and that it is enough to find a suitable person for love to explode with irrepressible force. Just to think of the need to understand the theoretical and practical bases of a science of love, makes it seem an arduous undertaking in the minds of the sleepy masses. As a result, most of them will continue to be content with poor imitations of true love. They will rationalize that suffering, quarrelling and frustration are all integral parts of love. They will continue to believe that no love is without suffering and that to love means to suffer.

Therefore, nobody is surprised by the drama of love. These phenomena are not considered exceptional, but as normal elements in human existence. As long as a human being does not really know what true love is and cannot master the laws of its successful practice, he will continue to experience a fantasy imitation of it. People will become resigned to being deprived of the genuine happiness and pleasure of the integral union between a woman and a man, which leads both to levels of joint and individual fulfillment, thus far unknown by humanity.

This union is the formation of the divine couple, who, having freed themselves of the supreme punishment which expelled them from Paradise, manage to return there, purified and spiritualized. We speak not of that fictitious dream-Eden to be found in an invisible, hypothetical heaven, but of the earthly Paradise, both material and spiritual.

Clearly, all this will be only a fantasy for those who do not bother to test it. The science of love is neither for intellectuals nor fearful scientists who shut themselves up within the shell of their own concepts so that their inner security is not threatened by truths which go beyond the cultural conditioning of humanity. They need to shield themselves with the superstition of the blind program of science, which claims to hold a monopoly on truth. They close their eyes to the evidence of their own evolution, to the irrefutable fact that what they know is like a grain of sand in comparison with the desert of what they do not know and that what remains to be discovered will not be invented by science in time, but will be something that has existed from time immemorial within Nature. The atom is not a modern invention but had already existed when the first rays of intelligence burst forth in primitive man. In the same way, we are surely in the first stages of glimpsing far more advanced concepts.

The intention here is not to convince or prove that there is a kind of higher love, which is unknown to the greater part of humanity; it is simply to show the imperfections of common love. We speak to an elite, not one of social lineage or economic status, but one of spiritual ancestry, for the truth cannot be spread to all because there are very different levels of evolution among human beings. As an aside, the scale of development goes from the extremely silly to the extraordinarily intelligent. Just as there are social classes, there are also classes of evolution, with stupidity and intelligence proliferating at all levels. Paradoxically, there are also "stupid geniuses," a typical product of our time; intelligent individuals who are totally devoid of human qualities or inner standards, unbalanced beings who are outstanding only for their mental brilliance in handling specialized techniques. Many of them are like foolish computers which, having been programmed in accordance with specific conditions, are incapable of modifying their programming as conditions change, repeating the message learned like talking machines. Unfortunately, society glorifies these "robots" and the masses think this is a highly desirable level to reach. This work is addressed to those who, while intelligent, are also able, to a certain extent, to withdraw from the blind conditioning of the human being. It also addresses those who can rise above the authority and suggestions of their social and cultural patterns to think without bias, with their own brains. These individuals are suited to receiving this message. It also addresses those people who, having already suffered intensely from love, have in practice proved some of the concepts we maintain. They will also understand these words. Those who are unprejudiced, those who do not imitate blindly, those who wish to have their own ideas, those who have not been distorted by vanity and those who anxiously seek genuine love, will best profit from this work.

There are those whose lack of inner enlightenment, will prevent them from seeing the importance of a philosophy which explains what love really is, because they ingenuously or perhaps with bias think that "philosophy is not a science" and that it serves no practical purpose. In reality philosophy is always one step ahead of science and philosophy is also the source which inspires science. In a separate work, we point out that Hermetic Philosophy is just as scientific as chemistry, physics or mathematics, but it is not a science for the masses because it is a type of knowledge that cannot be transmitted by the oridnary routes of communication in a culture.

True philosophy is not a source of mental games but is the real knowledge of objective truth. Hermeticism is the science of handling one's own instrument of consciousness, raising one's intelligence to levels of unsuspected wholeness. It is the science of raising one's awareness to a higher state of consciousness in which the neophyte acquires full use of the higher faculties of the species. Those who despise philosophy only know it in its traditional theoretical aspect. They are unaware that there is philosophical knowledge of an eminently practical nature which serves to raise the level of consciousness of the individual until he is master of a perfect mental instrument and able to master higher truth. They leave aside the irrefutable fact that intelligence is the real rudder of life and that if this faculty is not freed from alien interferences and raised to a higher condition of efficiency, awareness and clarity, people will lack a trustworthy compass that will show them the way to their higher goals. To overcome alienation in the individual and later attain complete deprogramming is one of the most important aims of Hermetic Philosophy. The spiritual fulfillment of the individual, an undertaking similar to attaining love is exalted here. Both subjects go together, because love is only possible through the correct handling of the human instrument, which must be polished and refined.

Love cannot exist with romanticism, neither can it exist without it. One must learn to see the difference between healthy and false romanticism and strike a happy medium.   Unfortunately, this knowledge lacks any retroactive effects. It is painful to squander the opportunities of an entire lifetime because the error made in this sense is irreversible. If one acknowledges one's error after the fact, it will only be worthwhile if the person is able to change his behavior for the future.

CORRUPT LOVE IS

FRIGIDITY AND IMPOTENCE

Frigidity and impotence are not aspects of corrupt love in themselves, but are results of physical and psychological disorders. They are instead causes of corrupt love which inhibit the manifestations of "natural" love. The term "normal" does not apply here, for it is normal for people to have all kinds of psychological conflicts. The word "natural" refers to whatever is within the standards of Nature. The unnatural is the natural perverted through human ignorance or corruption. Sexual incapacity affects women far more than men and statistics state that between 30% and 40% of women are frigid. This is an extremely alarming figure. This anomaly is a tremendous obstacle for a woman trying to attain her own happiness for, apart from making her incapable of achieving orgasm, it gives her an inferiority complex and feelings of frustration about her femininity.

To understand the problem of frigidity and impotence fully, its most common cause must be explained. Understanding the cause of this problem will shed light on a number of irrational attitudes.

Normally, frigidity is viewed as an inability to attain orgasm, but there are many types of frigidity, differentiated according to the degree of disturbance.

Typically, there are five degrees of frigidity:

1. Women who occasionally do not reach a complete vaginal orgasm.
2. Those who become excited but never reach orgasm.
3. Those who reach orgasm in the clitoris.
4. Those who are occasionally unable to become excited.
5. Those who suffer from total frigidity and blocked genital response.

The causes of frigidity are mainly psychological in origin, even though there are many cases of vaginal anesthesia and organic diseases of the nervous system such as multiple sclerosis, transverse myelitis, dorsal tabes and poliomyelitis, which bring on frigidity. The possibility of a cure in these cases, exists in direct ratio to an improvement in these illnesses.

Listed below are the most frequent causes of frigidity due to psychological origins.

1) Deficient adolescent sexual education, through ignorance or indulgence of the parents or because sex was presented as immoral or sinful.
2) The association of sexuality with danger.
3) Penis envy.
4) Masturbation.
5) Unconscious homosexuality.
6) Childhood traumas.
7) Foreplay that is too brief.
8) Partner's premature ejaculation.
9) Aversion to partner's physical nearness in some aspect.

1) Deficient Adolescent Sexual Education
A woman is very often given a false view of sex

when her education is based on misunderstood puritanism. In childhood she is usually taught to be a good housewife, a model wife from a social point of view, a magnificent cook and an efficient mother, but she is not prepared at all for the interaction in a love relationship. On the contrary, a woman is sometimes "educated" to fail in the sexual side of her relationship, to become frustrated, or to simply tolerate coitus as an unavoidable evil. In this approach there is no malice, but merely ignorance. A future wife gets detailed instructions on the art of cooking, the most efficient way of cleaning a house and is taught a great deal about every aspect of her probable future maternity. Nothing, or very little, is said about sex, and if anything is said, it is generally biased or erroneous information. Often a mother who has been frigid all her life will influence her daughter to accept this condition as normal and inevitable, as something which is part of a woman's destiny. Perhaps her grandmother and great-grandmother behaved this way.

This type of ignorant and prejudiced mother teaches her daughter a proud, puritanical and falsely modest type of behavior. She tells her, for her own good, that sex is wicked and should be suppressed at all costs, that to lose one's virginity before marriage is the worst thing that could happen to her. She is also taught that her future role in marriage will consist of respecting her husband, and obeying his will, keeping up the house, giving him healthy children and bringing them up. Discussing sexual relationships seems to be embarrassingly uncomfortable and preferably avoided. She is taught to put up with sex in order to keep her husband.

If a home environment has been excessively strict and if a girl has been threatened from childhood with severe punishment when she displays any interest in sex or in her own awakening sexuality, she will surely become frigid.

There are many times when a woman comes to marriage
ignorant, knowing nothing more of sex than what she has
asked of her school friends. They may be as badly informed
as she is, and may have told her threatening stories they
have heard from others.

2) *The Association of Sexuality with Danger*

This factor is part of a "normal" process in which a
woman, from the time of childhood, forges a link between
danger and sex. Many elements contribute to this, and the
main ones are:

a) Fear of the first sexual relationship

Many women have a general idea before their first
experience that the process of "deflowering" is
something terrible and shocking or painful and
bloody. An uninitiated girl develops a great fear of
sex. When the moment, in fact, comes for her sexual
initiation, her fear completely erases all likelihood of
enjoyment, especially if her companion is impatient,
inexperienced or tactless. The first sexual experience
is definitive, for it may cause frigidity, which is hard
to cure.

b) Fear of pregnancy

Many women also believe that childbirth will be a
terribly traumatic experience in which they become
like animals giving birth. She may be terrified by
shocking or vulgar accounts of childbrith which
profoundly terrify her and cause her to reject the
sexual act with all its potential negative
consequences.

c) Fear of sexual excitement

The sexual act may give the sensation that the body
is being invaded by strange elements which sweep
it to the fulfillment of the unknown, which is

perceived as threatening and dangerous.

d) A negative view of sex transmitted by some religions
Unfortunately, religions have surrounded the sexual act with an atmosphere of sin and corruption and have emphasized that God punished men and women for having committed the "original sin," expelling them from Paradise. The repression of the libido through the idea that the sexual act is sinful, is one of the most influential elements, not only in feminine frigidity, but also in the development of frustrations, complexes and mental disorders of all kinds. The concepts associating sex with dirtiness, immorality and vice are so incorporated in the collective unconscious of humanity that they have become ingrained in the human being. Thus a person, feeling the sexual urge, finds himself exposed to the dreadful anguish of being trapped between the sword and the wall, submitted to the terrible, contradictory impulses of two opposed halves of his personality, the Id and the Super Ego. The Id is the half with which the child is born and may be defined as a reserve of energy meant to satisfy instinctive needs without considering the consequences. The Id acts in an impulsive and chaotic way, heedless of logic and without the moral rules that allow the individual to tell good from evil. In contrast, the Super Ego is the individual's moral conscience in the sense that it is formed by cultural norms of conduct.

A large part of the Super Ego is "unconscious" in the sense that its influence on behavior is not perceived. The Super Ego can be called the "censure." As a result, a person is on one hand submitted to the impulses of the Id, and on the other, to the moral repressions of the Super Ego. As often happens, these tensions are opposed to each other and a conflict arises between them. The individual himself becomes trapped between both, under going the extreme anguish of instinctive, emotional and intellectual ambivalence. The sexual terrain is one of the strongest fields in which this conflict occurs because the sexual-religious-cultural concepts are an active part of the Super Ego. On the other hand, without the censuring process of the Super Ego, a human being would probably suffer far more serious problems. The permanent conflict between the Id and the Super Ego may be used positively only through a considerable elevation of the individual's level of consciousness, which will enable him to sublimate the Id and make the Super Ego reflexive.

e) Fear of being used as an object by a man
This fear is based on feelings of inferiority in relation to a man. A woman feels she must defend herself against him in order not to be abused. This point is related to the following one.

3) Penis Envy
Castration means the amputation of the genital organs in the male. The castration complex consists of a natural fear of being castrated felt by small boys. On the surface, this fear seems as absurd as expecting to be hit by an object falling from the sky, however, the fear of castration has a highly specific psychological base. There comes a moment in a boy's development when he becomes aware of his ability to control the urethral sphincter and, as a result, his flow of urine. Being able to urinate or retain the flow at will gives a boy a sense of power which is often displayed in childish competitions to see who can urinate farthest. This is the first relationship which a boy establishes between penis and power. Gradually, he sees that having a penis confers on him strength, prestige and dignity.

There comes a moment when a boy must face a most singular fact: that there are some children who do not have a penis (he has seen naked girls but cannot yet see that there are different sexes; for him, the girl is just another boy). When he observes these children without a penis, he infers that they have been punished by castration. This gives him great fear and anxiety that he himself might be punished in this way by his father. This fear is connected with the Oedipus Complex. The father appears as a rival for the affections of the mother and the son experiences a feeling of something forbidden and subject to punishment. The concern here therefore is what happens to a girl, for the idea of having been castrated is developed in her when she sees that a man has a penis which she lacks. A man seems to her to be a privileged being and she feels an envy which drives her to a type of rivalry. She may later turn into a "phallic woman," one who wishes to emulate men, and who has the fantasy of possessing or acquiring a penis.

According to experts on the subject, there are two types of penis envy:

> a) *Fulfillment of what is desired*
> This is the case with women who wish to be better than men and try to compete with them, adopting a masculine attitude and attempting to beat them in certain areas. Women who take part in feminist liberation movements, or participate in certain sports, or carry out activities pertaining to the male sex are often "phallic" in their orientation. They are unaware of the deep motivation of their behavior which they generally attribute to the need to free themselves from masculine slavery or male macho behavior. Masculinization in a woman leads her to reject her femininity, which will often lead her to lesbianism. It is understandable that when a woman

becomes masculine, domineering or authoritarian through her phallic aspirations, she cannot reach orgasmic climax. She may even be totally incapable of feeling attraction or sexual excitement for a man.

Both the Oedipus Complex and the castration complex affect all people at some point in their lives. In subsequent development some individuals may solve these conflicts, although some may fail to achieve an intelligent adaptation. If a woman cannot solve her anxiety over castration, she will unconsciously detest her own sex and will feel a profound envy of men. This attitude will make her discontented and insatiable as she adopts the behavior of a man.

b) The vengeful type

In this case, penis envy drifts toward an intense desire to exact revenge on the male (who is perceived more fortunate) by castrating him. The objective is to humiliate men before they humiliate women. In some circumstances, coitus is considered to be mortifying or disgusting to one or the other partner. Vengeance may have either a masculine or a feminine thrust: "I'll show you that I can be as masculine as you" (masculine response), or "because you've despised me, I'll make you admire what you've despised, but you won't get it" (feminine response).

Vaginismus, a spasm of the vagina makes penetration of the male organ impossible by causing severe pain. It is a clear manifestation of this vengeful type of castration complex in a woman. Unconsciously, a woman acts out her own type of revenge. She makes herself admired and desired, but at the same time she takes revenge on a man and punishes him by depriving him of coitus.

To sum up, a woman who feels castrated adopts one of two basic attitudes: either she competes with a man on his own ground and tries to surpass him, or she takes vengeance on him by trying to punish him, humiliating and destroying him in any way. The basic purpose of many domineering women is to castrate men and deprive them of their masculine attributes. This happens when a woman annuls him psychologically or seriously inhibits his liberty and individuality. It is painful to see couples in which a woman acts out the male role and a man is limited to playing an absolutely passive role. It is also sad that these unconscious attitudes in a woman limit her likelihood of achieving happiness in love.

4) *Masturbation*

Often, women who are used to masturbation from childhood set up a standard of sexual reaction which excludes natural relationships. These women usually become accustomed to clitoral masturbation, stimulating the clitoris and not the vagina. They do no more than acquire or reinforce a feeling of castration, as the clitoris is an atrophied penis. Its smallness gives a woman precisely the feeling of being castrated. There are other reasons why masturbation brings on frigidity which will be discussed later under the heading of magnetic sexuality. When a woman practices this solitary vice, she discharges her magnetic energy and thereby undermines her sexual potential, upsetting the normal flow of her libido. There is also a feeling of guilt associated with carrying out a "sinful" act in a hidden way. This strengthens even more, the link between sexuality and danger referred to previously. Later, when a woman tries to enter into a normal relationship, she merely feels coldness toward a man, or simply rejects him.

5) Unconscious Homosexuality

Unconscious homosexuality refers to the type of woman who, unknowingly possesses a masculine psyche. Her anomaly may be due to her upbringing with a weak and cowardly father, whom she unconsciously despised, or otherwise a harsh and punitive father who mistreated her. Perhaps her father wished to have a male child and constantly undermined her femininity, either by ridiculing her or by stimulating masculine behavior in her. This type of woman will grow in accord with her own femininity, although she will unconsciously have a masculine fixation. This is the outline of unconscious homosexuality; the father's manipulation acts to reinforce the masculine polarity of his daughter, who will intensely wish to have sex in the normal way but will always feel an unconscious check that frustrates her libido.

Only to the extent that a person manages to visualize or become aware of the dynamics of these processes and to discipline the self to influence the subconscious, will the person be able to overcome these conflicts.

6) Childhood Traumas

There are negative experiences in childhood which can quite easily condition a negative sexual response. When the moral standards in a home are too strict, rigid or puritanical, various threats are made to small children at the slightest display of early sexuality. If a little girl touches her genitals, she is told that she is bad and that God may punish her by "making her hand fall off" or other such threats. A little girl may have seen dogs copulating and ask about it, being told that the act is a sin and God will punish her if she does it.

This same prudish attitude triggers exaggerated reactions: if a little girl is surprised while spying on her parents making love, or if she has asked embarrassing questions about it, she will get a scolding or be punished. Once again, an association is made between sex and the illicit, between sex and danger.

7) Foreplay That is Too Brief

Considering the effects of the sexual relationship itself on a woman, the negative effect of too brief or too rough a sexual approach from her companion must be discussed. There are clearly marked differences between the sexes, both psychologically and physiologically. From a strictly physiological point of view, sexual excitement and resultant orgasm is mainly a medullar and reflexive act for a man, centered in the spinal cord. For a woman, sexual response is a more complex process because the cerebral limbic system (which is related to the emotions), as well as the spinal cord, is involved. For this reason, the sexual act in many men is characterized by a quick, mechanical behavior which almost immediately brings them genital satisfaction. For a woman, coitus must follow a slow process of stimulation. A man responds to a purely physiological stimulus; a woman needs adequate psychological and emotional petting which will awaken her erotic impulses. For a woman, coitus is the natural culmination of a coupling at an emotional level. A man, driven by his need to satisfy his appetite, disregards this sentimental communication entirely and only takes into account the physical assets of the female. It is common for a man to reach orgasm quickly, while a woman is still in the first stages of stimulation. When this situation repeats itself, together with the indifference displayed by a man after orgasm, it gives rise to great frustration in a woman. Gradually she becomes frigid and thinks: "why do I waste time on it when I can't manage to finish?" or "what do I get out of it by getting excited if I don't get any satisfaction at the end of it all?"

8) Partner's Premature Ejaculation

Premature ejaculation in a man is a variation of the above situation and presents a more serious problem for the male, because it not only stems from a medullar reaction, but also implies a special form of impotence. Premature ejaculation varies within a range from instantaneous ejaculation when the penis is inserted, to abnormal speed in reaching orgasm.

9) Aversion to Partner's Physical Nearness in Some Aspect

In this situation, it is quite likely that the sexual habits of a woman's companion are lacking in a minimum of delicacy and that he may take her clumsily, insensitively or aggressively. Certain aesthetic and anatomical characteristics may provoke a profound rejection on the part of a woman and she may unconsciously associate them with characters and experiences from childhood which disgusted or repelled her. The negative association of certain smells, like perspiration, certain heavily spiced food, or simply unpleasant body odor, also cause a woman instinctively to reject a man.

All of the above reactions may also be a means of unconscious revenge, motivated by the memory of possible conjugal infidelities.

This reaction also arises when a woman feels disgust or lack of attraction toward her husband, but at the same time, feels highly excited and reaches orgasm by thinking of another man. Whether the other man is real or fictitious, she feels more attracted to his image, which is in accordance with her ideal physical or sentimental wishes. She may need to have intercourse only in certain positions to overcome her obstacles to satisfaction.

It is common for the frigid woman, especially one

with penis envy, to display an abnormally combative attitude toward men, as if she were rebelling against her feminine condition. The most common ideas associated with this reaction are the following:

"The only thing men want is to go to bed with a woman."

"Men are awful."

"Men only think of their own selfish pleasure; all women know this."

"Once they've made love to a woman, they leave her because they're no longer interested in her."

"Sex is easy for men; they make babies and forget about us; that's why we've got to get everything out of them that we can."

"Men are perverse, dirty and immoral."

It is easy to understand that these beliefs make it difficult for a woman to find happiness in love, because her opinions and prejudices lead her to failure.

The psychological origins of masculine impotence are far less complex than a woman's reasons for frigidity. The following are the physiological causes for impotence in men: diseases of the genitals, urethra or prostate; endocrine disorders involving the gonads, pituitary or thyroid; other disorders such as diabetes, infections, damage to the spinal cord, excessive fatigue and chronic drunkenness.

The psychological factors in impotence are similar to those in a woman's frigidity. In both instances, sexual activity is associated with danger. Unconsciously believing that sexual activity is dangerous, a man adopts a defensive attitude and gives up sexual pleasure out of fear of danger. The basic threat is of castration, the fear that the penis will be harmed while it is in the vagina. There are two elements which cause impotence in men: *castration anxiety* brought on by fear of amputation of the male sexual organs and *unconscious identification* with the female sex through the Oedipus Complex.

There is a relationship between castration anxiety and the Oedipus Complex. The Oedipus Complex consists of sexually desiring the mother. The young boy wants his mother for himself and considers his father to be a rival. The feeling of profound jealousy is accompanied by a wish to eliminate him in order to be left alone with his mother. He develops an aggressive attitude toward his father. Nevertheless, he will love and admire his father while he also feels jealous, which causes him remorse, guilt and anxiety. Although he feels guilty, he does not know why. He fears his father will punish him by castrating him for having wished to take his mother away from him. This leads him to try to please his father by repressing his own virility. This situation leads him to desire the forbidden. He belittles and devirilizes himself, "becoming feminine" in order to please. These issues form the basis for castration anxiety.

From the fear of castration, a man will create mechanisms in adulthood that inhibit his sexuality. If he adopts a feminine identification, he will also inhibit his sexuality, but he will be guided by a desire to wash away his guilt and to please. What matters are the results. The man becomes psychologically feminine and is devirilized by repressing or rejecting his masculine condition.

It is interesting to consider the persistence of a sensual link with the mother, which leads a man to the following unconscious reflection: "No sexual contact is good enough because my partner is never my mother." At a deeper, irrational level, the following thought also occurs: "Any sexual link must be repressed, for any sexual partner represents or symbolizes my mother." All of this only leads to the problem of frigidity and impotence, that is, the adoption of an attitude which is psychologically opposite to one's sex. Both the masculine woman and the feminine man relate to others in this way, but the issue actually can be taken to a much more serious level, a concealed and little known one; the level of spiritual impotence and frigidity of the soul. All true virility is spiritual and any power to conceive flows from the woman's soul. The sexual organs are only the biological level of an infinitely higher force. The basis for this assertion will be explained in the chapter on the nature of love.

Common psychological terms are used here to explain phenomena with a profound Hermetic significance because psychology, unlike Hermetic terminology, has a language known to everyone, at least in its essentials and there is also a wide range of information on the subject. There is, however, an interesting phenomenon in the link between psychological and Hermetic knowledge. Psychology is "unaware of what it knows" and does not understand what it knows. Seen in Hermetic terms, psychology is unable to establish a relationship between the particular and the general, and does not recognize the need to project the particular onto the whole and to view the whole in the particular. Psychology, nevertheless, has a good descriptive system for the "mechanics of the beast." These "mechanics" operate by regulating the animal intelligence of *homo sapiens* which alienates and possesses human intelligence, enslaving it to its own interests. In this way, psychology, and especially psychoanalysis, may in some aspects be useful collaborators in the task of fulfilling the ancient and well-known Hermetic axiom of "know thyself."

Psychology should not be confused with

Hermeticism though, for the two subjects have the same likeness as a simple man and a wise man. Psychology is a useful tool, from the spiritual and esoteric point of view, only for those who know the Hermetic codes. For those lacking these codes, psychology should be kept on the level of its purely professional and orthodox importance. Psychology can be used as an efficient technique to receive benefit from the psychic faculties and for the therapy of certain personality disorders. Psychology is the cultural patrimony of humanity; Hermetic Science belongs exclusively to a small spiritual elite. One gains entrance into Hermeticism only through interest, humbleness, personal effort, deep motivation, adequate training, and personal experience.

CORRUPT LOVE IS

FRIGIDITY OF THE SOUL
AND
SEXUAL-SPIRITUAL IMPOTENCE

As life becomes more complex in its socio-cultural and economic demands, more and more men and women are practicing relations of the body, more closely related to animal mating, under the guise of loving. Women have limited their innate power to conceive to the narrow confines of their bodies and men have become animals led by testicles instead of by their brains. Femininity is confused with the uterus and masculinity with the phallus. The more "uterine" a woman is (that is, one who thinks with her uterus, instead of her brain), the more attractive and desirable she is mistakenly considered. The more phallic a man is, the more he seems to appeal to the feminine sex.

The common image of a virile man is but a caricature of true masculinity. The virile man is generally represented with great physical strength, scant or limited intellectual ability and almost devoid of emotional and spiritual sensitivity. His moral, spiritual and personal assets are overshadowed by his physical characteristics. He is often seen as an aggressive, bullying individual, but the true moral courage of the persevering man is unknown.

Similarly, the woman who characterizes the feminine ideal, posseses great physical beauty, a splendid anatomy and the capability of great passion, but her spiritual or human qualities are rarely valued. At the most, certain subjective and abstract observations are made, such as, "she is highly sensitive, very feminine, very capable," or that she is "on a higher plane." Sometimes her intellectual, professional or artistic abilities are discussed. Nothing is said of her soul or of her inner essence, perhaps because these concepts are little known and are very vague to most people. In general, people only try to discern "what an individual has" and not "what he is" from the human point of view. They refer to material and psychological possessions, but not to innate spiritual qualities. This mistaken idea of what true virility and true fertility are, leads people to imitate rather poorly femininity and masculinity, with particular emphasis given to the genital areas.

Genital love only causes the union between a man and a woman to lack power and is the equivalent of the mating of animals. The real crisis for the couple today is the loss or lack of a sublimating "spiritual force" behind the creative power of love. (Spiritual force means the attainment of a high level of consciousness. Functioning at this level of consciousness, to a greater or lesser extent, enables the individual to display the power of the "divine spark through his or her brain." The divine spark is the spirit itself, the spiritual essence of the individual, or the primordial intelligent energy which animates him.) As a result, a man and a woman progressively degenerate in a love union, rather than regenerate their forces. Degeneration is defined in the dictionary as "a decline in the qualities of the species, race, or ancestry." This describes what occurs when there is a love union that is not backed by a spiritual force. There is an inevitable loss of the higher qualities of the species, which become impossible to attain.

Materialists, who believe in the omnipotence of matter and who are not convinced by any abstract proof or reasoning, are far removed from grasping the secrets of happiness in love, and many will finally die believing that there is nothing beyond death. Love, for them, is only a fleeting pleasure, lacking any meaning other than that of reproduction or genital gratification. This message will not reach these people, but only for those who are able to go beyond superstition and fixed beliefs, and who honestly and sincerely seek to understand true reality. This message is for those who can rise above personal prejudice and reach the realm of integral comprehension and for those who possess deprogrammed intelligence that does not stop at the intellectual barriers of the species, but which penetrates the mystery of stellar knowledge. Stellar knowledge is infinitely superior to earthly knowledge and is reserved only for those who are truly spiritual. The means of attaining this knowledge is discussed in other volumes in this series.

Spirituality is not devotional mystic abstraction, nor isolated causes of hallucination. It is the highest degree of de-alienation, de-hallucination and evolution. It represents a quality that corresponds to the higher pole of the evolutionary path of *homo sapiens*. Spirituality is the ideal goal in the evolution of the species. Having spiritual force means realizing the true potential of the human species. This development is lacking in the majority of human beings, and lies in the collective intelligence of the animal species called *homo sapiens*.

As a direct consequence of frigidity of the soul, a woman gives only her body. Her soul is absent and far away, and it does not participate in the union of the couple. The most obvious result of this frigidity is the woman's profound dissatisfaction, as she seeks in vain her fulfillment through the misguided means of physical pleasure. Instead of bringing her lasting inner pleasure, physical pleasure alone leaves her emptier and emptier, forcing her to begin the cycle once more. She compulsively seeks inner happiness, but will never find it in simple physical coitus, because physical orgasm alone is not sufficient to fill her inner world. Only orgasm on the level of the soul, with the participation of the soul, can lead her to enjoy full feminine growth and to attain wholeness as a woman.

In the feminine sex, soul is defined as the "feminine energy of Nature embodied in the woman," which maps out her psychic structure as a female. The soul is the center of her elemental feminine condition. It is the highest level of her sexual differentiation. The body expresses biological dissimilarity but her elemental soul makes her a true woman and is the seat of her authentic femininity. This is why the participation or the absence of a woman's soul matters so much in a love relationship. Her soul's presence or absence makes the difference during coitus, between spiritual fecundity or barrenness of coitus, and genuine happiness or inner void produced by the act. If the soul does not participate in the union, it will only be physical, even when there is a deep emotional involvement. Here lies the secret of feminine happiness and the only remedy which prevents and cures feelings of frustration and disillusionment.

The role of a man, however, who has the same conflict as a woman, must be analyzed. In his case, the focus is on his spiritual force rather than his soul, for men and women have been given quite different qualities by Nature. A man represents the masculine element in Nature, the spirit, and a woman the feminine element, the soul. Just as her true femininity lies in her soul, the center of a man's virility or masculinity lies in his spirit, the source of his essential energy. Obelisks and columns of temples of diverse religions and philosophies throughout the ages denote this search for spiritual power.

As a result of materialism, we live in a world full of men without spiritual power and women without the ability to be fruitful. Ignorance of philosophy, superficial religious expression, and selfish, utilitarian behavior too often define human existence. This is why couples lack the necessary force to produce truly superior children to lead humanity to a more promising destiny. Couples transmit to their offspring the defective elements of mental states inspired by the concept of "an eye for an eye and a tooth for a tooth."

In her heart of hearts, a woman's most intense desire is to give her soul to a man, so that she belongs to him, not only in body but also in her higher femininity, which, although it is not to be seen, is intact in its fundamental state. This desire is purely instinctive, or perhaps intuitive, and she does not know how to go about it. She also faces the serious obstacle that, in order to achieve this type of higher relationship, she needs a companion of a level either similar to hers or higher, a man with "spiritual force." A man of this type is extremely rare. This is why a woman unconsciously and continuously submits a man to different psychological tests. She aims to detect whether or not the male possesses a certain amount of spiritual force, whether he is worthy of "receiving her soul." Despite this testing and life-long analysis, the result is generally negative and a woman dies a "virgin in her soul," that is, she dies with the frustration of never having been fertilized at the level of her soul. Had this fertilization taken place, it would have led her to her authentic feminine realization as a result of an integral union of Spirit and Nature.

What accounts for frigidity of the soul in a woman? Perhaps the most important factor is the lack of worthy men to give herself to, but another cause lies in a woman's selfish attitude of trying to use a man for her own emotional and economic gain. A misguided upbringing allows her to develop false modesty, self-love, and a sense of sinfulness in giving herself sexually, leading to diverse psychological disorders, which compel her to deny her condition as a woman. A woman may be perfectly normal from a physiological point of view, while she suffers from frigidity of the soul. This is a point which can be determined by her spiritual quality, the level of awareness of her intelligence and her individual state of consciousness. The act of giving oneself internally which is similar to the ability to conceive as an expression of the force of Nature, or the act of not giving of oneself, are matters of inner generosity or stinginess. If a woman has an unconscious materialistic concept of love, she will never feel the inner impulse of true giving, for there will not be enough money in the world to reward her adequately. Even if there were, the act of giving would be limited exclusively to her body, for in her mental world she has no concept of selling her soul, but only her body. Except in rare instances, frigidity of the soul is not an inborn condition, but is learned and formed by the particular circumstances in a person's life. The interaction of these elements, added to a woman's subjective state of mind, will give rise to the potency or impotency of the soul, and even if she has the ability to give her soul, she may not find the ideal man for this purpose.

True sexual satisfaction does not come, as is often thought, from genital stimulation, but from mating at the level of the soul. When this type of union occurs, orgasm is not only organic, but also psychological, mental and spiritual, reaching far more profound levels of the person's being. In truth, the common man and woman do not experience true sexual pleasure in love, for they focus on physical outlets which, at most, reach the emotional level.

The simple truth is that pleasure and happiness belong only to men and women who have a higher human quality and the fully developed spiritual power of real human beings. This state contrasts with the abundant examples of the species, who have not, to the least extent, been able to overcome their condition of *"animalis sapiens"* and who are really not fully human.

According to the Bible, the human couple was expelled from Paradise through original sin. Could this "original sin" mean no more than simple sexual contact? Doesn't the Bible refer in a veiled way to the sinful fact of losing spirituality in love, by degrading oneself through the purely animal sexual contact? Paradise cannot be regained without spiritualizing love, which means restoring love to its rightful place.

CORRUPT LOVE IS

HYSTERIA

Hysteria is defined as a disorder which causes a person to return to earlier stages of development and behave in a childish and capricious manner. An hysterical person, whether male or female, has a low resistance to frustration, as if he believed himself to be omnipotent. He unconsciously thinks that the world was made for him and that people must serve him and implicitly give in to his slightest whim. Domineering, demanding and selfish, the hysterical individual magnifies situations, making great problems out of little matters. He will not be contradicted and resorts to exaggerated laments, uncontrolled weeping, dramatic or theatrical attitudes. He sometimes seeks others' sympathy or attacks them with insults, with either emotional or physical aggression. At heart, he behaves like a spoiled child who will try, at any cost, to get his way.

There are many kinds of hysterical phenomena which may lead to the appearance of imaginary disorders or physical symptoms of illness, such as an hysterical pregnancy which shows itself in a swelling of the abdomen while there is no real pregnancy. Hysteria can also manifest itself in paralysis and blindness, showing how far a disorder of this type may go. The concern here is to study the way hysteria may hinder a love relationship, by causing one of the partners to act childishly and irrationally. Real hysteria, according to experts on the subject, is caused by a fear of incest, fear of having sexual relations with the parent of the opposite sex.

We can relate all this to the Oedipus Complex and fear of castration, mentioned in previous chapters, in order to understand the mechanism of attraction and rejection which can arise in the field of love. On the one hand, there is attraction toward the companion and on the other, rejection, when the companion in some way symbolizes the father image. These complexes also explain the theatrical and sensational nature of hysteria, in which a woman may, for example, need to unconsciously "draw her father's attention" and tries very hard to give rein to her hysterical outbursts only when she can count upon the right audience. The law behind this phenomenon is: there is no hysteria without an audience; the individual never carries on the "show" alone.

The hysterical woman, is far from being frigid. On the contrary she is highly passionate, due to her tremendous repression because the sexual act seems to her to be invested with the danger of incest. She therefore represses herself until she explodes in a way which seems unrelated to the cause of her conflict. The repression of her libido bursts out through her emotions.

From a Hermetic point of view, hysteria is simply a misguided flow of energy, as if the gas cooker at home were connected to the water supply and the force of this supply provoked a flood. The hysterical person's libido is blocked by repression and the individual accumulates such pressure that energy escapes in a way that is considered less dangerous (without incest) or inoffensive, that is, through explosive emotional states devoid of any mature, rational structure. In Hermetic terms, there has been a short circuit between sexuality and emotion, which brings on an emotional and nervous storm beyond the cerebral control of the person, as if the cortex had been inundated by a sudden rush of energy. Logical thought is pushed aside and the person acts irrationally. The repetition of this phenomenon forms standards of behavior which are more or less stable, and with the necessary triggering factors, the person will behave hysterically.

Due to this inappropriate inner contact, the emotional center "steals" the energies of the libido and the individual experiences orgasm in the emotional field. There occurs an alteration of levels in which orgasm, instead of occurring in the sexual area, is produced in the emotional area in a distorted way. Hysteria, according to Hermetic concepts, is an "emotional orgasm." As a result, the libido is tainted with the basic elements which are in the emotional "bowl." Ancient Greek philosophers said that before one can love, it is necessary to "clean the bowl." By this, they undoubtedly referred to the heart, for the emotional system is the center of the individual's passional states, where all complexes blossom, as well as fears, frustrations or perversions. Envy, hate, anxiety, fear and frustration, are currents of emotional energy.

Hysteria gives rise to sexual morbidity and causes distorted impulses whose origins are not necessarily in the energy of the libido, nor in the essence of the individual. They are simply a reflection of inner impurity. In some cases, hysteria can also lead to an extreme puritanism in a person. If he unconsciously realizes his inner contamination, he becomes afraid and imposes on himself the mandates of a puritanical order.

The libido is originally absolutely pure energy and it is the person who stains or corrupts it, often because he himself is too weak to resist the latent disrupting influences in his life. This process is clearly seen in cases of hysteria associated with relationships and is often associated with jealousy, which gives rise to destructive impulses. The jealous hysteric resorts to the worst insults and comparisons and will try to humiliate the partner, generating an intense, hidden and perverse sexual excitement, which reaches its paroxysm in an hysterical attack of jealousy.

The act of sublimation contrasts with hysteria. With sublimation, the libido is channelled through higher levels and gradually loses its "impurities," returning to its original purity.

According to Hermetic philosophy, hysteria is also an alteration in the magnetic polarity of a human being. For example, hysteria in women is caused by an "inadequate contact" between the sexual center and the heart because the clitoris, with its positive-masculine polarity, takes over control of the sexual system. In men, hysteria is controlled at the sexual level by the prostate gland with its passive-feminine polarity. In men, the heart has both polarities of which its feminine side is connected to the feminine element of the prostate gland, producing an inappropriate polarity. In women, the heart also has both polarities of which its masculine side is connected to the masculine element of the clitoris, also producing a mistaken polarity. Through these inadequate fluxes, people discharge animal magnetism which disrupts psychological equilibrium. Such a magnetic loss is at the same time provoked by a misguided use of creative power. When an individual represses himself to the point of blocking his libido, he causes a problem similar to stagnant water which decomposes due to lack of oxygen. The personal magnetism of the hysteric is a sick magnetism and lacks any higher vital properties. This state can be perceived intuitively by those who encounter it.

The best remedy is to "clean the bowl," in other words, to cleanse oneself by self analysis and will power of all the negative sentiments which might be felt for others and oneself. It is also necessary to carry out a sexual sublimation through the spiritualized sexual act, one which is natural, conscious and pure. What is a pure act? It is an act carried out after having carefully cleaned the emotional bowl, and an act that is free of inner contradictions; the person does not mix sex with emotion nor imagination as happens in "inappropriate" physical contacts.

PART TWO

WHAT IS LOVE?

The moment has come to reveal what love is and to provide deeper understanding. This subject is not the stuff of poets and romantic dreams, nor a matter for scientists, who would most likely relegate it to hormones. Love is not self-deception, nor as many dreamers maintain, "born of the heart." This approach to love will not follow the well-worn path of *homo sapiens*, but instead will be like reading the book of Nature, whose laws are constant and perpetual.

Nature is beyond time, culture, science and morals. Nature is the matrix in which nothing can be invented, for everything has existed from the beginning. This is the mystery to which Egyptian initiates referred when they said, "I am what I am, what has been, what is, and what will eternally be." Regardless of human perception and interpretation, rain has always fallen on the earth, the force of gravity has always existed, the sun has always lit up the planet, there has always been an atmosphere made for breathing, and there has always been animal, vegetable and mineral life. The earth continued to be round even though men thought it was flat. The greatest doubts do not in the slightest alter Nature's equilibrium because natural truth is atemporal, immutable, invariable, imperturbable and immortal. This is why natural law, contrary to cultural ones, is the only type of wisdom which can withstand the passing of time. The science of the earth is only local. The laws of Nature make up a "stellar science" called Hermeticism in honor of Hermes Trismegistus, the wise and ancient sage who established all the fundamental rules for humanity.

We will follow the thread of Hermetic wisdom or "stellar science," in order to discover the mysteries of love, asking the essential question we have been waiting for: What is love?

To understand the subject, all its possibilities will be covered:

Love as Universal Energy
Love as universal energy is a valid creative force in the cosmos. We will call it "Eros," the vital generating energy which is the essence of life and is what maintains the existence of everything in the universe.

Love as Telluric Energy
Love manifested as telluric energy is Eros which is specific to the planet Earth. We will call it "Human Eros." It is the force which produces the manifestation of love.

Love as a Primary Need
Love is a primary need of the human being. In fact, the impulse to be affectionate and loving toward other people and to receive love in return is an appetite incorporated in the collective unconscious from the remotest antiquity. This gregarious instinct gradually leads a person to appreciate and need emotional contact with others. People are born with a hunger to love and to be loved.

Love as a Sexual Need
Love as a sexual need of the human being is the natural result of the Human Eros itself. This telluric

energy is what provokes physical desire.

Love in a Relationship

Love in the form of the couple's relationship is the manifestation of Human Eros projected on the need of both sexes for complementation.

Love as a Romantic Fantasy

Love as a romantic fantasy is only the action of the "daydream phantom" or idealized image within the individual. When an individual abandons himself to illusions to comply with subconscious demands of the "daydream phantom," then love occurs as a romantic fantasy.

To reach an integral understanding of love as energy, one must recognize two basic and inalterable principles in the universe: life and death. Both correspond to concrete forces and not to abstract ideas. In psychoanalytic terms, Eros and Thanatos refer to the life and death impulses, respectively. These terms will be used here for they are well known, but with the provision that in Hermetic knowledge, the terms correspond to objective and subjective energies and not merely to psychological concepts.

Eros and Thanatos are physically concrete energies which operate throughout the whole universe. Cosmic Eros is the universal creating principle and Human Eros is that part of Cosmic Eros which acts on the person to give rise to diverse manifestations of love. Love is not only an abstract idea; it is also a concrete type of energy which is identifiable in the human being, even when science does not relate this kind of energy to love itself, and believes instead that love is only an abstraction. The force of love, is a particular type of magnetic energy operating in man with its center located in the spinal cord. Actually, rather than say "I love you with all my heart, " one should say "I love you with all my spinal cord!" The energy of love is a magnetic force from which the impulse to love relating to the emotions or feelings, rather than from thought, is born. The following diagram represents the Cosmic Eros and Human Eros, and displays their analogies:

FIGURE 4

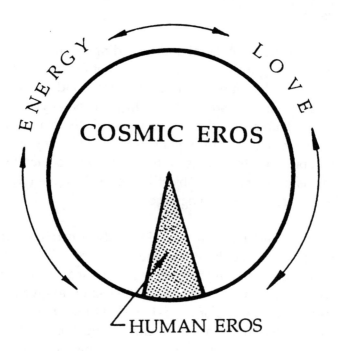

Erotic energy is only a part of the Cosmic Eros, which acts at the human level by producing the impulse to love. Sex and Eros are not the same thing, for the genital organs correspond only to one of the levels of manifestation of Human Eros, which expresses itself through the following levels. These levels can be seen as a spiral which grows smaller as it rises upwards, ascending from the sexual towards the spiritual.

1. Sexual
2. Emotional
3. Intellectual
4. Mental
5. Spiritual

These levels determine the differences in the quality of love and its degree of connection with an animal or truly human nature. For the moment, leaving aside the concept of false or true love, we will analyze the possibilities of union in the human couple. Within the spiral of love, there are different positions, as the examples below will show.

The majority of people of the human race who know only physical love are found at the base of this spiral and represent the first sexual level.

A bit further up the spiral, there are those who join emotion with physical sex and have a higher type of contact. They are on the second level.

Around the third level, couples communicate sexually, psychologically and intellectually with awakened inner awareness, which is quite rare. Couples whose relationships function solely at the intellectual level are not included in this level.

On the fourth level are the couples who are advanced Hermeticists and who have achieved integral communication in all aspects of the self, but who have not yet attained a profound spiritual communication.

Finally, at the fifth level, there are only highly evolved Hermetic couples who have achieved perfect spiritual and integral communication. The love of this type of couple is the relationship between two beings whose spirits manifest through their brains and whose relationship is therefore experienced in more elevated vibratory frequencies.

Each of these levels corresponds to a vibratory frequency which measures degrees of perfection in love and which can serve to specify how true or false the contact of those in love may be, from the point of view of "ideal perfection." (see figure 5)

These levels of expressions in love are also related to degrees of selfishness. The more sexual the relationship is, the more selfish and vice-versa, but one should not fall into the trap of defining false love as selfish and true love as altruistic. If there were a synonym for genuine love that revealed its true character, the term "consciousness" would be more apt, in the sense of being more aware, more judicious and wise. A more conscious individual naturally becomes less selfish, not because he is so programmed, but as a logical consequence of his elevated inner standards.

The five levels described above do not represent rigidly defined ranks but levels which actually overlap and touch each other because they symbolize degrees of expression. The second level, for example, does not begin at a point imagined as zero, but at the degree immediately above the one at which the first level finishes.

FIGURE 5

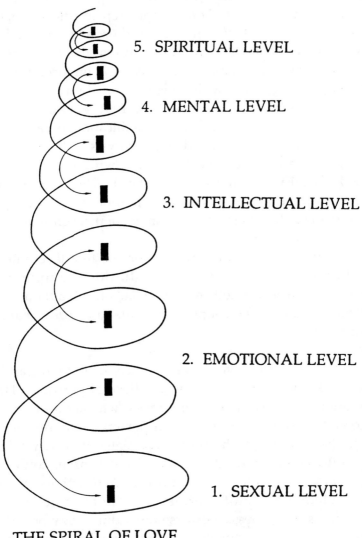

5. SPIRITUAL LEVEL

4. MENTAL LEVEL

3. INTELLECTUAL LEVEL

2. EMOTIONAL LEVEL

1. SEXUAL LEVEL

THE SPIRAL OF LOVE

If the first level were to finish at ten degrees, the first degree of the second level becomes eleven. All this helps us understand that there are gradations within each level and each one is equivalent to a greater or lesser elevation in the spiral. For example, replace the stages of the levels with divisions in numbered degrees; for example, level one goes from one to ten; level two from eleven to twenty-six, and so on. What is important is an understanding of the wide range of possibilities existing within each level. A couple at the first level cannot be assessed in a hurried qualitative classification, because the level is merely a basis for deeper analysis. There can be people with a healthy modality, and with an unhealthy modality all within the same first level. The same occurs up until the third level. This format applies to the couple and to the individual in an assessment of their growth.

What happens if a woman on the first level unites with a man on the third level? In this example, the situation tends to stabilize at the man's level, although in certain instances the couple may come to a sort of happy medium.

Within the love spiral, on each level, there can be found sexual, emotional, and intellectual persons. This location on the spiral does not reveal whether a person is good or bad because the sexual person of the first level may be good despite his instinctive center of gravity, while an intellectual individual, say on level three, could be perverse. A person's cultural training in the sense of knowledge and not morals, does not influence his goodness or badness. Perverse individuals may be either very ignorant or highly cultured, for knowledge in itself, is not specific, but is instead, neutral.

FIGURE 6

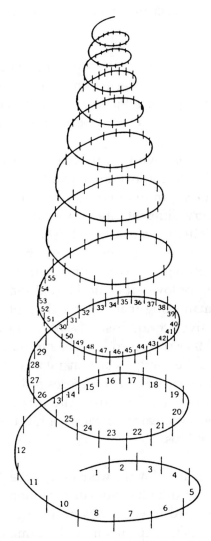

DEGREES ON THE SPIRAL OF LOVE

The same situation exists on the love spiral. It is neutral in itself, but it places people at different erotic levels, at greater or lesser vibratory frequencies, which makes individuals react in accordance with their internal development.

The neutral nature of the spiral disappears on the fourth level, because in order for the person to possess a mind, he must first practice the laws of universal harmony, which in their essence prevent any perverse or malign act.

The spiral of love reveals the secret of love. It explains that all types of love are equal from an energetic point of view, being motivated by one sole energy, but manifesting at very different vibratory levels. Any type of love, including fraternal, altruistic, Christian or maternal, is basically erotic love, because Eros is the driving force behind each, which impels one to create within particular planes of the manifestation of love. It could be said that there is no work of the human being that is not a child of love. Even the most destructive acts are basically inspired by this force, albeit in this instance corrupted in its manifestation. Love is the life force; it is the energy which maintains the metabolic and cellular processes; it is what imposes order on the laws of the entire universe. Thanatos, the force which only destroys in order to recreate new forms of life, is nothing but the counterpart of Eros.

A mediocre man loves a woman with the "same love" as an individual of a higher human condition. His erotic energy flows toward lower levels only because he lacks higher qualities. This explains how the same energy that gives a delinquent the impulse to steal, or impels a coarse person to enjoy being lecherous, also makes a Leonardo da Vinci rise to the heights of scientific, spiritual and artistic creativity. The only difference is that Da Vinci took advantage of Eros' generating power to rise on the erotic spiral. He carried out a sublimation which allowed him to create children, not children of the flesh, but children of the mind.

Creative or erotic energy is not sex, but is instead, the generating power which makes a person have sexuality. It is one more element in the ensemble which makes up physical life with all its biological and psychological processes: emotion, thought, intelligence, spirit, soul and consciousness. Part of this generating force is beyond the individual's will and is what maintains life, but a considerable portion flows through channels under the individual's direction, in accordance to his human quality. This force either elevates or debases the individual, depending on his actions.

Therefore, love is all of these things:
1. A primordial energy and creative force.
2. A type of relationship between a couple.
3. A type of relationship with the environment.
4. A need of the collective unconscious of humanity.
5. A particular situation in which the individual is placed in relation to the erotic spiral.

As far as the relationship between a couple in love is concerned, there are three possible situations:

1. Equilibrium
2. Imbalance
3. Perturbation

These points refer to the quantity and quality of the flow of energy in human beings during the sexual act, which is a phenomenon independent of the levels of love just described, and which generates, as a consequence, various possibilities of erotic communication in the couple.

Genuine love is the integral communication between persons of the opposite sex, who, by means of their contact, come to form an androgynous being in which they themselves are complemented, but in which each of the parties keeps his and her own identity and capacity for self-fulfillment. Emotions, instincts, thoughts and states of consciousness born of this union are not love, but are the children of love.

This reveals the secret of true love: love is not the fusion of both partners into a single being, but is their complementation to form a third individual, the androgynous being who is the mysterious child in which the couple are fused without either party losing his or her individuality. To achieve this, a couple has to attain perfect communication in the sexual, instinctive, emotional and intellectual spheres. Sexual communication does not mean only coitus, because if it did, any one who were not capable of coitus would lack this contact. Sex occurs on an energetic plane, as well as a physical one, through the sexual organs.

A couple who has reached higher fulfillment handles the creative force to generate and regenerate themselves constantly, thus avoiding magnetic stagnation. Their personal magnetic energies are renewed when they come together proportionately and harmoniously in the sexual act, in either a physical or energetic expression. This balanced type of intercourse may be symbolized in the following diagram which represents the proportionate flow of erotic energy through the sex, the heart and the intellect, bringing about an integral contact. The illustration shows how an energetic flux of one third of the total Eros energy is assigned to each of these channels.

FIGURE 7

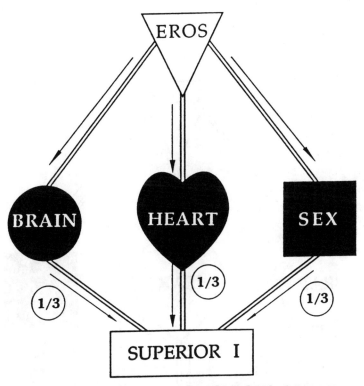

BALANCED OR HARMONIOUS COITUS

The following diagram, represents the imbalance caused by a disproportionate union where most of the erotic energy flows through the genital organs to the detriment of the emotional and intellectual sensitivity. In order to illustrate this example, an energetic flux of one third of the total Eros energy is assigned to each of these channels.

FIGURE 8

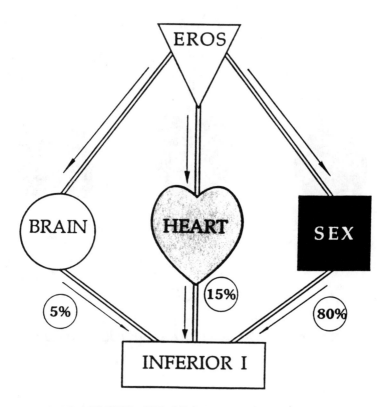

UNBALANCED OR UNHARMONIOUS COITUS

On the strength of the above explanations, it is clear there are two types of sexuality: one which is organic or physiological and one which is "invisible" or internal, whose true nature is magnetic and which refers to the flow of Human Eros within the individual.

Physiologically, the sexual act, which is explained in detail in many text books, always has the same mechanics. All people react in a similar way to physical sex. A simple physical examination of an individual is enough to know whether the person is male or female. Something very different occurs with magnetic or internal sexuality though, because an individual of the male sex may be, magnetically speaking, feminine, or vice-versa, depending on the vibration which the individual himself transmits to his magnetic field.

The quality of the organic sexual act is measured by the simple pleasure of coitus, in its psychological characteristics, its duration and simultaneous occurrence and depth of orgasm. There is, however, another unknown sexual act which unites physical coitus to "magnetic intercourse." It is from this integral act that true erotic fulfillment is derived; otherwise one would only experience momentary pleasure, followed by an inner void or malaise, a clear sign that an appropriate magnetic union had not taken place. Magnetic coitus in its higher modality is possible only for a few, because the product of a certain kind of learning is not acknowledged by the cultural legacy of humanity.

Just as there are characteristics pertinent to physical sexuality, such as the size of the penis or its capacity for erection in response to certain stimuli, there are also conditions which pertain to magnetic sexuality. Bear in mind that the sexual organs are permanent, that is, they are an invariable part of our anatomy and have their origin in our biological heritage. Magnetic sexuality is not inherited in the sense of quality; it only exists in a human being at a primitive level bearing a certain likeness to what is called "animal magnetism." The individual possesses Human Eros within, but in an undeveloped or larval state, capable only of animal reactions. We may say that there is a "magnetic sex in potential" in this condition; an invisible penis or vagina which are undeveloped and childlike in nature. This is why an individual, lacking a developed magnetic sexuality, exaggerates the importance of the physical, emphasizing the genitals, trying in vain to find fulfillment in love at the integral level, through sex at the purely animal level. The genitals, in fact, are animal. Magnetic sexuality, on the other hand, at a high level, is "human-spiritual."

This same point leads directly to the problem of "sexual sin." In fact, this fault lies only in the physical coupling without a higher magnetic presence. In purely physical coitus, there are also strong magnetic currents, but these are of low vibration, like those of animals. Highly developed "magnetic sex" is quite different and refers to magnetism produced by a higher state of consciousness in the individual which is pure, clean, uncontaminated and charged with a higher vibration. This force is powerfully polarized. Its gender is clearly defined, and is either totally masculine or perfectly feminine. This energy is the secret of the first attraction between the sexes. When "sex-appeal" is spoken of, it refers to the presence of a considerable magnetic force, which is not, however, necessarily superior from the point of view of consciousness.

Magnetic sexuality gives rise to a series of curious and interesting problems which will be discussed in later pages. For the moment, the previous explanations can be summarized in this way:

1. There are both physical sexuality and magnetic or "interior" sexuality.

2. Magnetic sexuality, which is not cultivated is unconscious and of a childlike and primitive nature, scantly defined and with a low vibratory quality.

3. Integral sexuality is composed of organic sex and fully cultivated and developed magnetic sex.

We can diagram the case of a disturbed love relationship, in which the erotic current flows through the wrong channels, provoking a series of disorders, such as the previously analyzed cases of hysteria. Figure 9 shows how the emotional center "sucks" all the erotic energy which comes to the sex, using it for its own stimulation. This may happen during the sexual act or regardless of it. In coitus, physical sexuality follows its normal course, but magnetic sexuality, if it is disturbed, bypasses the natural channels and reaches orgasm through the heart. This brings about masculine devirilization and a loss of femininity in the woman because the necessary ratio of energy is disrupted. Everyone has magnetic sexuality, but only those who have cultivated themselves Hermetically reach full maturity, elevation and development. This is the secret of true virility: magnetic sex saturated with the conscious energy produced by a higher evolution. True femininity also lies here.

A great number of the perversions of the libido are really diseases of a magnetic sexual nature and they can corrupt those who come in contact with it, because magnetism is something which is projected and penetrates into other people.

FIGURE 9

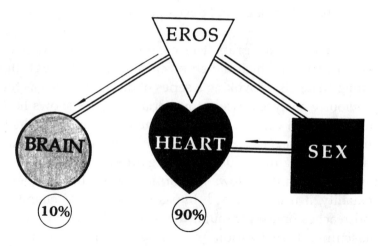

PERTURBED SEXUALITY

MAGNETIC RELATIONSHIPS

BETWEEN MEN AND WOMEN

All people possess magnetic sexuality, even though it may be in a primitive and uncultivated form. Genuine "magnetic coitus" is the integral sexual act, accomplished through both a physical and a magnetic exchange. People who lack knowledge of this can only achieve a primitive sort of "magnetic contact" between the sexes. This type of "primitive magnetic coitus" is merely an imitation and caricature of true magnetic union.

Primitive magnetic coitus has a certain similarity to an integral union. In both cases, there may be a magnetic sexual contact without knowing it and without any physical contact whatsoever. Only through bodily nearness, many men and women relate sexually.

A woman has a constant need of a man's magnetism, while he has a need of her physically. Magnetically speaking, a woman receives and the man gives. It is difficult for many to understand the meaning behind the word vamp in reference to a flirtatious sensual woman. She in reality absorbs masculine magnetism and is nourished and rejuvenated by it. The men who admire her do not realize that part of their personal magnetic charge has been taken away.

Not all magnetic exchanges however, are of a vampiric type. The exchange of magnetism is normal, and occurs even with two people of the same sex, though not always at a sexual level. Two men just shaking hands, meeting each other or spending time together, exchange magnetism of the same polarity. In this case the sexual exchange does not occur, but rather a manifestation that is similar to the counteracting of decomposing stagnant water, by analogy. Through this exchange of magnetism of the same polarity, the "stagnant waters" have circulated and have become "oxygenated" so to speak, renewing and rejuvenating the magnetism itself, provided there is a friendly harmony between the two and on the condition that they are people with healthy, balanced psyches, free of defects or negative magnetic charges.

A woman has a permanent need of masculine magnetism and her need fulfills the law of life in the Hermetic sense in that "life" is the clash between two magnetic forces of different polarity. A woman, whose magnetism is passive or feminine receives the active force of the male, which in turn generates new energy for itself when it meets its feminine counterpart. A man fulfills his need of the passive feminine force only through physical contact with women, because contrary to them, he can only absorb a tiny amount of magnetism directly, through physical proximity.

We will mention in passing that sexual contact for the man, when a condom is used, from the magnetic point of view, is simple masturbation, because he does not receive any kind of magnetism in this way. By contrast, the woman receives magnetism because she, as we have shown, does not necessarily need to be touched physically to absorb magnetism as she can absorb it simply by osmosis and just by being in close proximity. This should not discourage however, the use of a condom in cases of risk.

The damage caused by masturbation not only lies in the creation of "magnetic demons," but also in the fact that a great quantity of magnetism is expelled, which is irrecuperable and is the opposite result of normal coitus, in which equilibrium is produced. Onanism causes a strong drain of magnetic energy which causes an increase in the risk of contracting certain grave illnesses due to the weakening of the vital forces.

There are many disorders in those groups of women who for some reason or another are deprived of male company because women regularly need masculine magnetism. As women's nature is receptive and not projective, when they only share their magnetism without any exchange, all types of neurotic and hysterical disorders result. Their magnetism, as it lacks an active or positive stimulus, becomes stagnant and "dammed up." The oxygen their magnetism should have received (from masculine magnetism) has not had the chance to penetrate them. Due to this lack of masculine magnetism, small or large groups of women, isolated from men, exhibit intense rivalry amongst themselves which is latent even when they are good friends and esteem one another. Generally their unconscious antagonism is so great that it is difficult to keep harmony and cohesion and it is not uncommon for bitter quarrels to break out. By contrast, in male communities, apart from natural exceptions, companionship, mutual aid and a healthy competition prevail.

The aphorism which refers to women as "the apple of discord," is generally misinterpreted as male rivalry for a female, when in fact, the problem is actually one of magnetism. When there is a hunger for masculine magnetism and no supply, as happens in groups of women living together, a nervous imbalance is produced in which the women unconsciously try to effect a "masculine imitation." They bring to the surface their 25% male factor and become highly aggressive. On the contrary, men alone generally devote their efforts to telling smutty stories about real or made up sexual adventures and thus imaginatively replace the physical need for a woman. An interesting phenomenon occurs under the influence of alcohol. The part of the opposite sex which we all carry within us is stimulated. When women drink to excess, they become inordinately aggressive (masculine) and men become unusually sentimental (feminine) and often cry.

It is interesting to note what happens to a man who is the only masculine member in a group of women. In his day-to-day relationship with his companions, he experiences a gradual deterioration of his psychological virility or magnetic sexuality and will little by little become effeminate, indecisive, weak and irresolute. If this situation continues for long, the effects will become so accentuated that impotence could occur. In this case, the male has become the sole source of masculine magnetism among that group of women, who, due to their intrinsic need of the positive pole, absorb his magnetic force, leaving him empty and depleted.

This example becomes far more dramatic in the family environment when a married woman with a domineering nature has excessive control over her husband and male children. The problem begins almost inadvertently when the head of the family is shy or diffident and the woman is of a strong, commanding nature. She gradually begins to absorb her husband's magnetism and he becomes more and more effeminate and timid. His wife, on the other hand, becomes masculine, despotic and demanding, for the magnetic power she has pulled from her partner acts on her psyche in an unbalanced and exaggerated way.

Exactly the same thing happens to the male children of such a mother. If for some reason they are not especially resistant, they will develop a feminine character and may even become sexually deviant. This situation is far more serious when the father is missing, when one or more male children live with a widowed or divorced mother who bears the whole burden, mastery and control of the home, while she herself is also of a domineering nature. It is also true that there are other problems, such as the Oedipus Complex or fear of castration, which might have an influence in the devirilization of a man through other channels, causing him to assume a passive feminine role which makes him gradually discharge his active magnetism.

When an appropriate equilibrium exists between a man and a woman in marriage, the disorders mentioned do not arise. It is far more likely that both the couple and their offspring will develop harmoniously.

A woman depends on a man's magnetism and he on sexual possession of her. The feminine sex has a profound need for active magnetism. The male feels a powerful physiological urgency to possess a female and thus find an outlet for the force of the Human Eros accumulated within him. When this energy is repressed or stored too much, it may overflow and express itself in the form of emotional or imaginative morbidity or else through the devious channels of sadism and masochism. Chastity is much easier for a woman than for a man, for she constantly derives satisfaction from her receptive type of magnetic sex which is stimulated by the forces taken from the males around her. The same thing does not occur in men though, who are incapable of absorbing considerable amounts of magnetism without actual physical sexual contact. Celibacy is a hard deprivation for a man to bear because the erotic pressure gradually accumulates in him, reaching levels which can affect his nervous and hormonal equilibrium.

The human female subconsciously knows these phenomena, because they are the true origin of female coquetry. She tries to make herself as attractive as possible, dressing herself, making herself up and adorning herself as seductively as possible, not with the aim of trapping a husband or a man, but with the real aim of "catching" magnetism. In fact, the desire to be admired, not only hides the simple wish to keep up her self-esteem, but also the subconscious intention of absorbing masculine magnetism which she gets when she becomes the focus of male attention and admiration.

Some women are in fact "vamps" who seduce men with the sole aim of sucking their magnetism. On certain occasions, in a manifestly dramatic way, a man is left emotionally and psychologically drained and destroyed. This situation is made worse when the "vamp," seeing that the man is left inert and empty, immediately leaves him for he is no longer of any interest to her. It should be emphasized that a woman's longing for magnetism acts, in practice, in accord with her inner quality as a human being. If she is of an elevated human condition, she will never be a "destroyer of men." On the contrary, if she is ambitious, unscrupulous, materialistic and lacks higher feminine qualities, and if she is physically attractive, she could quite easily become a "man-eater." She does tremendous harm to herself by this behavior. If her main purpose in a relationship with a man is to take over his magnetism and his wallet, she debases the feminine archetype, the divine conceiving force of Nature. As a natural result of her behavior and not as a punishment, she will sooner or later have to pay in exchange for her covetousness. This type of woman "loses her soul." She must content herself with a poor substitute of a soul, made up of dispersed, patched or stained remnants of those forces which she has taken over. Here we come to the need to explain the mystery of the feminine soul, which will be done in the following pages.

Within the sphere of magnetic relationships between men and women, the phenomenon of magnetic polarities and their influence must be considered by analyzing the instinctive, psychic and cerebral polarities. Masculine and feminine qualities are expressed differently in the organs of each sex. In reference to the brain, for example, in women it is active and masculine, while in men, it is passive and feminine. Furthermore, women are feminine in the sexually instinctive sense, but they have a masculine polarity in their clitoris. Men are masculine in the sexual sense and have a feminine polarity in their prostrate gland. The heart of both men and women is androgynous, having the qualities of both sexes or polarities.

This key to the mysteries of a couple's relationship reveals why a man depends intellectually on his companion. The brain is the man's matrix and he remains intellectually barren until he receives a woman's psychic fertilization. This could be one of the reasons why, the knight always sought a lady to serve in the times of chivalry. The intent was that she be feminine and that she inspire the noble knight and adequately fecundate his intellectual matrix, making him fertile in the world of the mind. This dynamic also accounts for the seeming disparities observed in the artistic creations of certain poets and writers when they are, for some reason, separated from their previous partners and take up a relationship with another woman. The effect is sometimes so obvious that they completely lose the brilliant touch that had characterized their work before their separation from a particular woman. Afterwards, depending on the content of the new woman's brain, the man's work is reduced to a ritual act, not as far as culture and technical or professional training are concerned, but as far as quality, sensitivity, understanding and depth. Speaking hermetically, a man is not a creator in the world of the mind and needs to unite with a woman in order to create in that sphere. Conversely, a woman is not a creator in the instinctive realm and needs masculine power to become a creator in that sphere.

This explanation shows that there are many possibilities of generation between men and women, apart from the procreation of carnal children. This view gives a glimpse of the great importance of training a human couple who, in proportion to their possession of knowledge, harmony, human concern and quality, may generate sublime or destructive effects. The perfection of energy in a couple can either elevate each individual to heaven, cast him or her into hell or keep them indefinitely in the most insipid purgatory. Many men can never reach certain goals, for they lack the necessary support to apply their will power to the action of fulfillment. When Archimedes said "give me a means of support and I will raise the world," he was not referring to a physical phenomenon but to an esoteric Hermetic concept. The lever in this analogy is man's will and his means of support is the woman.

THE MYSTERY OF THE FEMININE SOUL

The ancient symbol of the Sphinx signifies caution and secrecy, therefore prudence dictates how much of the Hermetic secret of love can be revealed. It would not be appropriate to display Isis naked before those who do not value her. One may only catch a glimpse of her eternal and immortal beauty, the goal pursued by eternal "lovers of truth," philosophers of all time. Though her mantle be thin, Isis must remain veiled. Hermeticism's task is to lighten Isis's veil. In order to see her face to face, one must be a true Hermeticist, having passed through the arduous, painful and lengthy tests Nature demands of those who seek the naked truth.

From now on, we invoke the hidden guardians of the secrets of Nature to blind the sight of those who are unworthy, so that they may remain unaware of the essential knowledge transmitted in this book. They may only attain the empty and programmed understanding of the "word" and not the deeper, living meaning.

The great symbols of universal duality are always found in relation to the human being. Hermetic tradition sustains that "God does not exist beyond man." This cryptic statement does not negate a Higher Being, but, on the contrary, it gives Him a more rational and concrete

existence, an existence no less mystic on account of this
relation to the human being. To go fully into this subject, it
must be noted that everything in the universe exists in
pairs: masculine and feminine, active and passive, light and
darkness, life and death. Accordingly, the egg is the symbol
of woman, who is the passive conceiver of Nature, and the
sperm is the symbol of man who is the active principle of
Nature. Male and female are only halves of a whole,
contrarily similar, but not equal. As the Bible says, God
created Adam from dust, but Eve was not born in the same
way, because she was made from one of Adam's ribs, taken
out while he slept. In this simple and symbolic tale, part of
women's mystery is hidden for it may be inferred that man
and woman were created in different ways. In some way
Eve came from Adam himself. In this respect, the Bible
certainly does not refer to her corporal existence, but rather
to that of her soul. There have often been arguments about
whether a woman has a soul or not and great thinkers, such
as St. Augustine, had serious doubts about this issue.
Hermetic tradition, whose wisdom has existed since the
times of Atlantis and Lemuria, holds that a great mystery is
hidden behind this dilemma and we shall try to unveil it a
little.

The significant secret is the fact that there is a
transcendental difference between a virgin and a woman
who has already had her first sexual relationship. This
disparity is so great that the virgin, in fact, lacks a soul and
acquires it from the first man who possesses her sexually
and breaks her hymen. Before this event, the virgin has
only a collective soul, not an individual one. She possesses
a soul in common with all virgins, which is really the soul of
Nature embodied in her. The hymen is Nature's seal. It is
the protection which Nature has placed in her living
temple, the woman. When this seal is broken through
sexual initiation, life is given to a force which will remain

alive in her forever and that is her human soul. At first, she had only a primitive soul, formed from Nature's elemental substance.

A woman's soul will be of a higher or lesser nature, giving her either happiness or grief in life, depending on the quality of her first sexual union, because this event, to a large extent, determines her future destiny. It depends mainly on the level of evolution of her initiator and on the states of consciousness he experiences during coitus and on the delicacy or roughness of his advances. If a man possesses an inferior and passional nature, with his psychological center of gravity in his stomach and testicles, or if he is passive and feminine, or complex-ridden, a woman will most certainly receive a tremendously negative force which will lead her to an unhappy, ill-fated existence. In the course of her life, if she has sexual relationships with other men, she will not basically modify her original soul. She will only add new elements to it which are additions to the main nucleus of what she received at her initiation. As an example, if the first man was coarse, immoral or depraved, and the second a true saint, the influence of the second man will not be enough to wipe out the stamp of the former, which will be kept forever as the main element of the soul.

Sexual initiation is really the most crucial and decisive experience for a woman because it determines her happiness or unhappiness, her elevation or debasement. In addition, she will continue to be psychologically united to her initiator, even though she may never see him physically again. It cannot be otherwise, for she received her soul from him, just as the man received his from God. The virgin initiated by a man of higher development, who is consciously aware, positive, intelligent and balanced, will be receptive to all the elements needed to achieve a happy and prosperous life, apart from her own spiritual elevation.

It will surely be argued that this is a great injustice, because a woman is thus branded by her sexual initiation and should this experience be negative, it will prevent her future happiness. The intrinsic character of Nature is amoral, beyond good and evil and is basically indifferent to morality or immorality, because it is above these concepts. Nietzsche defined his own philosophy as "amoralism" and said that the "superman" could not keep to the conventional norms of morality. Moreover, human ethics only represent the norms of behavior considered acceptable to a certain society at a given historical moment. Nature, is infinite and eternal, beyond good and evil and keeps only to the fulfillment of the rules of the game set by the Creator. People suffer when they violate these rules. The most serious problem is that human beings have deviated from the path of spiritual evolution, and have replaced it with the frenzied search for pleasure and sensual comfort, which has made them forget the rules of the game, if ever they knew them. Such rules do not belong to the cultural records of humanity and can only be discovered through motivation, effort and personal desire.

Regardless of the individual quality of a woman, the positive or negative influence of the male who first possessed her, will prevail in her sexual initiation. The validity of this statement, whether it be fair or unfair, can be tested simply by personal observation. Grave danger is involved in a woman's first sexual contact, because at this moment, she is born into existence as a "human soul" and abandons her elemental realm. Her vestigial elemental soul, which is without any individuality, does not perish however, but is molded and adapted to the vibratory energetic schema given by the man. If the man is, for example, a pessimistic type, the woman's elemental soul is stamped with this impression, just as clearly as a photograph is developed from a negative.

What happens to a woman after her first sexual experience? How does she handle her relationships with the male sex in general? These questions lead us to other mysteries of Nature, such as the concept which symbolizes woman as the egg. Like the earth, she conceives all the "seeds" which penetrate her, whether they are good or bad, positive or negative. Mother Earth does not distinguish between poisonous and wholesome plants; she lets them both grow. Likewise, a woman is a true egg or magnetic uterus, which conceives all the seeds which penetrate her and which come from the active irradiation of a man. This is a great problem for the "huntress of magnetism," because she receives indiscriminately so many different types of vibrations that she loses her psychological identity completely. These vibrations are incorporated into her soul generating varied and complex emotional and psychological states.

The soul of a woman who lost her virginity is made up of three levels:

1. The elemental or collective level (Nature's original soul).
2. The human soul received from the first man.
3. The psycho-sexual vibratory emanations received from the masculine sex in general.

As Figure 10 illustrates, a woman can be visualized as a container or bowl. Imagine her as the bowl itself and the contents as the soul she was given by the first man in her life. Now imagine that the bowl has two different levels; the first, which corresponds to the soul received is sealed and therefore watertight in the bottom part.

FIGURE 10

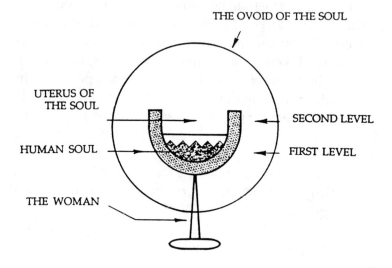

However, there is still a second level above this, open to the reception of new or future forces. This second level is protected by a magnetic circle or ovoid and is comprised of energies, which although powerfully influence the woman, do not modify her primordial content, but instead make her the bearer of ill-fated or fortuitous vibrations and events.

Sometimes, a woman transmits these forces to those men with whom she unites sexually, transmitting positive or negative vibrations which came from the men with whom she had intercourse in the recent or distant past. This is the reason why a woman's soul is so complex and variable and why it is so difficult for a man to understand. The truth is that she herself feels sudden impulses to do things which she does not really want to do, or else, she experiences negative emotional states without knowing where they come from. They come from the forces which she receives in her "bowl," in her magnetic uterus and also from the men who have looked at her with desire or admiration.

There are some women whose contents may have become contaminated and corrupt through the fault of certain men, to the extent that those men changed those women's true natures into "garbage containers." There are still others who contain only positive forces. This situation does not only depend on what is received, but mainly on what is accepted or allowed to enter. The magnetic ovoid of a woman's soul, which is the protective lid to the bowl, is only opened when something intimate in her feels attracted to the force trying to penetrate her. In this way she either accepts or rejects this force, depending on her degree of inner evolution, spiritual elevation and psychological equilibrium. A woman may be pure at the age of sixty, even after having lived through many experiences, or alternatively, she may be contaminated and perverse at the age of fourteen. It is the force of her spiritual quality, her inner ancestry, which can save her from a negative initial sexual union, even though she may be young and inexperienced. This quality is a mixture of what she has inherited from her parents, her education, her own effort, sense of responsibility and personal concern.

Truly intelligent people will understand that the feminine sex is the bearer of the karma of humanity, that is the bearer of the causes which later, when they are transmitted to men, will show themselves in concrete effects. A woman mentalizes the man in her brain and he carries out everything that she transmits to him from the contents of her bowl. The destiny of the world is not in the hands of men, but is truly in the hands of women. There is only one way to better the spiritual and human condition of *homo sapiens* and that is by recognizing and giving back to women the place which really belongs to them as "Mothers of the World." To be worthy of this dignity however, women must first free themselves of the chains of mens' macho behavior, which is but the expression of man's spiritual and virile impotence. Women must achieve equality with them and shoulder their responsibility as conceivers of a better world. This is true, higher maternity and is a different option to the procreation of flesh and blood children. Women's power to conceive has been castrated by the codes of behavior which society imposes on them and by the rigid, hypocritical morals which oblige them to constantly and neurotically repress their libido, as if "sublimation" was not an option. Morals need urgent reinforcing, not in a repressive way, but in a way that comes from individual's inner awareness in response to what is inappropriate, by terminating all the hypocritical moral norms which make lying and deceit necessary and by replacing them with a greater openness and clarity in people's lives.

It seems that certain insidious currents exist that have a vested interest in keeping women in an inferior position at all costs, without giving them the chance to rise to the same level as men in their intellectual training, individual liberties and responsibilities. There seems to be a special wish to keep women subjugated and thus to prevent any chances of creating a better world. There are groups which would no doubt be harmed in a world with less selfishness, more spirituality and more fraternity.

It is commonly thought that it is men who rule in life. On the contrary though, a man carries out a woman's mental orders, because she causes him to conceive with her masculine brain. She plays his game though, and helps to keep up the illusion that it is he who has the power, but things have gone so far that the right hand no longer knows what the left hand is doing. A woman has become so divided into two clearly defined halves that she herself does not know which half she belongs to: the half that submits to the male and who obeys him, which is the outward appearance, or the inner half who, out of a desire for rebellion, insensitively dominates a man without him realizing it. Simultaneously, she keeps up an appearance of obeying him. One has to wonder if a man's decisions are his own or if they are born of the female brain. Based on this scenario, it is questionable if a man's decisions are his own or if they are born in the female brain. Of major concern is the need to end the fiction of male superiority and for men to drop their chauvinistic attitudes. Women must abandon their feigned condition of defenseless adolescents. If women really have the same rights as men and are educated to truly develop their intelligence fully and diverse skills and not just their biological ability to bear children, there will be a chance to instruct them in the correct use of their mental and conceiving powers, so that they may thus assume their role as creators of a better world. Otherwise, trapped in the roles of "female bearers of children" women will always be kept from the higher works of the spirit and intelligence. It is understandable that if women are educated as a type of "wet-nurse," their first concern will be marriage since they are educated to have children. For this same reason, they have neither the opportunity nor the wish to develop themselves in other fields of human endeavor which would considerably widen their inner world. Women's capacity to conceive has been diminished to mere procreation and they are also kept ignorant of the fact that they can fulfill themselves through a wide range of possibilities which go far beyond what a profession or artistic skill can offer.

Of course, there are many women who have not chosen the role of motherhood and who have become outstanding professionals, artists, or leaders of various causes. However, an equal or greater danger exists for the intellectual woman more so than that of the mere conceiver of children. The danger is the gradual distancing and eventual withdrawal of her own femininity, as she is driven by the urge to compete with the masculine sex on equal ground. One can observe a great percentage of women who have a highly developed intelligence, who have allowed their femininity to atrophy because they do not know how to maintain their inner equilibrium. To illustrate this problem, there are two contrasting types of women:

1.   The instinctive or "uterine woman."
2.   The intellectual woman.

An instinctive woman is one whose motivational center of gravity is not in her brain, but in her womb. Incapable of intelligently analyzing diverse situations, she reacts passionally like an animal; she is a slave to her instinctive impulses. The intellectual woman, on the contrary, analyzes everything and shapes her behavior accordingly because her thoughts are more powerful than her inferior impulses. She may however, often react to people and situations in an insensitive and unfeminine way.

FIGURE 11

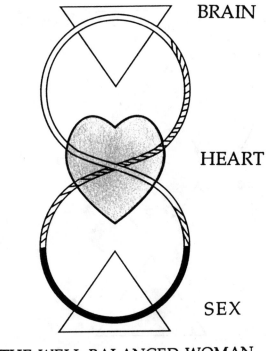

BRAIN

HEART

SEX

THE WELL-BALANCED WOMAN

FIGURE 12

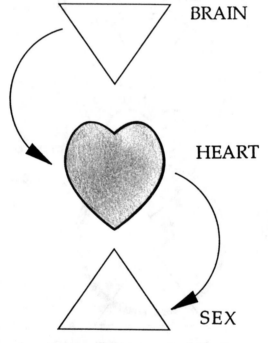

THE INSTINCTIVE WOMAN

FIGURE 13

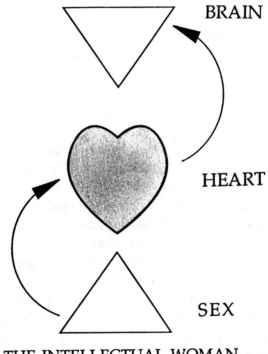

THE INTELLECTUAL WOMAN

There is a third type, which may be called a "balanced woman," who consciously uses her heart to strike a balance between her instinct, her emotion and her intellect. Her esoteric symbol is the number 8, which denotes that the intellectual and instinctive currents cross and regulate each other in the middle, in her heart. The balanced woman is not at all uninterested in maternity, because if she wishes to be a mother, she simply does so freely as one of her means of self-fulfillment. If she does not wish to, she will focus her power to conceive in the world of philosophy, art and science, education or other areas of expression. Correct development of emotional sensitivity, self-control and dominion, are what allow a woman to become an integral being who can transcend the instinctive forces of Nature which circulate in her interior.

It is of extreme importance to understand that woman is the primordial cause of a family's happiness or misfortune, as well as that of different countries and of the world at large. She projects her emotional states through her own brain from which she fertilizes a man's brain in a positive or negative way, depending on the quality of the vital and imaginative states in herself. The type of woman already referred to, who always puts economic interests before love, has an inner life of very low vibration and is ruled exclusively by "animal" selfishness. She also makes a man conceive selfish thoughts, materialistic behavior, insensitivity, harshness and inhumanity, thus laying one more brick in the building of a selfish, violent and corrupt humanity.

Women do not realize that, because they are like the earth, whatever they conceive or project will also return to them. In fact, the individual whose thoughts are fertilized by the inferior thoughts of a woman, will inevitably turn against her in due time with the same selfishness and lack of love he received. A woman makes a man conceive, but receives something equivalent from him in return. This is the reason why women, who sell their bodies to one or several men, must in exchange pay the price of being considered an object or a "thing" which can easily be discarded or replaced. On the contrary, a woman who gives love to the man worthy of it will always be loved in return. The exception to the rule is the woman who gives herself to a man of low human quality, who will trap her in the sensual world of inferior passions without giving her love of any kind whatsoever.

Attentive readers who know how to read between the lines and go beyond simple literal interpretation will discover in these explanations profound mysteries of human existence. They will grasp the secret of happiness in love, unless they have closed or inflexible minds or are caught up in strict religious or cultural programming. In this case, they will understand nothing at all. Those who blindly discount everything they cannot understand, will not comprehend what this work intends. As with all our other works in the series, this book may be a door for some leading to something of supreme value, or else a threshold to nothing.

THE MYSTERY OF KARMA

The last chapter pointed out that the woman is the bearer of karma, the bearer of the vibrations deposited in her not only by men who have possessed her sexually, but by all those who have looked at her with a sensual desire. Contained in her bowl are not only the vibrations of healthy admiration decent men may have felt for her, but also the lecherous vibrations of the men who felt disturbed or distorted impulses toward her. In her state of "taker" of masculine magnetism, she may easily be defiled if her inner morality is not sufficiently solid and if she does not possess integrity. It does not matter how attractive and clean a woman may appear on the outside. What really counts is the inner beauty and purity of her soul inside. Qualitatively, a woman is what her soul exudes. Normally, one only sees the outer wrapping of a woman and is totally unaware of her content, which could be either positive or negative. In fact, what madness would move a person to drink from a bowl without knowing what it contained? A bowl that we drink from may be very beautiful but may perhaps be filled with poison. Of course, as far as the woman is concerned, this happens unconsciously, without any malice on her part. It is well known that there are women who bring bad luck and others who bring about all kinds of positive and happy events. This depends on the contents of her "bowl," in other words, on the karma which her vessel contains. When a man unites sexually with a woman, he never knows if he will receive the kiss of death and failure or the breath of life and success. As a consequence of a woman's intercession, a man receives the seeds he conceives, which later bear their fruit in the form of actions or material creations. Women are the generating minds and men, the hands which carry out material creation. Women rule in the world of the mind, and men in the world of matter.

When a positive woman has been married for a long time to a highly positive and prosperous man, and he suddenly dies, she may often later remarry. If so, one can verify how the new husband, although he seems to have been an unlucky or negative person, undergoes a surprising transformation, becoming little by little more forceful and more positive, until he gains a status similar to his wife's former husband. The first husband was really the one who had deposited a higher positive vibration in her "bowl." The opposite case is also quite common however. There are women who do, in fact, transmit "bad luck" and even "fatality" to their men, such as certain women who have been left widows for the fourth or fifth time, all of their husbands having died violent deaths.

The negative forces which a man transmits to a woman are not in the form of karma, but are in the form of vibrations which penetrate into her as a sperm into an egg, leaving her defiled, purified or simply unchanged. The possible harm a man may do to a woman is of a different nature, for it mainly involves her soul, contrary to a woman's action whose aim is mainly directed toward the material sphere. A vicious or negative man degrades a woman; a negative woman destroys a man materially.

The real importance placed upon a woman's virginity at marriage does not lie in the physical fact that she offers a hymen to be broken, but that she does not thus bring any negative karma to the union. For a male, this means the certainty of not having to bear the destructive karma of other men.

It is interesting to analyze what happens in prostitution. A prostitute receives the magnetism of many different men, who use her really as a sort of waste-bin to unleash their lowest, coarse and morbid impulses. Receiving so many vibrations, her soul is made up of myriad facets, to the point that she has no individuality, a feature ever visible to others' eyes, however well-groomed she may be. The prostitute has fallen very low on the human scale, but there is also hope of a way out when in certain instances, she is freed by a man who falls in love with her. By a kind of miracle of Nature, love redeems her to the point of enabling her to help her lover to better himself economically. She has fallen so low that she has "reached the bottom" and now with a companion who gives her his love, she cannot do otherwise, but raise herself up. Another mystery of love is the fact that a man has the power to raise a woman spiritually, but that a woman utterly lacks the power to redeem a wayward individual who, except in rare instances, will remain as is. He will merely exploit his companion emotionally and materially and she will waste her whole life bent on the chimera of his salvation. *A woman can only influence a man's material life, but not his instinctive one.*

There is also another type of woman, who has fallen even lower than the prostitute on the human scale. She is the one who has been led by a surplus of luxury and comfort and who has perverted her sexuality by fervently seeking new sensations because the abundance in which she has lived, has led her to sensual exhaustion after having tried out to excess, all possibilities of pleasure. This is how she can become corrupt enough to carry out acts against morality, and go to any extreme in her aim to revive her exhausted sensuality.

At the other extreme of femininity lies the example of noble and patriotic women who have become mythological figures in the history of their countries and have elevated their libidos on the wings of humanitarian and unselfish ideals. These women occupy an important place as representatives of the higher feminine conceiving power.

In antiquity, there are examples of civilizations with broad philosophical knowledge, such as the ancient Greeks, who used prostitution in a higher way, with the exclusive purpose of raising the conceptual and spiritual levels of its citizens. There were women in certain temples who had been specially trained to be "high priestesses of love." They had to be highly cultured, refined and had to master the technique of one or several musical instruments, as well as possess philosophical and artistic knowledge. They lived in a building adjoining the temple and undertook to sexually satisfy travellers or those who sought their company. This type of sexual exchange however, was free of any animal, coarse or pornographic nature, such as that displayed today by sexual commerce. On the contrary, making love was considered to be a sacred act, a chance to unite with divinity. The art of these priestesses lay in directing all manner of erotic and sexual relationships to higher levels. They never had intercourse without first reaching a psychological and sentimental rapport, all surrounded by the greatest delicacy, elevation and refinement. This type of relationship was not kept to the mere erotic, either, for the priestess questioned her transitory companion on the circumstances, duties and problems of his life. She advised him in everything for which she was properly trained and conversed with him on art, science and philosophy. Through this practice, Greek civilization reached the levels which continue to echo today. All solar civilizations and cultures have known these secrets, and from there came, for example, the mystery of the "sun virgins," priestesses who were not intended for the practice of higher love, but who were to act under the control and direction of the forces of Nature. In traditional Japanese culture, geishas have also occupied an important place in guarding certain spiritual norms, a role which western man has never been able to understand. Great civilizations such as those of Greece and Egypt decayed when their spiritual and political guides lost the magic keys which tradition had bequeathed to them.

Today, no spiritual or psychological discipline which has the purpose of improving the human species, is currently being taught and practiced. There exists only the concern for feeding a·child properly and offering him an appropriate emotional environment for his upbringing and development. There exists no special discipline for pregnant women to practice, even though this period is the time when the foundations of the child's psyche are being laid. In fact, all vital and nervous states experienced by the mother during pregnancy later shape the child's emotional nature. This is how parents pass on their own karma to their children ignorantly and irresponsibly. A couple almost never thinks of what they have to offer their child, apart from their own pride, expectation and satisfaction as parents. There is a Biblical maxim which states that "the sins of the fathers shall be visited upon their children." Its cryptic message explains how during the act of fertilization or generation, the spirit of the individual to be born, penetrates through the crown of the father's head and runs through his cerebral ridges and spinal cord to enter the mother's womb. On this journey, the spirit collects all the intellectual and spiritual influences it will receive from the father, incorporating into itself an extract of his psychological conditioning. Later, during the pregnancy, the child-to-be receives its mother's influences. Because of this, she should live through these nine months in a purer, more elevated, peaceful and relaxed way, so that she can imprint the highest emotional states upon her offspring. If the mother has a happy and peaceful pregnancy, constantly surrounded by the positive, harmonious influences of good music or the contemplation of beauty in any form, her child will receive their beneficial influences and will develop in a higher way.

It is important for people to become aware of the indispensable need to withhold all sexual activity during pregnancy, because the high potential of psycho-sexual discharge which occurs during this activity, irreparably harms the fetus' delicate nervous system and later shows itself in the form of various nervous disorders and upsets in adulthood. Usually, out of ignorance and lack of knowledge of these facts, none of these precautions are taken. There is a remarkable carelessness regarding the activities and emotional states of the mother-to-be and coitus, for example, is not stopped until right up to the last months of pregnancy. In such cases, a strong negative karma is often transmitted by the parents to the child which is something like a Biblical curse, and will pursue the child throughout his life unless, in certain exceptional cases, he can manage to acquire the necessary knowledge to neutralize this negative inheritance.

The first thing a couple should ask themselves before they decide to have a child is: "What can we offer a child? What kind of psychic inheritance will we give a child? Can we educate a child positively?" At the Hermetic level, the question to be asked is this: "What type of karma will we give to our offspring?"

"Karma" is the oriental name given to the law of cause and effect, an expression which is used often and is quite well known. The relationship between cause and effect must be understood, for everything is governed by causality. A person's karma is the ensemble of causes pending in his life, which will inevitably show themselves in lucky or unlucky effects within natural lapses of time. Through the mystery of karma, it is possible to understand how an individual sets various causes in motion; and how these causes accumulate, joining those of other members of his family and then, those of his village, city, and country and then form a collective karma which can lead to destruction and war or to prosperity and peace. Fatality could be interpreted as the inevitable harvest of a cause set in motion by the individual himself and free will as the liberty to generate new causes.

Since children have been mentioned, the time is appropriate to point out the need to eliminate, for all time, the myth that children love their parents to the same degree that their parents love them. The truth is that children do not learn to love their parents until they become adults. Before adulthood, they merely need their parents. All the enchanting gestures which parents observe in their offspring and interpret as displays of love, are no more than the child's attempts to manipulate them in order to get what he is used to having from them or what he wishes to get. A child learns to behave affectionately towards his mother as the most effective way of being able to count upon his mother's attention. He imitates the attitudes of his parents because by doing so, he discovers that he not only keeps alive the stimulus he has received, but can also get extra "rewards." Only when a person reaches maturity, does he learn to genuinely love his parents. Before this, he merely puts up with them as something necessary. One of the greatest errors committed in the education of a child is when a couple, blinded by self-adoration through the mirror of a biological form born of their own flesh (the child), mistakenly believe that their child loves them for who they are. What the child really does is echo their pampering. Parents sometimes experience tremendous disappointment due to this erroneous belief. Parents should not expect too much from their children and should maintain this point of reference as they provide their children a proper upbringing, which will help them to shoulder their own social responsibility.

This view of children brings to mind the comment made by Fromm in relation to the difference between true and false love, when he says, "I love you because I need you" (false love) or, "I need you because I love you" (true love).

Bear in mind that parental love is seldom free from selfishness. Parent's affection for their children, especially in the first years, is generally a matter of loving themselves through their offspring.

Finally, the cycles of "bad luck" generated in marriages through quarrels must be mentioned. Any quarrel which goes beyond a certain limit and becomes a real emotional, intellectual or verbal aggression, sets in motion negative causes which sooner or later will certainly bring about unfortunate events, illnesses, economic problems, obstacles, frustrations and failures. The clash of psycho-sexual energy between a man and a woman always gives rise to "energetic children," products of the couple's primitive and uncultured magnetic sex, these energetic children being forces which vibrate around them with tremendous discordant energy and negatively influencing their destiny. An intelligent couple will take great care not to fall into destructive confrontations which generate

"demoniac" offspring, who will later keep feeding on
their parents' energy. With this type of discord, fate will
often show itself in certain persons' lives in the form of
true "strokes of bad luck," which are the effects of the
negative causes generated by the couple.

Another problem is the disastrous habit some
women have of addressing insulting or undermining
remarks to, or about their husbands. Since they are
creators in the world of the mind and the word, they are
poisoning their husband's brains with negative seeds,
which in time will in fact reduce them, in this form of
negative witchcraft, to the level of timorous, inhibited,
failed and destroyed creatures. Of course, Nature's
reaction cannot be held back and this type of woman
soon reaps the same for herself. What she projects
through her force brings her equivalent illness, grief,
disillusionment or frustration. One reaps what one sows.
How often have we heard a woman complain about her
husband, saying that he is a failure, a good for nothing, a
fool, when in fact she is driven by jealousy, hurt pride or
overriding ambition? Such a woman does not know that
not only is she making success impossible for her
husband, but she is also accumulating a tremendously
negative karma which will sooner or later come down
upon her own head.

Something similar happens to the type of
chauvinistic man who, in an attack of anger against his
wife, covers her with abuse. Despite the fact that a man
does not create in the world of the word and in the mind,
he acts instinctively and therefore sends poisonous
energies into his companion's energy field (bowl), thus
dirtying and debasing her energy. Such a man is also
unaware that by this type of behavior he is setting
himself up against Nature and that life may become very

painful for him. Even more serious is the act of physically abusing one's wife, for the only reward one can get from this, is to make oneself a slave of Nature, a toy of the tide of life with no chance at all of reaching a higher destiny.

FURTHER DIMENSIONS

OF THE NATURE OF LOVE

Unless people learn what true love is, they will continually commit new and lamentable errors without realizing it. They will only be able to learn the true nature of love by comprehending its rules, defined in the most precise way.

There are three basic points for discussion concerning the issue of the nature of love:

1. Is human love a purely subjective phenomenon in which an individual projects an emotional crystallization onto the lover, or is it perhaps an emotional state in which the qualities and values of the loved one are revealed?

2. Is love founded on a psycho-physiological structure or a purely physiological one? Is it founded exclusively on sexual desire, as Freud believed? Does love exist independently of organic processes, particularly where love may be incompatible with them?

3. Is love an inalterable process based on the nature of the human being himself, or is it a purely human invention which arose at a certain moment of history, perhaps as a result of literary creation?

The answers to these questions are sometimes far simpler than might be imagined. In their desire to know the truth, men are not primarily concerned with training their minds. As a result, rather than solving problems, people often infinitely complicate matters. They are not satisfied with simple solutions, because all knowledge which is not highly complex, is often underestimated. In fact, the more difficult and convoluted a concept is, the greater the guarantee of authenticity it acquires in the eyes of the masses, who mistakenly identify extreme complexity with truth. Truth is always simple and should be presented in terms that are within the grasp of the average intelligent person. Paradoxically, the simpler the language used to describe certain phenomena, the harder it is for scientists to understand what is said, as if simple words were really a sort of cryptic system, designed more to conceal than to reveal.

These questions on love will be answered in simple language, but first it must be repeated that wisdom is not the product of heated debate or the result of exhaustive studies in specialized texts. Wisdom is simply the corollary to Hermetic discipline which allows one to "read the open book of Nature" with the proper effort and at the proper time. Hermeticism is not a static science, passed on from mouth to mouth, in which the instructor merely repeats what he has heard from another. This knowledge is creative and dynamic, for it constantly renews itself and remains the same only in its basic or fundamental codes. Every genuine Hermetic master is autonomous and transmits the knowledge he himself has acquired. This teaching must be evaluated within the historical and social context to which it belongs, in which each respective master works on a path consistent with the aims he has set for himself.

The discussion on love will continue in the form of a series of questions and answers on its origin and nature:

What Is Love?

Love is the universal magnetic energy. The universal principle of creation is called Cosmic Eros and the part of the Cosmic Eros which acts on the human being, to produce the force of love in a couple, is called Human Eros. Love is not an abstract idea. It is a concrete energy which, when it manifests itself in the human being, makes him behave in a certain way, driving him to mate either for reproduction or for the pleasure in union with a person of the opposite sex.

Is Love a Sentiment?

Love is not a sentiment. It is the potential of the primordial principle of life which flows through different channels, including the feeling of empathy toward certain people, sympathy, tolerance and good will toward one's fellows and extreme identification with a person of the opposite sex. Love in itself is not a sentiment, yet sentiment in turn is produced by love. Attraction and repulsion, sympathy or hate, all are products of love.

Are There Several Kinds of Love?

Love as a force is unique, but may be demonstrated in several ways depending on an individual's free choice. Love has different levels of manifestation and exteriorization, and many means of fulfillment.

Is Love the Same as Sex?

Love is not sex, but sex is one of the manifestations of love. Human Eros can flow through the following levels, from the most physical to the most subtle:
1. Genital expression
2. Higher sentiments of sympathy for individuals of opposite sex

3. Fraternal, filial and paternal love
4. Sublimated love which leads to higher manifestations
    of spiritual, philosophical, intellectual or artistic
    expressions

Is Love a Biological Need?

Love is a biological need because it is the pressure
of life which drives the individual, in accordance with
his human quality, to focus this force on simple sexual
pleasure, reproduction or higher forms of self-
fulfillment.

Are There People Who Do Not Love?

All human beings love, even those who appear to
live for hate; for in truth, what they do is distort the
primordial energy of Human Eros, according to their
individual free choice.

Is Love Good or Bad?

Love in itself is neither good nor bad. Love is
basically pure energy and it is non-specific. It is the
human being who focuses the energy of love on
goodness, creativity and fraternity or on hate, fanaticism
and destruction.

Does Love at First Sight Exist?

Love at first sight is simply a type of love energy
which provokes a magnetic attraction. It does not mean
that a true love relationship between two people exists.
True love is always the product of a conscious and
directed process, never the result of a first contact.

Is Love Located Physiologically?

Love is located in the spinal cord and from there the
flow of energy is produced which later reaches one or
another of its possible ways of fulfillment.

Do Animals Feel Love?

Animals, like vegetables, minerals, planets, stars, and galaxies, feel love, as they were born of love, live for love and die for love.

What Is the Purpose of Love?

To create and maintain life.

Is There a True and a False Love?

With the energy of love, there is only one category in the whole universe. With couples, there are many degrees of love from the lowest to the most perfect. False love takes the most imperfect form of union and communication between man and woman. True love represents a form of higher union for a couple, producing a balanced and harmonious relationship, which entails an integral experience for the individual.

How Can One Distinguish between True and False Love?

True and false love do not represent absolute degrees, but are relative degrees of growth and perfected development in a human being. In corrupt love, the quality of falseness is based on a distancing, distortion or perversion of natural principles. Generally, love is true when a couple feels deep affection for each other, when there is a total absence of hypocrisy, when the lovers have no need to lie because they fear each other. Love is true when, despite their profound union and communication, each person preserves the liberty to fulfill oneself as an individual. When a couple can be separated for a long time without ceasing to love each other, when they "need each other because they love each other" and not when they "love each other because they need each other," then love is true. In true love a couple shares responsibilities for themselves and for the other. True love is the higher flux of the Human Eros. False love is the same Human Eros flowing through the expression of inferior passions such as sexual abandon, jealousy, vanity, hypocrisy, deceit and irresponsibility.

Should Love Be Selfish or Altruistic?

True love is altruistic, while false love has an intrinsic nature of pure selfishness, which uses the other for self-gain and pleasure. In selfish, false love, the main ingredient is jealousy, a sort of "psychological cannibalism," which one of the parties develops at the expense of the other. However, altruism should be rational, conscious and controlled. It must not fall into the opposite extreme of harming oneself to please a lover of low quality who lacks personal merit. The altruism we speak of must be practiced by both parties. For its part, selfishness is more closely related to sexual possession than to love.

Is Hate the Opposite of Love?

No. The opposite of love is death, because love is the primordial energy of life. Hate is the opposite of feeling affection or fondness for a person and is only one of the many manifestations of love.

These simple questions and short answers are meant to offer a basic orientation to certain classical questions on love. The rest of this work will considerably broaden the knowledge contained in the answers above.

The "love spiral" is a depiction of the Cosmic Eros, relative to the magnetism associated with the earth and the atmosphere surrounding it. This telluric magnetic field is the Human Eros, or the record of inferior and superior vibrations which all human beings generate and project through their instincts, feelings, thoughts, passions and actions.

The Cosmic Eros is pure and non-specific, while Human Eros is shaped by man. This magnetism has the same properties as a photographic film, though instead of printing images, it stamps vibrations. In the magnetic field of the earth, all man's experiences are stamped. It is the storehouse of the vibrations of humanity since man first appeared on the planet. An immense range of vibrations lies there like a gigantic keyboard that goes from the lowest tones to the sharpest or highest. The human being constantly contacts this storehouse, connecting with the lowest and most destructive tones, or with the sublime ones, depending on his or her emotional and interior state, because these two vital centers act like electrical adapters. If the individual is depressed, the lower frequencies are open to him; if he is in a highly positive mood, he connects with the highest. In this magnetic storehouse, there are thousands or millions of stories of the dramas of people's loves, which are acted out according to their own love patterns, but whose themes have generally been taken from two main sources:

1. From films, poetry, romantic literature, love stories and the imitations of living models.

2. From the magnetic records: everything that has been, is and will be, is recorded in these magnetic records and stored for all eternity.

We live submerged in a sea of magnetism, saturated with an enormous amount of different vibrations, which in turn are constantly captured by people, whose degree of giving in to or submitting to these forces depends solely on the strength or weakness of their own Ego. The lowest and most morbid passions are often unleashed when a person unwittingly contacts a decomposed, corrupt or depraved focus of magnetism, which will lead to aberrations. This accounts for the origin of emotional contagion in the masses. An example of this phenomenon is often experienced when a wave of panic is unleashed, sweeping in its wake all weak wills which lack a stabilizing force of their own. Thus, epidemics of violence, religious mysticism, fervent patriotism or revolutionary vehemence are generated. When there is an environment of negative magnetism, most contagious illnesses are incubated and spread, because disease is bred more by magnetism than by viruses or bacterium. Explaining magnetism in this way, helps one to understand the healing process of "laying on of hands." The healer transmits his own energy to the sick person, and when possible, neutralizes the corresponding disorder. The action of the mythological figure of Cupid, who "pierces the lovers with his arrow," can be explained as a magnetic irradiation coming from one individual who fascinates another, or rather as Human Eros which captivates both, causing a strong, mutual attraction.

Magnetic energy is the decisive factor not only in love, but also in the mutual sympathy or antipathy between people. There are people for whom we feel an almost instantaneous profound aversion upon meeting them. This happens when the vibrations of their magnetic fields are not in harmony with our own. Each individual possesses his own magnetic irradiation, an energy which comes from what an individual absorbs from the Human Eros. In addition, the body also makes its own magnetic force which combines with that of the earth in such a way that each individual has a particular magnetic quality. This particular magnetic quality is defined by the individual's degree of consciousness attained, human quality, knowledge and evolution. Therefore, the higher a man's level of consciousness, the more accelerated the vibratory frequency of his magnetic field.

The magnetic field of the Hermeticist, who is an highly evolved individual, is formed from the following materials:

1. From the Human Eros, whose vibration is speeded up through an awareness of this force.

2. From personal magnetism generated by the individual himself.

3. From a combination of the above two forces.

As a result the Human Eros and personal magnetism make up the magnetic ovoid of the Hermeticist and this configuration in turn makes up his field of force and his sexual magnetism.

To a certain extent, it is possible to know how evolved a person is and to classify his vibratory condition merely by tuning into his magnetism and intuitively analyzing it. Magnetism accounts for the way the planets influence our destiny because the earth is constantly bombarded by cosmic rays which carry a magnetic influence, which in turn is transmitted to individuals, causing specific effects.

A group of people gathered together in the same place radiate a collective magnetism formed from the joining together of separate vibrations, the sum of each individual's contribution. If we come into contact with one of these groups' vibrations, we immediately receive a high energetic impact of a positive or negative quality, according to the quality of that group's magnetism. Magnetism is not only projected, but also penetrates into solid bodies and stays there as a permanent element. For this reason, there are places where we feel an indescribable sadness or intense depression, which is the product of negative vibrations acting there. People who frequent clubs or bars where defeated or sick people gather to drink, are contaminated by these negative forces and bring "bad luck" on themselves. These people open themselves up to emotional upsets and misfortune, and it becomes very difficult for them to direct their lives toward happiness, success and spiritual progress. Studying the mystery of Human Eros in depth, reveals the existence of Satan in the world of man, because Satan is the portion of perverse vibrations of telluric magnetism. This is one of the reasons why Satan has been represented in the form of a serpent which crawls over the surface of the earth. The symbol of the serpent however, is not always negative. There is also a luminous serpent, Satan's counterpart, which was the symbol the Pharaohs bore on their foreheads to represent the sublimated, spiritualized Human Eros. The ancient Hermetic symbol of the serpent biting its tail accurately represents the "love spiral" or telluric magnetism.

Fraternal love, because it is unselfish, is placed at a fairly high level on the scale of love, even though it does not apply directly to a couple's relationship, but to the emotional communication with others. This love has a basically altruistic nature, which breeds harmony and easy communication between people. Fraternal love becomes deplorable when it is one-sided and allows one person to take advantage of another. There is an element of danger in blind altruism, the admonition "do good to all," because this action can mean in many cases a violation of people's free will. There is a risk that Nature might visit on the helpful person the same suffering he is trying to alleviate in the affected person. One should help people as far as possible, but only when they really deserve to be helped; otherwise, instead of doing them a favor, one not only harms them greatly, but one might also harm oneself.

Why does a man seek a woman and vice-versa? Does

he perhaps do so driven by sexual urge? Or is there something deeper behind it? In the majority of cases, a man undoubtedly seeks a woman out of sexual need, while a woman is drawn by a need for economic security and the need for a man's magnetic energy. There are higher motives however, more closely related to love than to sex. These are the needs to perfect oneself and to become a complete being in possession of both sides of the truth in its masculine and feminine faces. When an individual man and woman, who are each separate halves of a whole, are united, they can acquire a knowledge and fulfillment which they could not have imagined. This certainly happens when a higher type of union takes place.

THE EFFECTS OF TELLURIC MAGNETISM

Telluric magnetism has a fundamental importance to the process of love and an analysis of the decisive effect of it on a couple's life together and on an individual himself follows.

Magnetism in Love Charms

There are many people who experience great disappointment in love because they are not loved in return. Often, in cases like this, they have been known to resort to the aid of seers or fortune tellers to force the faithless lover through a spell to return or to show interest where there had previously been indifference. Sorcerers will work some sort of charm in exchange for a suitable fee. Within the limitations of their scant and sometimes distorted knowledge, they unwittingly use their own inferior magnetism. Their own magnetic force is of low vibration, simply because there is no higher purpose of a spiritual nature in the type of transaction that obliges an individual to feel artificially attracted to another. This tactic may in fact either succeed or fail. It does not matter what the result is, however. The individual does great harm to himself by seeking the seer's aid, because these consultations are generally a focus of inferior, decomposed magnetism. The clients on the whole, are those who come to empty themselves of the misfortunes, suffering and "bad luck" of their lives, which are really the effects of causes they themselves have created. Each new client not only leaves behind his own negative forces, but also absorbs the ill-fated magnetism he encounters in such places.

In many instances, the seer may be an honest, well-meaning person, but who rapidly becomes saturated with destructive forces. There is great irony in the fact that an individual, by seeking such help, may in fact receive a much heavier burden than the one he brought with him. In certain cases, the individual may temporarily solve his original problem, in exchange for another far more serious one of a completely different type. In the use of love charms, the seeker sets negative causes in motion by trying to enslave another person through the use of magnetic forces. This generates karma, which will sooner or later come back to the person who created it because it is not possible to go against an individual's relatively free will with impunity, for to do so is to go against Nature, and is a mode of corrupt behavior. Sorcerers of a low nature who practice an elementary type of black magic are always surrounded by entities which thrive in the world of low vibrations. Hell really exists in this sense. Its description corresponds to the world of lower energy; the energetic plane which is the storehouse of low vibrations generated by the animal passions of the human being.

Magnetism and Lower Entities

Any display of Human Eros is creative, even when physical offspring are not conceived. "Magnetic offspring" are formed from the individual's electric fluids. When the creative expression is bestial, animal offspring are created which take on truly devilish forms that are neither wholly animal nor human, but rather a monstrous cross between both. This is the true origin of demons. They are the children of man and wield so much power over him. They need energy to survive and their only chance is to absorb it directly from people. They can only do this with individuals who are going through negative passional states, otherwise their vibrations would not be food, but rather, poison. These creatures cannot withstand the higher vibrations of positive individuals with balanced psyches and strong wills, for they mature in the shade of those poisoned by sadness, depression, envy, frustration, resentment, hate and vices. Demons attach themeselves firmly to these types of persons in order to suck their vital fluids which nourish their elementary lives. Demons in hell do not torture their victims out of sheer perversity, but to feed upon the energies discharged through their suffering and passion. There are individuals who have become true hosts to demoniac larvae, which may also cling to those who keep their company, like horrifying leeches. This is precisely what happens in the consulting rooms of seers and sorcerers. Such settings become the center of attraction for these magnetic demons who find there the adequate means for feeding themselves.

Once the mechanisms of magnetism are viewed in this way, it is possible to comprehend the ancient traditions and assertions of the existence of "incubi" and "succubi," (invisible demoniac vampires born out of the activity of masturbation, who copulate with their victims in their sleep). These demons provoke all kinds of erotic dreams through which orgasm is reached. The powerful energies of orgasm are taken over by the "incubus" who later seek fresh victims in order to survive. Such experiences also provoke an uncontrollable anxiety to masturbate in certain individuals, thus corrupting them and sucking their magnetic energies from them.

At present, scientists are skeptical about these phenomena, just as they were about hypnosis in the early days, which before it was adopted by medical schools, was termed a superstitious practice. But the time will come when these entities will be generally acknowledged. As an aside, hypnosis was a common practice among Egyptian initiates who carried out feats through hypnosis which modern science could not imagine, nor explain. Certain scientists have commented, reasonably enough, that if telepathy and clairvoyance "really existed," they would be known, because it would be impossible to keep them secret. They do not, however, stop to consider that if a man were really telepathic or clairvoyant, his state of consciousness would have changed to such a degree that his motivations, thoughts and desires would be impenetrable and that he might thus not be willing to get involved in matters of this world.

Returning to the subject of magnetic demons, they are responsible for many cases of obsession and madness. These demons manage to completely take over an individual's subconscious, using it to express their own vital impulses and to take from him the energy they need to survive. In many instances, electroshock therapy does not really act on the person's brain but repels and expels the obsessive entities. Unfortunately, through this pratice, the individual's defenses are left weakened and after a certain time he will be possessed by the entities once more. These entities cannot live at great altitudes however, and mountaineering is the best therapy for ridding oneself of them. They cannot survive above an altitude of ten thousand feet and will disintegrate in a maximum of ten days. This is the reason why the Incas, who possessed great esoteric knowledge, built the city of Machu Pichu and its temple at a high altitude, to liberate their consciousness from the negative influence of magnetic parasites.

The monstrous beings which dipsomaniacs see

during their attacks of delirium tremens are not imaginary. They really exist in the world of energy and become visible under the effects of heavy alcoholic intoxication. Something similar happens with the effect of hallucinatory substances, which causes people to have access to the world of energy, but which connects them with vibratory states in harmony with their own psychic conditions, having either horrifying or beautiful visions and dreams.

The positive, balanced individual is naturally protected against inferior entities, but intense emotional and passional states open up his defenses and leave the door open to the possibility of possession.

Magnetic Tension between a Couple
We shall study the effects of magnetic exchange on the human couple further and use as a reference, the attraction or repulsion which its polarities may arouse. Men and women represent the opposite poles of magnetism: positive and negative, respectively. Beyond the human level, and in a greater sense, one may say that the secret of universal life consists of the attraction between two poles of energy, the phenomenon which generates vital energy. For this force to be really powerful however, each of the poles must firmly maintain its own inherent condition; the positive should remain fully active and the negative, passive. In general terms, this principle is the basis of attraction between men and women which may cease if there is an alteration in the condition of the poles. The attraction is based on the continuity of a proper tension between them. If this force is extinguished, the same thing happens with the power of attraction. Once the tension disappears, the attraction is finished.

This leads to one of the most commonly accepted misconceptions regarding married life and that is, that it is necessary to share the same bed, to ensure conjugal harmony. This belief confuses physical proximity with psychological and amorous communication, maintaining that to sleep together, means union. The truth is just the opposite, because when a man and a woman share the same bed, they constantly exchange magnetism, thus diminishing the tension between their polarities and as a result, their attraction for one another. Slowly, the sexual attraction fades. An uninterrupted exchange of magnetism hinders an adequate recuperation of this loss, therefore the positive pole is saturated with negative energy and vice-versa. Although this does not change their fundamental gender, it considerably diminishes their power, tension and attraction.

Even when a couple might not have intercourse for a month or so, "magnetic sexuality" still exists and operates, energetically speaking. All that is necessary for this type of union is close proximity. Intercourse, organic or magnetic, involves giving energy from one's own polarity and receiving energy of the opposite gender. During sleep, an individual will weaken himself by losing part of this force and will receive a discharge of the opposite polarity which diminishes his own, even more. With time, each member of the couple loses their polar stability to a great extent and both become united at a single extreme, where they are placed in an intermediate situation in which there is almost no magnetic tension. This leads to a loss of sexual attraction. What comes of this loss of attraction depends on how much emphasis the couple places on sex, because if their relationship has been mainly physical, their union will be destroyed. If they communicate well on other levels though, the problem may not influence them on the whole.

To understand this problem fully, the relationship between sex and love must be studied in more depth. For the moment, we will focus on the marital bed and insist that it could be the cause of death of magnetic attraction between many couples. Bear in mind that there is a difference between magnetic attraction and magnetic symbiosis. Attraction, which is natural, consists of the force produced between two opposite poles and is maintained through an appropriate degree of tension or separation. There are couples in which this polar attraction has totally disappeared, but who have sexual relations just as frequently as they did at the beginning of their relationship. This may seem contradictory, but it is only apparently so. What seems to be real attraction, is no more than an automatic type of sexual relationship, more like a program of physical conditioning on the part of the couple. There are married couples who regularly have intercourse every other day, but in a totally mechanical and habitual way. Intercourse out of habit must not be confused with its true counterpart, which is a natural and logical consequence of profound attraction. There are many people who think they are highly virile due to the frequency of their copulations, but the truth is that these are only conditioned reflexes, and not the result of natural attraction. True virility is of a magnetic, not organic nature.

When a couple becomes habituated to frequent and mechanical coitus, there comes a moment when their union is no longer one between two beings of different gender, but rather, a sort of masturbation carried out by a symbiotic being in which two parties have been fused.

Individuality in a relationship can be lost not only psychologically but in a physical sense, through the sexual union itself. Natural sexual attraction should not be confused with the type of masturbation that results from the fusion of two opposite poles joined at some midpoint. By losing their polar individuality, two lovers become one single being of indefinite gender as far as their polarity is concerned and their union lacks the characteristics which define coitus as the copulation of a male vibratory principle with a female force.

To maintain attraction in love, each party must develop and keep his or her individuality. They must be able to preserve their own magnetism in order to keep their personal batteries well charged. An effective way to recover and maintain one's own magnetic tension is to observe regular periods of solitude and isolation, in order to be alone with oneself. Polar magnetism is replaced and strengthened in this way, and the attraction between the couple will be kept forever. If the goal is to preserve the relationship, this recommendation is more logical, because to try to keep the two members in a forced type of union in order to avoid separation, violates one of the basic requisites of love - that nothing can be demanded; one can only give. If love is not entirely voluntary, it is not really love. Otherwise, one falls into the unfortunate situation of trying to unite through pressure and external rules and not by love. Love is an inner process which cannot be manipulated from the outside, because if this occurs, its vital essence is destroyed.

Human sensations are spent if they are monotonously repeated without necessary intervals of rest. Even the sensation of pain will disappear if it has been felt uninterruptedly for too long. Sleeping together in the same bed is not only impractical in terms of differences in sleeping habits, but will extinguish the attraction between a man and a woman through habit and will cause the destruction of their individual magnetic polarities. It is more novel and exciting to visit each other from one bed to the other without sleeping all night together and this will not produce the negative effects outlined above.

Many people are so lost and disoriented regarding the significance of love when they believe that by binding two people of the opposite sex through legal, social and religious obligations (one of which is the double bed), they will be bound internally. This is a fanciful concept, for physical proximity and erotic suggestiveness are no guarantee of true communication. In fact, there are couples who live apart for many years, separated by thousands of miles, but whose union is far deeper and more stable than others who share the same bed. The greatest obstacle is that people do not realize what a genuine and profound union exists between the sexes and instead try to create an artificial one through obligation and material commitments. Hermetic philosophers are concerned with what really matters, the inner union, because when it exists, it is the achievement of a true union of the couple bound by love.

Philosophically speaking, a high percentage of marriages are not "legal" under Nature's laws. They are marriages set up and maintained by legal and social obligations, which lack the energy pattern of the "matrimonial ovoid" that can only be formed by Nature herself when a couple is truly harmonious. Just as one cannot bring children into the world solely by decree of a state law (which disregards Nature), no marriage can be authentic only on the strength of having been granted legal, social and religious approval. This approval springs from the creations of man and not of Nature. For a marriage to be an authentic one, both the legal and natural laws must be united. Natural law is the law of science and the law of science is the expression of God's mandate.

Society is not able to form a real marriage. It can only legalize a couple's union with the intent of protecting the structure of the family. This protection is only the outer aspect of the bond, but what really matters is the inner, natural union that only couples themselves can attain.

For this reason, Hermeticists differentiate two types of marital unions:

1. The legalized marriage, which is a legal marriage under man's laws without inner or natural union.

2. Integral marriage, which is also legal, but achieved through the union of the laws of Nature. It is thus doubly authorized by both human and natural law.

For those who are reading this work closely, it will be obvious that it's intent is to teach people how to form a doubly legal marriage, one which not only obtains approval by man, but also by Nature's laws. This is the secret of true happiness — knowing how to obtain Nature's blessing by complying with her laws.

A marriage is formed in accordance with the laws of Nature when a couple, through a harmonious relationship, profound empathy and a large capacity for communication, form a common "magnetic ovoid," a sort of invisible child whose existence proves the formation of the natural bond. This bond legalizes the marriage according to natural laws. The Creator established the rules of the game in the universe and these rules are the laws of Nature. There are legal marriages of many years which have never managed to attain the stamp of legality from Nature, because they are not valid in the eyes of the "tribunals of Nature." The reason this type of acknowledgement has not been obtained is due to the non-existence of the "matrimonial magnetic ovoid," which is irrefutable proof of the effective consummation of the bond. Although there are no known physical systems of observation and proof of this phenomenon, this fact remains.

When a couple is approved by the "tribunals of Nature," this fact is evident in itself through the level of communication, love, union, power and happiness obtained. When Nature's approval is lacking, it is also quite evident simply by observing the lack of harmony, indifference, hypocrisy, and unhappiness. The difference between these two situations seems as if one had been blessed by God and the other had not. It is also possible to test the veracity of what is being said here for the matrimonial ovoid can withstand any crisis or problem. Each partner preserves their individual equilibrium and integrity, however difficult or dramatic the problems might seem. It is also important to note that although a marriage may be non-existent in the eyes of Nature, this does not mean that it cannot change. On the contrary, if both members try hard enough in their practice of the science of love, they can succeed in legitimizing their union under natural law.

There is another important difference between a legal and an integral marriage. Integral marriage has a generating power all its own in the world of causes and acquires the magical facility to manifest material effects through the causes which it consciously sets in motion. The legal couple, on the other hand, can only generate children of the flesh, and should restrict their creations to this area.

A legal matrimonial status is no guarantee that a spiritual bond of love has been formed in the couple. In an integral marriage, the bond is formed at the beginning and after it has been formed, it is completed by human legality. Such a union is far more profound, rational, human and in harmony with Nature's laws. There is no guarantee that a couple will manage to achieve a more spiritual and profound union later, than at the beginning of a marriage no matter how long the marriage has spanned. The tedium of daily routine often destroys the scant possibilities a couple has of attaining higher communication.

Only the double legality of the integral marriage can lead to an alliance which, transcending its common conditions, leads a man and a woman to a high degree of love, happiness and fulfillment. Their spirituality, evolution and satisfaction are not experienced by common humanity. The divine blessing of marriage, a gift from God, cannot come solely from belonging to a particular faith. This type of consecration can only be obtained through constant respect for the natural law and through spiritual merit from the practice of virtue, self-control, responsibility, moral perfection and through one's spiritual evolution. The individual who pleases natural divinity, does so, not as a result of admiration or penitence, but through his own effort.

FURTHER DIMENSIONS OF SEX

Sigmund Freud said that the basis of everything is sex and included affection, fondness, tenderness and fraternal love within the definition of sexual life. He described love as "sex deviated from its original sexual object." In one aspect however, he left his theory incomplete, either out of a lack of knowledge of its complete structure or in order to hide a truth for which humanity, at that time, was not ready. The Science of Love speaks of love as magnetic energy or Human Eros and one of its possible manifestations is sex. Freud, although not totally correct about this concept, was not far off when he classified love and sex as the same phenomenon, for sex is really love, although incomplete, because love represents far more than sex. Both are of the same substance, but love encompasses the total range of possibilities of which sex is just one part. Understanding the concept of Human Eros means understanding the sublime mystery of love.

Human Eros is the generating power which is the source of energy for sex and which in turn is the propagator of life. In fact, life in the human being depends upon sex and death occurs when that force is extinguished. Sex therefore, with respect to the life and death force, can be considered to be like the genital organs and the spinal cord. Death is always an orgasm; one dies in the same way as one is born. We are born through the orgasm of our fathers and we come to be the father of ourselves at death because we die through our own orgasm. In this way, it is always the father who has the orgasm that gives either life or death. Death and life are the polar extremes of a single energy, that energy being the Cosmic Eros or the Universal Generating Power.

If a person dies of old age, his sexual battery is consumed as slowly as the flame of a candle, but when he dies violently, there is always a sexual spasm. One should analyze the analogy between orgasm and death, for when an orgasm occurs, one dies a little. It should not be thought, however, that abstinence is the most appropriate way of not wasting energy. On the contrary, a magnetic pole weakens without its opposite. The solution does not lie in coitus interruptus either, which involves greater danger, but rather in maintaining a higher level of consciousness during the sexual act.

One must be aware of the correct relationship between sex and love, in order to know the characteristic differences between a relationship of love and one of a purely sexual kind. Love is sex; but it is much more than sex. The following diagram symbolizes the role of sex within love and represents the Generating Power or Human Eros, whose center of accumulation and projection is sex, which flows through emotional, intellectual, mental and spiritual levels or vital centers.

These areas make up the whole, which is Love or the Generating Power. Sex is not synonymous with love, but is an appendix of it and is formed from the same substance. Generally, a couple's love relationship has as its basis, sexual or emotional contact, or a mixture of both.

FIGURE 14

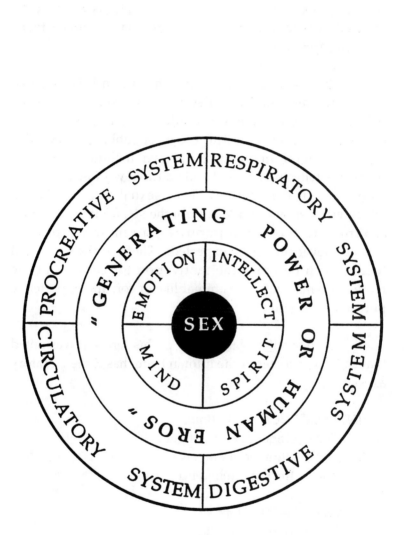

There is a clearly marked difference between sexual and emotional tendencies; a sexual emphasis is generally directed at obtaining sexual pleasure; an emotional focus pursues happiness.

The sexual impulse diminishes when it is satisfied, while the emotional impulse increases the desire to be together. There are many modalities of sexual union, however, from the lowest to the most sublime. Nevertheless, an integral union should always include the sexual, psychic, intellectual, mental and spiritual worlds in order to be perfect. It is important in the sexual act, to establish which vital centers should control the act, for if the instincts are freed to their own impulses, a relationship of an elevated level cannot be expected. There is always a vital focus which becomes the motivation for coitus and the motivation may either be animal-like or corrupt, or perfectly pure and beautiful.

In <u>The Stellar Man,</u> (Vol. 2 of this series) it was noted that each vital center of the human being has three vibratory aspects:

INTELLIGENCE — The Brain
1. The intelligence of intelligence
2. The emotion of intelligence
3. The instinct of intelligence

EMOTION — The Heart
1. The emotion of emotion
2. The intelligence of emotion
3. The instinct of emotion

INSTINCT — The Sexual Organs
1. The instinct of instinct
2. The emotion of instinct

3. The intelligence of instinct

In a purely sexual relationship, the focus is on the instinct, which has four possible instinctive levels which indicate its quality or lack of quality:

1. A purely instinctive level
2. An instinctive-emotional level
3. An instinctive-intellectual level
4. An instinctive-emotional-intellectual level

At all these levels of instinct, sex controls the act, but the quality of the relationship varies according to its expression, whether it is limited to pure instinct, or includes the emotions and the intelligence. The same analysis applies when the emotions or intelligence take control over coitus, which can take place at any of the four levels. None of these types of sexual relationships are the highest, but are modalities within the grasp of the man without Hermetic training. Although these modalities may not be fulfilled at their highest levels, the possibility is well within the range of the individual's normal potential.

Higher forms of coitus are only for those who have attained advanced states of consciousness, because they require the use of the mind as the directing force. In other works, we have explained that the average man lacks a "mind," in the true sense of the word. This possession is not an inborn one and is not part of the human being's normal development. The "mind" exists as the product of Hermetic initiation, work and development. In the higher forms of love, the flux and reflux of the Human Eros are controlled by the Superior I, which is the individual's permanent and absolute center of gravity and which allows him to form part of an integrally united couple. Genuine love, in its higher expression, is the relationship between a man and a woman who make up one integral and complete being.

"Sexual sin" consists of the unthinking, animal use of sex, when the sexual act enslaves the individual's integrality in a bestial and purely libidinous relationship. There is no "sexual sin" when the creative force is at the service of higher consciousness. To participate in sex in this way, however, the individual must first develop his consciousness.

Relationships based solely on sexual interest cannot lead people to happiness or to true inner satisfaction. However strange it may seem, neither will they lead to sexual satisfaction, because satisfaction does not lie in the genitals, but in developed magnetic sexuality which is the result of personal growth.

A strictly physical sexual relationship, which is what the great majority of human beings experience, is very much like the mythological ordeal of Tantalus, the son of Zeus and the female Titan Pluto, whose torture was to have before him what he ardently desired, without being able to reach it. Tantalus was dying of thirst while standing in a pool of water, but whenever he approached the water to drink, it receded. There were tree branches with succulent fruits over his head, yet when he reached to pick them, they withdrew. This analogy depicts sexual thirst which can only be temporarily satiated in the physical sphere, while the inner, magnetic desire is left unsatisfied. For this reason, sex in itself is never satisfactory, but constantly engenders new desire which one attempts to appease with greater erotic activity, thus creating a vicious circle. This tendency is perhaps much greater in a woman, because the nature of her sexual response is more complex than a man's. There are many women who, without being frigid, have all the sex they could wish for, but who remain permanently unfulfilled. A man in turn easily slips into orgiastic activity as a means of deceiving himself and thus, conceals the anxiety of his profound dissatisfaction.

Quite the opposite occurs when coitus takes on a higher modality, in which the Superior I of the individual takes control and brings about an organic, magnetic, instinctive, emotional, intellectual, mental and spiritual relationship. This contact is truly pure and sacred and can lead a couple to a real paradise. Although this statement may seem quite simple in theory, in practice it requires great tenacity, perseverance and dedication to attain a Superior I. True love and genuine sexual satisfaction do not belong to the masses, being reserved for those who triumph in the process of spiritual selection carried out by Mother Nature. Nevertheless, the door is open to everybody, but most people are however deprived of love and happiness through their own design and choice. Life itself, is competition and selection and those who waste their time blaming others keep themselves from success, whether it be material or spiritual. Nature only makes human beings unequal in order to later delight in grouping them by means of the process of selection.

The secret of many sensations resides in sex, because all stimuli are sexual and sexuality is innate. A small baby has sexuality which it displays through the senses, especially in the act of sucking. In maturity, sexuality spreads to other areas, but the senses remain eminently sexual. Hearing, seeing, touching, eating, chewing, sucking, smelling and tasting are all sexual stimuli. People go to the movies, lead a social life, eat, listen to music and feel sad or content through the erotic stimuli which these activities imply. There are many ways of stimulating sex apart from the purely mechanical, physical way and they are connected with the emotions, the imagination and the sensations of the five senses. The person who enjoys his chewing gum, little suspects that the relaxation he derives from it, might come from sex and not from the nervous movements of his jaw or the taste of the gum. Social gatherings also excite magnetic sexuality, as do the pleasures of eating, stimulation of pop music and the influence of aesthetics and visual stimuli such as colors, forms and lights. It is quite easy to test the erotic power in a certain tone of voice or a special perfume. Eating with one's hands has a profoundly sexual connotation, for it adds to the perceptions, the tactile sensation, which may bring great pleasure. The same happens with the smell of food. This also explains why drinking a cocktail in an ordinary glass is far different from drinking a cocktail in a glass of a special shape and color. The colors of clothing and the response to their textures are direct messages to sex. The contact between a man and a woman's hands goes immediately to the libidinous sphere by means of touch.

Furthermore, the individual who feels sorry for himself does no more than experience a morbid masochistic sexual pleasure. People's aggressiveness also has a profound erotic significance, from a sadistic point of view, because the person enjoys hurting others by word, deed or in a concealed or open manner. Analyzing this issue in depth, it can be concluded that the libido governs the life of the human being in an unbelievably broad sense.

At this point it is relevant to examine the issue of non-organic masturbation, which is felt through the senses and is a common practice for many people. To understand this phenomenon one must make a distinction between "normal," meaning, the way things should be and "abnormal." It is perfectly natural for an individual's sexual field to receive stimuli from the senses, because if it were not for that, its energy would be extinguished and he would probably die. The abnormal and pathological reside in the sado-masochistic behavior applied to the sexual senses and it is necessary to note that sado-masochism, which is pathological, has now come to be considered normal, as a general standard of behavior. What is normal is not necessarily healthy; "normal" has been altered to the point that "normal" is actually sick or distorted, without anyone noticing it.

Sado-masochism, applied to the senses which feed the sexual impulse, exists when a person enjoys rapid and constant emotional fluctuations between the sensations of pleasure and pain. This type of pleasure is not natural, but morbid and distorted. If this leads one to conclude that all human beings are somewhat sick, it is not a reason for sorrow, but on the contrary, a challenge to rise up to. The full meaning of the expression "degenerate" is revealed in this context. "Degeneration" is when a person distorts his human condition through the misuse of his generating power, using it to masturbate through a continuous fluctuation between pleasure and pain. There is always a chance for an individual to "re-generate," to create himself again in a higher level by the intelligent use of his creative power. Humanity, as we know it, is "degenerate," because it has deviated from its path of evolution and replaced that path with the search for comfort and sensual pleasure, a fact which can be seen by anyone through simple observation.

The best example of how inorganic masturbation works is in gambling, where an individual fluctuates sharply between the pleasure in the expectation of winning and pain at losing his money. This evokes strong sado-masochistic excitement, which can make a person become easily addicted to "the vice of gambling," which should instead really be called the "vice of inorganic masturbation."

As the gaming table becomes a center for the projection of psycho-sexual energies, it also becomes a place of attraction for magnetic demons. These demons find, in such places, the ideal conditions to feed upon the energies given off by the gamblers who are later left empty, in terms of energy. However grotesque this description may seem, the gambling room is a sort of "milking shed" for magnetic demons, in which the gamblers provide the vital nourishment. Exactly the same situation occurs at race tracks, where a person may lose his family or home because of his uncontrollable urge to bet. The individual who becomes addicted to gambling not only loses his magnetic energy, but finds this loss reflected in his daily affairs. He will be unable to revitalize himself and it will be almost impossible for him to carry out any type of project.

It is essential to be aware that magnetic demons delight in the suffering of people and that they therefore possess a primitive type of intelligence which is directed toward causing pain, failure and suffering in their victims. It should not be forgotten that these children of darkness feed on lies, failure and suffering. Their victims go through highly destructive emotional states and give off magnetism which feeds the demons.

Another form of inorganic masturbation is the fondness for highly dramatic stories such as those seen on television, where the characters go through all kinds of misfortune, humiliation, pain, sickness and suffering and which are also often rewarded by strokes of luck, love at first sight and the triumph of good over evil. What is of concern here is the viewer's attitude. The viewer is caught up in the emotional fluctuation of suffering and pleasure in the ghastly scenes and generally cannot miss the next episode, because he is unwittingly stimulating his own sexuality. The individual gets used to these habits and unknowingly establishes negative standards of sexual behavior, because he will subconsciously try to repeat in his own love life or marriage, those painful or morbid situations which stimulate him through inorganic masturbation. A person who, in good faith, gets used to sado-masochistic fluctuations of pleasure and pain, perverts his sexuality to the point of becoming a seeker of sick sensations. He resorts to the distressing, but "pleasurable" drama of jealousy or the masochistic delight in feeling deceived, despised or humiliated. If these situations do not exist already, then the perverted individual will surely invent or provoke them.

Almost all matrimonial quarrels brought on by jealousy are based on this reflex of inorganic masturbation through conflicts, in which insults and praise alternate. One partner fluctuates between being the humiliated and the humiliator; the other morbidly seeks to lower himself and to cover himself with dirt, or else throw mud at the partner and even give or exchange blows. These situations cause an intense psycho-sexual excitement in the individual, which acts as a sort of reinforcement of the perverted standards of behavior and thus tend to become habitual forms of reaction. The pathological becomes normalized and is no longer noticed, nor cause for concern. Couples thus fall into melodramatic patterns, leading them to unhappiness, because they confuse these factors with the concept of "living intensely." Often, certain adolescents who wish to live as intensely as possible, fall into the trap of spoiling their lives by acting out patterns full of melodramatic alternatives, in which there is the presence of drug addiction, alcoholism, laziness, disease, ill-fated loves, hunger, poverty or delinquency. People do not stop to think that when they seek new and stimulating sensations, all they do is to spur on their own sexuality, thus displaying their profound erotic dissatisfaction. The more an individual "seeks sensations," the more evident his sexual discontent will be, because genuine satisfaction can only be achieved through magnetic sexuality.

The religious ecstasy of the saints is no more than a state of sexual "nirvana," although it is a sexuality which is sublimated toward the spiritual through a long process of development and elevation of consciousness. Any person who develops his conscious awareness and practices a genuine spirituality will find true sexual satisfaction which will show itself in his life as a feeling of plenitude, peace and inner satisfaction. Human beings are eminently creative beings and their erotic impulses must attain their creative goals or else be frustrated. This is why artists, scientists, researchers or philosophers achieve inner sexual satisfaction through their activities and feel thus fulfilled.

What a human being so zealously seeks through all these hidden objectives, is really his sexual fulfillment, even when he is unaware of his motives. The desperate search for power, fame, glory, prestige, wealth, love and pleasure is really hidden sex or erotic energy which seeks the survival or perpetuity of the individual through something transcendent and through the attainment of inner sexual satisfaction.

All human beings at heart have the same goal, that is, to find sexual fulfillment. Unfortunately, lack of knowledge, daydreaming and a fantasy-building nature makes an individual confuse sensual pleasure with inner satisfaction. This is especially true when he does not realize that fulfillment is achieved through the education and control of his sensual nature. Such control is indispensable and is a requisite to achieve sublimation of the libido. One should not however, confuse sublimation with repression, because repression is mere stagnation and decomposition, while sublimation means directing the flow of the Human Eros toward higher levels of expression.

The power to generate life is a power which either debases or saves a person, depending on his sense of responsibility, consciousness and concern. All human beings have the same chances to elevate or debase themselves. It is the individual's choice which decides his future destiny and it is his own ability to appreciate reality or to live in fantasies. Nature subjects human beings to inexorable trials, and whether they succeed or fail, defines their spiritual or bestial nature. The overcoming of great ordeals in mythological tales, for example, such as the labors of Hercules, refers not to the deeds of warriors, but rather to the internal conflicts in the human being and to moral and spiritual ordeals undergone by those wishing to mold their characters to attain self-knowledge and the true path of *homo sapiens* who has often deviated from the path of evolution to pursue comfort and sensual satisfaction.

Consequently, a great majority of people focus on the pursuit of illusions, without ever fulfilling them and when they believe they have attained them, they melt away in their hands like soap bubbles. By the time people understand the causes of their lack of fulfillment, it is usually too late to change course and too late to work toward concrete goals and not imaginative ones. Many people crawl painfully through life, going from illusion to illusion and never realize the irrelevance of what they pursue. Very few people wish to face their own reality, because an overwhelming majority resorts to a variety of escapist tactics aimed at dissolving their Ego, perhaps killing it forever, by fusing it with the mass consciousness or by dissipating it in constant orgiastic exaltation. Hermeticism teaches an opposite approach, advocating the conscious training of the Superior I. In this training, a person's greatest capacities are tapped and concentrated upon, allowing the individual to reach total self-realization. This path of self-realization is the opposite of the dissolution of the Ego, which is a process that leads to death.

Since people constantly deceive themselves, they confuse the search for happiness with the pleasures of the senses and they try anxiously to get maximum pleasure, believing that they will ensure their own happiness before it slips by. In doing so, they resort to indiscriminate sexual stimulation and think that they are enjoying life.

Cigarette smoking is a form of subconscious sexual stimulation. A person enjoys the sensation of sucking and the taste of tobacco, deriving sexual pleasure in the guise of "inorganic masturbation." Most often, the smoker has deep sexual complexes caused perhaps by a conflict between his libido and Super Ego, which makes him consider coitus sinful, but smoking on the contrary, as something with no erotic content and significance. In reality, he is enjoying disguised sex. The practice of finding hidden sexual pleasure of this type has become a common behavior in a humanity intoxicated by the idea of sexual sin. When the erotic is considered sinful, people resort to disguised stimuli, where they can enjoy sexual pleasure without feeling guilty.

Smoking is a hard habit to stop, because the individual is possessed by a magnetic demon born of the sexual magnetism released by the stimulus of the act of smoking and its emotional states. This entity, rather than the individual, will refuse to stop the vice. If a person were really aware that he was nourishing a being alien to himself, it would be easier for him to have the will power to stop smoking. It is not the person who needs the tobacco, but the magnetic demon who does.

Probably at a certain point in the history of humanity, the pejorative concept of sex may have been an artificial boost to the morale of the times, but the moment has come to appreciate sex for what it really is: the concentrating battery of the vital energy of the universe, of the Cosmic and Human Eros. Each individual can either pervert or purify sex. The sin lies with the person and not with the act itself.

THE SEXUAL ACT

Union through sexual intercourse plays an extraordinary role in an individual's life, either elevating or degrading him, not only in his spiritual evolution, but in his material existence, his happiness, prosperity, misfortune or sickness. This fact remains unknown to orthodox scientists who only concern themselves with sexual problems related to impotence or neurotic and hysterical frustrations.

The most important thing about coitus is its intrinsically creative nature. The Human Eros, in its twin polarity of masculine and feminine, has a creative objective and its aim is invariably fulfilled. There is no coitus without offspring; when the ova are not fertilized, invisible offspring of a magnetic nature are created, which in time, become the individual's "invisible descendants." These invisible children are responsible for the couple's happiness or misfortune, according to the essential quality with which they were created. Sometimes, when the sexual act itself is of a higher quality, these descendants may become real angels. In other instances, which are more frequent, demonic beings are engendered through the individual's corrupt sexuality. These invisible offspring constantly torture their parents, fostering discord, jealousy, hatred between them and causing them to undergo painful experiences so that these "vampires" can feed on their parent's pain. This is why the sexual act should only take place under very special conditions and should never be intended to give free rein to inferior desires. It should be a conscious act, without inhibitions and should be submitted to the control of the higher faculties of intelligence.

The potential of a woman conceiving a "child of Satan" as seen in movies, actually describes a highly concrete possibility. Of course, it is not Satan in person who fertilizes a woman, but his influence is manifested through the man who possesses her. The demon child born from this woman only exists in the world of energy, because the carnal child may, at least in appearance, be quite normal.

Demonic children are often begotten when coitus is limited to the expression of the corrupt animal passions in an individual. By corrupt and animal it is meant that which has not attained a genuine human condition and, although no longer completely bestial, is corrupted through a lack of a stable and mature Superior I. Only the mature Superior I can withstand the degenerating influences of an emotional and violent world.

A wild animal which kills its prey in order to eat is not corrupt but pure. The most perverse animal that exists is *homo sapiens*, who goes to extremes of refinement in wickedness, cruelty and rapacious actions that no other beast in its natural state does. Only man kills out of cruelty and avarice and such corruption engenders invisible "satanic" children. Only when spiritual power prevails in a couple, can they procreate an invisible child of a higher nature.

This discussion, so far, refers only to invisible offspring. With children of the flesh, the situation is not very different because they are usually biologically human and psychologically animal and in some cases also possess demonic souls. Parents are usually responsible for these types of offspring for they pass on their own "satanic" energy, corrupted animal energy, to their children, making it impossible to control and educate them. Rather than having control over their children, parents of demonic children are manipulated or conditioned by them. This represents only the prolongation of a situation which existed before conception. Before conception, the satanic energy, not yet projected on the offspring, was contained within the parents and controlled them instead. After conception, the children are extensions of this satanic energy. Only those parents who achieve perfect mastery and training of their own animal souls, will be able to educate their children properly. Otherwise, they themselves will be conditioned by their offspring.

The importance of proper conditions for coitus thus becomes apparent. Coitus should be carried out, not by the force of passion, but by the force of love expressed in sexual balance. Only when these conditions are created and a couple is in perfect harmony, is sexual union advisable, otherwise it may greatly harm those involved. It is not the energy of excitement that should unite a couple, but the force of attraction of love. Sex in itself, has nothing bad or dirty about it. It is the individual, in his condition of "corrupt animal," who perverts his own sexuality. He grows accustomed to reacting in an "impure" or perverse way; not through the harmonious attraction of love, but through a simple uncontrolled physical impulse. Just as it is useless to be intelligent when intelligence is not submitted to the control of reason, genital sex for the sake of it, without any union with the individual's total being, becomes something which is not only dehumanized, but animalized.

An extremely important phenomenon occurs at the

moment of orgasm. The individual's invisible defenses open up. At the beginning of coitus, a man and a woman are united in a magnetic ovoid similar to the matrimonial ovoid, but one which is temporary and inferior in quality. It is as if each partner unites his energy to that of his companion while coitus lasts. When orgasm is reached, an opening occurs in the magnetic ovoid, and superior or inferior vibrations penetrate through it according to the spiritual and sexual state of elevation attained by the couple.

Two possible types of feeling can result from this union: one of indifference or repulsion for one's partner (a result of the low quality of the act), or another of happiness, a sense of permanence and of profound union, the natural result of a higher type of contact. The real effects go much further however, and affect the couple's future, because by uniting sexually, they set in motion a creative psycho-sexual energy which generates causes in the world of energy. In time, these effects manifest their positive or negative effects. The couple not only engenders invisible offspring, but also causes Nature to conceive and yield her fruits according to what is sown through the energy of Mother Earth.

Again, a reminder that those who have eyes to see and ears to hear will fully understand. For others, the entrance to wisdom will remain sealed, for they are not prepared to transcend terrestrial science and attain stellar knowledge.

There is very little hope of "regeneration" for those who approach coitus as a ritual act in a purely mechanical way and as a reflex, because they will never be able to reap the fruits of the "tree of the science of Good and Evil," the tree from which God told Adam and Eve that if they ate, they would become like gods.

Unfortunately, human beings have distorted the sublime act of generation and made it a vehicle of pleasure and reproduction, granting it importance only as a physical act and totally ignoring the tremendous effect that it can have on their lives. The spiritual or animal quality of sexual contact determines its effect. Certain types of behavior are perfect demonstrations of what "should not be done," because these types of behavior can harm those who practice them. Forms of coitus which are expressions of corrupt love are:

1. Orgiastic coitus
2. Coitus during illness
3. Coitus during menstruation
4. Anal coitus
5. Coitus under drunken or drugged conditions
6. Coitus when depressed
7. Coitus immediately after a quarrel
8. Coitus done out of habit or as a reflex response
9. Coitus while upset with one's partner
10. Coitus by force or obligation

Sexual orgies are in reality, a cover-up for the individual's inner conflicts. The individual subconsciously seeks to fight the intense anxiety he feels of inner solitude and forlornness. This state of mind alone, immediately destroys any possibility of an "act of love" and a person is reduced to compulsive behavior as an attempt to help himself in the emotional problem he is going through. This physical relief will temporarily appease his anxiety and make him forget his problems for the time being, but has nothing to do with a genuine sexual act motivated by love.

When a person is ill, coitus does no more than harm both the sick person and the partner. A sick person's vital vibration is very low and his magnetic force lacks sufficient power to carry out an integral union and is restricted to mere orgasm. Sex under these conditions wastes the vital energies needed by the body to recover from the illness itself and attain balance in health.

Sexual contact during menstruation is really the most ominous and corrupt practice imaginable, for during this period, a woman discharges the negative forces she has accumulated. In the same way as a human being discharges waste material through the anus, a woman eliminates all the residues of her feminine metabolic activity through her menstrual blood, as well as the chemical products of her negative psychic states. This blood is highly charged with residual magnetism, which from menopause onward, has to be processed differently. When a woman has intercourse during her menstruation, she conceives a very powerful demon, a satanic being that will torture and persecute its creators, bringing them all kinds of misfortune. Exactly the same happens in anal coitus, for this is the way in which fecal magnetism is eliminated. If a man ejaculates in this part of the body, a couple will conceive demonic and monstrous forms in the plane of energy, which may come to incarnate in the form of subnormal, perverse or deformed children. These are serious matters which warrant profound meditation, because harsh reality inevitably proves them to be true.

During intercourse, under the influence of alcohol or drugs, an individual may open up the plane of the lowest and most negative vibrations and in turn pass on this low energy to his invisible or carnal offspring. Many children go through extremely serious problems in life because they were conceived in a state of drunkenness. This does not refer to those defects which medicine traditionally ascribes to the children of alcoholic parents, but to problems of karma and psychological defects. These types of children are the unwitting bearers of tremendously negative forces alien to themselves, which will be serious obstacles to their material and spiritual advancement. Drugs, the same as alcohol, may put the individual into contact with forces which are hostile to human life. The vibrations of these forces will inevitably bring about fateful effects for the individual himself.

Coitus in a state of nervous depression has exactly the same consequences as does intercourse after a quarrel. In this instance, not only are the negative forces conceived which were set in motion by a quarrel, but orgasm will act as a reinforcement of this behavior, being subconsciously interpreted as a reward and becoming a reason for the quarrelling. Quarrels will tend to be indefinitely repeated, as their mechanism is associated with a subsequent pleasurable act like coitus. A couple may thus undertake a destructive rhythm of serious quarrels which will bring into their lives obstacles, problems, illnesses and ill-fated events in general. If they have children, the children will take on all the negative forces and will most certainly fall under their influence, reaping harmful effects. "Bad luck," mental retardation, rebellion, irresponsibility and delinquency are typical results in these cases. Similar conditions occur when orgasm is reached while a couple is experiencing disharmony caused by resentment over conflicts which have not been resolved or when there are real or imaginary grievances. This lack of harmony is reflected in the results generated by the sexual contact.

Finally, sex performed out of habit is a purely animal act; not a product of genuine love and communication, but rather a product of physical excitement, from which no higher types of results may be expected.

The generating power of sexual intercourse is not

limited to visible or energetic offspring, because coitus also extends to the intellectual and instinctive spheres. This is how a woman makes a man conceive in his brain and how a man in turn fertilizes her in the world of instinct. He conceives ideas and she, impulses. Both are compelled to carry out materially what they have generated in each other.

In this way, a man and a woman "regenerate" or "degenerate" each other through coitus, according to the elevation or baseness of their act. They influence and shape each other, reaching either the sublime or the infernal. Their conceptual capacity, knowledge, sense of responsibility, love and concern, dictate the results. In the same way, the energetic space of a human being becomes peopled with magnetic monsters, the offspring of millions of couples. Again, if one is to generate "angels," there must be a very harmonious and elevated union which can only occur in people who have evolved sufficiently through awakening, through raising their consciousness and who have attained an appropriate level of spirituality.

The materialism of our time is the worst hangman of humanity, because people have become accustomed to thinking that nothing exists except that which can be seen and touched. People are deprived of the wise knowledge of the Hermetic masters, the heirs of stellar science, the Science of Man. Hermetic wisdom states that "as it is above, so it is below." This means that man is analogous to the universe and that the whole cosmos is within him on a tiny scale. Unfortunately, *homo sapiens* only directs his attention to the exterior. It is as if he were afraid to contemplate his inner world, even though true wisdom, happiness, humanity and evolution depends upon knowledge of this inner world.

When humanity emerges from this period of spiritual darkness in the course of its development, it will perhaps be ready to adopt certain Hermetic codes of higher generation. At the present time, only those who are able to think for themselves, transcending the cultural norms of humanity to attain their own intellectual individuality, can manage this. Only in this state can a person give himself to meditation on Hermetic knowledge and perhaps come to understand what is being said in this book. If an individual is a slave of his cultural programming, he will lack true intellectual capacity, because he will think with the collective brain of the masses, which is the melting pot of mediocrity, rigidity and superstition. Really, only the person who escapes from the herd and attains his true individuality, is free to reshape or direct his life at will.

In this Hermetic analysis of sexual attraction and coitus, it is of great interest to consider what happens in old age, when desire fades. Since life resides in sex, it might be thought that the individual would die when sexual excitement goes. One might also wonder when the generative forces are extinguished if the amorous attraction of love also ends.

There usually comes a moment when sexual desire fades away or becomes almost imperceptible. This does not mean that the generating power no loner exists, because sexual expression is only one part of it. When sexual desire fades, the accumulating battery of the Human Eros, or sex, is internalized. The life force contained in sexual desire turns integrally toward the interior of the individual, with the specific aim of maintaining the equilibrium and strength of organic life. Instead of working in order to generate, it begins the job of maintaining life. This does not mean at all that the couple's attraction for each other ends, but simply, that their love evolves into deep affection, tenderness, companionship, friendship, intense sharing and understanding. This only happens to those who, to some extent, have had access to genuine love, because in other instances when sexuality fades, boredom, indifference, lack of communication, misunderstanding, repulsion and even hate may arise.

For the couple who really love each other, a relationship in old age may be the most beautiful, peaceful and full stage of their lives, in which joys and sorrows, triumphs and worries have united two beings in a way no passion could ever have. Passion, without love, is doomed to die, but love without passion does no more than strengthen itself when freed from the ballast of possessive egoism.

Another point with regard to coitus, is the problem of reproduction, because semen is invariably ejaculated, even when a couple wishes only to conceive invisible offspring, instead of children of the flesh. If the ovum is fertilized, then the original intention is thwarted and the act is reduced to a mere reproductive act, producing carnal children. With individuals of certain religious groups, such as the Catholic Church, the taboo of birth control is invariably upheld, even in extreme cases where a woman needs to be sterilized to avoid a future threat of death caused by pregnancy. It is not our job to advise anyone on this because others' ideas should be respected, but we believe we can offer certain food for thought on this matter. Nature understands nothing of human religious or philosophical morality, and when the human population exceeds a certain number, she sends the "Four Horsemen of the Apocalypse" (which Blasco Ibañez referred to in his famous novel), in the form of famine, disease, war and death. Thus equilibrium is periodically established. It is the price one has to pay for respecting religious "illegitimacy" of birth control.

Thomas Malthus, in his well known Essay on

Population written in 1798, explained that if we did not have these periodic checks, the birth rate would so outweigh the death rate, that the multiplication of mouths to feed would outpace any increase in food production. He said that while the population increases in a geometric ratio, supplies do so in an arithmetic ratio. Time appears to have proven his theories.

When economic, racial or religious interests prevail, it is assumed in certain instances that the economy profits from having more obedient consumers and that certain racial groups tremendously increase their power and influence by augmenting the number of their members. Naturally any religious group would anticipate a dramatic increase in its influence and power, from an increase in the birth rate of its congregation.

However, beyond all these arguments, there is still the problem of the balance between mouths to feed and food supply, which so far has no solution, and on the contrary, will over the years, become far more serious and considerably increase the threat of war. The great historian Will Durant states that "war is a nation's means of feeding itself," an accurate definition which should make us reflect profoundly.

The ideal procedure to avoid the possibility of conception, is sexual abstinence during fertile periods which constitutes both an infallible contraceptive system and excellent training for character and will power.

Referring to the sexual act, one very important question remains: how should sexual relationships be entered into without becoming sinful, corrupt or implying the creation of malign entities?

The higher act of sex should only be carried out as

the culmination of a process of strong magnetic attraction. The higher act of sex is conscious and under the control of the will; the higher act of sex is meant to produce harmony, deep. communication, understanding, affection and fondness. The couple realizes that a sacred or divine act is being carried out and that this relationship will inevitably engender either carnal or energetic offspring. Once this condition is fulfilled, coitus should be carried out without the least concern for reaching orgasm but with the greatest inner delicacy and modesty. One should maintain awareness of oneself as a being who possesses the divine spark and that one is not a mere animal.

The act should involve no emotional upsets, alcoholic influence, or overeating. Spiritual serenity and calm should go hand in hand with physical ardor. There should be a peaceful mental and emotional atmosphere, in order to eliminate morbidity or sado-masochistic disorders. The couple should lie completely naked for total magnetic exchange and they should be sure that they are not interrupted or bothered meanwhile. Coitus should begin gently, delicately, playfully, shifting one's focus from the goal of reaching orgasm, for orgasm should come naturally, as if there were no predetermined aim.

This is also an excellent method for overcoming impotence and frigidity; to be sexually united almost without moving, trying to prolong this state for as long as possible and without the least concern for orgasm. One should however avoid getting into the habit of coitus interruptus, a practice in which the act of intercourse is voluntarily interrupted when the man reaches the point of ejaculation. If this particular practice is continuously repeated, it may cause a narrowing of the urethra or an inflammation of the prostate gland.

Tender manual and emotional caresses should be an

integral part of this process of love-making, especially where the woman is concerned, because she only reaches full excitement with the involvement of the limbic system, the cerebral mechanism of the emotions. A woman's cycle of sexual response is noticeably slower than a man's, and she thus reaches her climax at a moment when her companion is perhaps tired. This is also one of the most important reasons for prolonging the process prior to orgasm. Certain marriage manuals recommend manual stimulation of the clitoris to speed up the process of excitement. From the Hermetic point of view, there is nothing wrong with this, but only physical sexuality is stimulated by this method, and not magnetic sexuality, which is the most important factor in the sexual relationship. Magnetic sex is only stimulated when a man projects an adequate stimulus from his own magnetic virility, if he has that virility. This virility is not inborn but the product of the individual's conscious evolution. When a woman receives the radiation of this magnetic virility, her own electric sexuality is aroused. Like the man, a woman is not born with magnetic femininity, but must acquire it through Hermetic work on herself. Like the man, she has a primitive or elementary inorganic sexuality, which is very rarely activated and which is set in motion with masculine magnetic virility, causing in her an excitement in the magnetic sexual realm, which does not however, exclude physical sexual excitement.

For a higher type of sexual intercourse, there should be a union of the magnetic sexes, even if the magnetic sexuality in question is only an undeveloped primitive sexuality. This type of sexuality benefits from prolonged stimulation, when a couple stays sexually united without hurrying their orgasm, and, on the contrary, carefully retards it. Union may last for thirty minutes to an hour and it may or may not culminate in orgasm. It is possible to test the genuine result of this type of relationship by the degree of inner satisfaction or frustration felt at the end of the process. If there is inner peace and satisfaction, the magnetic exchange has been appropriate. On the other hand, if the woman for example, is still excited and frustrated, its purposes have been crossed. As far as the frequency of coitus is concerned, the act must not become an empty and mechanical ritual or a simple reflex activity. Each couple must determine the natural rhythm which suits them best.

As this book is not meant to be a manual on sex, but a work on the profound significance of love, it will not discuss the positions suited to sex as there is abundant literature on the subject. Magnetic sexuality, rather than organic sexuality is our concern, because sexual union may debase or elevate a couple according to the quality of their union. What is more, this union may be the elixir of life or the breath of death. In fact, the secret of life is rooted in the existence of an adequate tension between two poles, and sexual contact is an excellent manifestation of this tension. If this tension is maintained, it can give life, if it disappears, it can bring death, not in the physical, but in the energetic sense. A woman should therefore be a modern day vestal for a man, that is, she should attain an inner attitude of purity, to prevent the "sacred fire" from being extinguished in the man. Virile power, the "sacred fire," is extinguished when a person practices absolute chastity or when he is a libertine. Organic sexuality may sometimes be kept up normally, while the real fire, which is the symbol of magnetic sex or generating power, "goes out" or loses its force. A man thus becomes an individual who is organically male and energetically female.

These pseudo-males are eunuchs in the world of the spirit, even when they carry out genital prowess. Their virile impotence is noticeably displayed in their chauvinistic attitudes, in violence, aggression, lack of self-control, premature ejaculation, emotional instability, low resistance to frustration and abuses of power. Certainly, the opposite qualities are no indication of masculinity, for there should be a balanced dose of aggression, strength and power in a man. A truly virile individual should be capable of controlling these faculties without abusing them. There are very few who possess true virility and who are strong enough to wield the legendary Excalibur, the mythical sword of King Arthur, who directed the brotherhood of the knights of the round table, the seekers of the Holy Grail, the sacred goblet which legend says Jesus Christ used in the Last Supper. According to tradition, the mysteries of the Holy Grail were only revealed to sufficiently pure knights; their search is the subject of many ancient legends, featured in Chretien de Troyes' Perceval, in Wolfram de Eschenbach's Parzival and in many English folk tales. Wagner's occult opera, Parsifal, is based on Wolfram de Eschenbach's poem.

What concerns us in these tales is the phallic symbol of King Arthur's sword and the lance recovered by Parsifal. Arthur wins all his battles with the magic sword and, like St. George, even manages to kill a dragon. Parsifal, for his part, snatches the sacred lance from the wicked Klingsor and kills him with it, turning him and his castle to dust. These are evident symbols of the Hermeticist's higher will, based on his magnetic virility, while common men are deprived of this strength because they constantly seek leaders to support them in order to overcome their own weakness. True will power should always be based on magnetic virility and be an expression of it. A woman, for her part, should base her will power on Nature, for she herself is Nature, and does not need the same conditions as a man in order to carry out her work.

The masses, who lack virile will power, act passively and merely go with the current. This is why any individual who wants to excel and develop a more spiritual state of consciousness, should begin by attaining psychological and intellectual individuality to enable him to think as an autonomous being.

Materialism is the dominant attitude of our time. It is a clear demonstration of the passive, feminine character of present day men, who, being psychologically female, are "fertilized" by the force of matter which acts as the male. The spiritual person, on the contrary, is masculine, for instead of being fertilized by the force of matter, he makes matter conceive by giving it consciousness through intelligent usage. Although all giving is feminine in nature, when the act and quality of giving is present in a man, it is a masculine attribute, and while all self-control is masculine in nature, in a woman, this state only increases her femininity.

Possession through passion is also a type of giving, for the individual is fertilized by an irresistible force which obliges him to possess a woman violently.

Despite the fact that the common man is energetically feminine, he may become masculine as he gradually achieves self-control. Self-control is not only a character building discipline, but also means the recovery of one's own masculinity.

To return to the problem of energetic tension between two poles, which maintains life, let us analyze misguided forms of behavior which may lead to the diminishing or extinction of the attraction between the two individuals in a couple.

These types of behavior are:

1. Misuse of sexual contact
2. The purely mechanical sexual act
3. Loss of the lovers' psychological individuality
4. Symbiotic fusion
5. Weakness in the man's character
6. Male chauvinism
7. Psychological rigidity
8. Lack of individual solitude
9. Characters which are too similar

All of these types of behavior diminish the tension between the poles, which results in a loss of magnetic attraction, and consequently, in the extinction of vitality in love for a couple.

In some cases, such as sexual misuse or the mechanical act, there is a magnetic saturation and a loss of polar vibration. In other examples from the list, it simply happens that there is not a suitable polar separation, a basic element for adequate tension. This is true of the third point, the loss of psychological individuality, because it represents the definition of each individual's polarity. When this polarity disintegrates, it destroys the attracting magnetic tension. Exactly the same happens in other instances. Weakness in a man's character causes him to lose his polar distance and definition. The male chauvinist absorbs the woman into himself and loses his polarity. The psychologically rigid individual becomes static and does not radiate the energy inherent in his polar condition; the individual without sufficient solitude becomes saturated with his counterpart's magnetism and loses his polar distinction. When characters are too similar, there is simply a lack of adequate distance between the extremes.

If a couple sleeps in the same bed for years, they exchange so much magnetic energy that their individual polarity weakens, diminishes or is extinguished. As a result of excessive or uninterrupted coexistence, this magnetic saturation often causes sexual fatigue.

Witness the Hermetic wisdom of Khalil Gibran's lines on marriage:

> "Let spaces grow around you.
> And let the winds of heaven loosen their dances among you.
> Love each other devotedly, but do not make a bond of love;
> Make love a movable sea between the shores of your souls.
> Fill each others' cups, but do not drink from the same cup.
> Share your bread, but do not eat of the same piece.
> Sing, dance and be merry together, but let each of you be independent.
> The strings of a lute are separate though they vibrate to the same music.
> Give your hearts, but not so as your companion becomes master of it.
> For only the hand of life can hold hearts.
> And stay together, but not too much together.
> For pillars hold up the temple, but they are separate.
> And neither does the oak grow in the shade of the cypress nor the cypress in that of the oak."

This lovely poem expresses the need to keep a certain distance to preserve magnetic attraction.

In couples who live too much together, encouraging each other for many years sexually, emotionally, intellectually and physically, what once "gave them life," (their mutual stimulation), may, in a figurative sense, "give them death" due to magnetic saturation. Constant repetition of certain stimuli causes mutual psychological poisoning, inadvertently and tragically emulating the classical oriental torture of the dripping of water. By constantly listening to the same things, by having similar agreements and disagreements, by repeating the same physical and emotional caresses, what was once so pleasurable may become irritating or even hateful. This does not indicate a lack of love, but a simple tiring of the senses. This same fatigue is akin to the well-known phenomenon of difficulty in seeing or appreciating oneself. For anything that takes up too much of our attention will finally disappear from view because the stimulus is "spent."

Boredom in marriage can be avoided with prescribed intervals which interrupt sexual and psychological contact between the parties, with the goal of resharpening the senses. Uncontrolled intensity is the death of pleasure, which then becomes indifference, guilt or suffering.

Each couple must strike an adequate balance in this matter, by wisely adopting the maxim of the potter's kiln which says, "neither far enough in to get burned, nor far enough out to freeze."

Emotional intensity, which so often arises in love and which also extends to sexual projections, is based mainly on insecurity. The spouses mistrust their ability to keep their partners and try anxiously to absorb the other person. This lack of self-confidence in itself is the main obstacle to the necessary rest periods that are vital to keeping up the attraction. A mistaken belief dictates that temporary separation can somehow damage the love relationship. This concept could only be true when love does not exist.

LOVE IS

AN ACT OF WILL

In order to see the nature and the practice of love in the correct perspective, it is essential to understand that love cannot be the child of chance nor a spontaneous event, but instead, a product of the individual's will to love. Love, to be real and happy, should be planned from beginning to end, otherwise one must resign oneself to living out romantic fantasies and illusions in an unproductive romanticism which leads only to frustration, unhappiness and a lack of love. A love relationship between two human beings cannot be left to chance and instinctive impulses, but must be an act of a person's will.

This concept might seem to be the antithesis of what people believe love is, because people often believe love is involuntary, a result of "love at first sight" or of an electric contact which pierces them with the ray of passion. The examples in Nature have made them think that the individual should follow the example of animals, who, at a given moment, feel an uncontrollable urge to mate. They may also think that something like the pollination of flowers or the courting of birds should happen to them. Perhaps illusory examples of love offered by history, literature, poetry and the movies arouse in them the insane desire to experience a romance in the style of Romeo and Juliet, Cinderella and her prince, etc. There is a belief that successful loving is an innate ability of the human being, just as natural as breathing or eating and that one only needs to find an outlet for an emotional impulse to encounter love. Thousands of lovers have lost their way in pursuit of the illusory chimera of "spontaneous" love, seeking a sort of wind-borne seed which chance will drop in the right place where it can germinate and grow.

People do not recognize the true nature of love, and spontaneity is unfortunately confused with animal instinct. People do not for an instant think that there is a need to learn a technique in love in order to happily enjoy Cupid's gifts. At most, there is a recognition of the need to master certain sexual techniques which provide the right degree of pleasure. The very idea of acquiring knowledge and skill in a science of love as a means of success in love, seems incompatible with the cultural notion of love as a spontaneously generated force.

This myth should be dispelled once and for all; one should study the science of love with the same care and devotion as that given to learning any profession or art. It is impossible for an individual who does not know himself at least a little, and who also does not know his partner, to achieve true happiness in love, unless he is willing to settle for love as only physical pleasure.

Fortunately, there is a science of love; a profound system of knowledge which offers an understanding of human nature. The basics of this science are being presented in these pages. A human being is an instrument of love, and without true knowledge of love, he will not be able to scale the heights of happiness. Tuning and controlling this instrument, he will be able to create the melody of happiness in love, which is not a gift of Nature, but a composition brought to life by a human being.

The real cause of the crisis in love and in the dynamics of the human couple, is that man has almost completely forgotten his inner world in the pursuit of external fantasies. The disintegration of the couple is the crisis of mankind; this disintegration means losing the path to spiritual evolution which is an internal path that leads to the most profound wisdom, spirituality and integrality. By rescuing love and reinstating it to its elevated place, the higher values of the human being are also recovered and fortified.

Making love an act of will does not mean to force or artificially create a situation which does not exist naturally, but rather to place higher consciousness as the focus of the whole process. Using reason and consciousness in love does not take away the warmth and ardor of the union. On the contrary, the more faculties developed in the process of love, the greater will be the pleasure and happiness derived from it, for it will be possible to cover wider and deeper levels within the individual.

Sentimental love, which operates in a reduced sphere, is equivalent to playing a tune on a piano with only seven keys. If one has access to all musical possibilities, one can interpret a melody in all its power, depth and color. The sentimental and sexual alone are only a small part of the keyboard of the instrument of the human being and when a person is limited only to several notes, he will never come to know the depth and splendor of true love. This is why we cannot say that "love is blind," for this expression only refers to a caricature of love and not to the genuine relationship conducted with one's eyes "wide open." Animals may practice blind mating, but for human beings, one hopes for something more.

Previously, we have stated that true love is "the

relationship between the integrality of two people of the opposite sex." This can be understood perfectly if we consider this integrality as the total range of the senses, from the densest and most material, to the ethereal and spiritual. Love itself however, is not ethereal, but is a highly concrete process.

The Superior I of a person must manage the complete scale of his sensations in a conscious and intelligent way to be able to unite with a partner in the most complete way possible, in a relationship that is rooted in potential and actual reality.

Through a realistic, conscious and balanced attitude, an individual must be able to destroy unproductive fantasies which may lead him to a subjective and illusory experience in love. It is quite painful to see people become so addicted to their own pleasurable dreams which are totally disconnected from reality, and to see them living in a subjective world as if they were constantly drugged. There is nothing strange about this, because people drug themselves with their dreams and fantasies in the belief that this habit surely could not harm them too much. Fantasy usurps reality and the inevitable consequence of this experience is to indefinitely hope for events which are never fulfilled, except in the dreamer's imagination. This deprives a person of a chance to really live.

The will to love should not be expressed with a person with whom one does not feel the right sort of harmony. The process must be directed in the most intelligent way possible so that love brings about the best type of communication and the greatest possibilities of success. Before achieving that success, one should make an effort to understand the other party without premature judgment. There is no love at first sight, only sexual attraction and the "falling in of love" which are products of simple animal magnetism and the influence of the "daydream phantom" or idealized image through which one sees the image of one's dreams in the individual one has just met. This is why we must interact with a person who interests us for quite some time before getting to know him or her properly, to determine whether the other person may be the object of our love, and whether that person is able or willing to return it. Throughout this process, one should avoid premature conclusions and "sexual tests." This does not mean that sexual contact should be forbidden, but that this contact cannot be the basis for judging the feasibility of proper communication. It can only show the degree of sexual compatibility which is just one of the couple's points of contact. It is a mistake to trust the evidence of satisfactory coitus as a test of the possibilities in love. A person, through an act of will, should try to put aside appearances in favor of the essential. Knowledge of the other person includes a perspective that goes deeper than his or her mask. Getting this knowledge is no easy task, for each individual has a large repertoire of masks and never shows his true face. Only at moments of crisis can the true face show itself. This often makes quite an impression as the true face may really contradict the other face we are used to looking at.

Each person attempts to give the best possible impression and to project a good image, particularly in love. Inner reality or ugliness can only be seen at moments when a person becomes stuck or dissociated in his or her psychological programming on account of sudden or unexpected events. A special type of patience makes it possible to penetrate peoples' inner worlds and to come to know them as they really are, however this process, may take years.

Teenage love, for those involved in it, is thought of as a delightful drunkenness to give oneself to in body and soul. They believe that the ecstasy felt is the highest proof that they truly love each other. In truth, the experience of "falling in love" is not caused by love at all. The expression "to be in love" is wrongly used to describe what is usually a mere magnetic intoxication. By close contact, each of the lovers increases or doubles his own "mass energy," a magnetic force inherent to corporeal matter. Each feels an electric exaltation which makes them go through intensified emotional states. This, however, is not true love; it is only one of the densest and most animal-like manifestations of love energy. This excitement has the serious drawback of dying down when the two bodies are no longer close to each other, leaving not the slightest trace, but perhaps only the sensual desire to feel it again. When there is a pressing need to be absorbed in each other, it is not love, but "mass energy," which impels bodies to seek each other to increase their magnetic potentiality for a while. When this state passes, only fatigue and an inner void are left, a feeling like that of an engine which has suddenly lost half its horsepower.

Interestingly, Freud considered falling in love to be a sort of hypnosis, a concept which is accurate and in line with our theory of mutual magnetization. We have also analyzed the close relationship which has always existed between hypnosis and magnetism to the point that traditional hypnotists were also called "magnetizers." Oddly enough, until now, there has been no satisfactory scientific explanation as to how hypnotic magnetism is produced, even though in the Hermetic environment, this is well known.

People avidly test what is going on with a certain person and use caresses to analyze sensations, believing that by analyzing the sensations, they will be able to see whether what the other person feels is love or not. Love is often confused with sexuality or feeling and decisions in love are built on a very fragile basis. Only those who understand the true dimension of love as a science which enables them to attain integral union at all levels and profound communication together with real sympathy, affection and companionship, may be successful in the search for this sublime relationship.

A man's expectation of finding a perfect woman, "made to measure," is a fallacy and a clear demonstration of the need for the use of the will in love. In a mad search for love, there are many who end up destroyed by deceit or poisoned by the conviction that "women are stupid" or that "they are no good." If we remember that a woman's soul always comes from a man, then what a man really wants to find is a woman with a suitable soul, even having been formed by another man. The fact that the soul has come from another man is not an obstacle. The difficulty lies in the improbability of meeting a woman with a suitable soul. It is therefore more reasonable to understand and to adequately motivate the woman who is pleasing to him, with the aim of drawing out the best in her. However, a certain selfish attitude in a man drives him to the desire to obtain the best of her without giving the highest part of himself. A man must deposit in his companion's container the highest personal virtues available to him with the aim of helping her to conceive a superior individual life. At the same time, he needs her to help him attain his own intellectual fertility, an impossible goal if there is not a perfect mutual collaboration. One must accept the fact that man alone is nothing; he is merely half of something, as is woman. Only if there is a higher "will to love" can they be led to the ecstasy of polar integrality, to the joy of fulfillment of oneself as a total being who possesses the two fractions of the whole.

One of the most important things to bear in mind about true love is its intrinsically active nature. The individual gives of himself just as the sun gives off its own rays. False love, on the contrary is eminently passive in its motivation. It follows the ebb and flow of life, just as the actions of ordinary humanity. To explain this more fully, reflect on the word "passion" and recall that it is derived from the word "passive." The word describes a condition in the person which is compulsively motivated by forces alien to him. He feels affections or impulses, independently of his own will, and experiences diverse thoughts and actions. He remains "passive" in relation to an energy which takes possession of him and obliges him to feel, think or act in a certain way. Passional or "false" love is the vehicle through which an external force, alien to the Ego, takes possession of an individual and drives him on toward an emotional or sexual storm; an individual participates in the storm much like a ship driven by a hurricane. Pseudo-love is obviously characterized by extinction when the external impulse which motivated it stops. This is an experience which happens to some people. When their partner stops loving them because the external impulse has died, these people will say, "he was very good and affectionate before, but something happened and everything changed completely." The truth is that the individual did not change at all; it is simply that the external motivation disappeared.

This circumstance leads to a definition of love as being "self-motivated," that is, a relationship which begins as an active affection in the Ego itself of the individual. True love is not based on passion, but on the will. In love, an individual loves consciously, actively, with the strength and power of his own Ego. When love is based on passion, an outside force is at work, not the conscious control of the will. Unfortunately, love for many people is based on passion and passive involvement and is only a shadow of the sublime experience of genuine love. Only a few people achieve the expression of the sublime relationship of true love in their lives.

Those who search for love with the same focus as those who hunt prey are far removed from the right approach; their actions bear the same relation as love does to an African safari - none at all. Love and the hunt for prey are quite alien to one another. Selfishness is also antithetical to love, not because love should necessarily be altruistic, but because selfishness is not a force which radiates like the sun, but an energy which gobbles to feed itself. To allow oneself to be loved is only one expression of the impulse to feed oneself emotionally or sexually through another person, without compromising one's Ego in this act. The key to false, selfish love is that people become unable to give themselves, because they do not intend to compromise their own Ego. They want to remain apart from the process of love, receiving without giving. This is not only a denial of love, but also a display of the person's essentially childish condition, because he confuses his partner with his mother's breast as a source of security, support and well-being.

There is a golden rule in love: if love is self-motivated and actualized, it is certainly authentic; if love is based only on passion, then it does not actually exist. The problem is that very few people have the necessary wisdom to judge a particular love situation. As long as a person has not become a "master of love," he will lack the necessary discretion to judge these situations precisely. Summed up in the guidelines below, are a few very simple rules to make these discretionary judgements (which should be used with caution).

The following lists define in the first column, the golden rules of love and love's genuine qualities, while the other column defines the opposing traits and absence of love.

TRUE LOVE	FALSE LOVE
Is giving, asking for nothing	Is demanding and intolerant
Is unselfish	Is basically selfish
Is self-motivated	Is compulsive, based on passion
Is the product of a process	May happen at first sight
Is experienced with open eyes	Is hypnotic
Does not manipulate the partner	Manipulates the partner
Allows one's individuality to flourish	Denies one's individuality
Does not depend on sex to survive	Depends on sex for its survival
Has continuity	Has no continuity, instead interruptions
Can survive prolonged separations	Dies out with prolonged separations
Is wise	Is impulsive and ignorant
Is mature	Is infantile
Does not bind the partner; has only the desire to give of oneself	Rests on obligations and oaths
Is flexible	Is rigid

Is not utilitarian in approach	Depends on how useful the partner is
Brings peace, confidence, security	Generates anxiety, discontent, conformity
Generates happiness	Gives only fleeting pleasure and enjoyment, or causes misfortune
Increases with time	Decreases with time
Is absolutely sincere; both partners know each other	Needs hypocrisy, lies and pretense
Communication exists on several levels	Communication exists at only one level
Allows for individual equality and liberty	Is unequal, exploitative and allows no individual liberty
Has no limits	Is limited
Is renewed and strengthened by inner changes	Is destroyed by changes counter to its intellectual and emotional programming
Stimulates and develops individual potential	Limits and inhibits individual potential or causes one person to develop at the expense of the other
Is fertile and productive intellectually, emotionally and spiritually	Is fertile only in the realm of emotions and procreation

Tends toward the integral evolution of each partner	Does not allow each partner to grow and is rigid and static
Inner or magnetic sexuality is active	Only physical sexuality is active
Is governed by tolerance, mutual respect, perfect communication and the deepest affection	Is governed by pride, jealousy, vanity, selfishness, obligations, and the dictates of society
Has its own original pattern	Conforms with social, conventional and cultural patterns
Is active and creative and constantly renewed	Is passive and governed by habit and inertia
The couple shares both errors and successes	The couple designates "guilty" and "innocent" parties
Has its own dynamics	Is programmed and static
Reaches perfect union at all levels, while it maintains the individual's inner space	Requires symbiotic fusion, with no inner space for the individual
Is the result of the use of the will and conscious reflection	Is the child of improvisation
Is not disturbed by the day-dream phantom, because it is realistic	Brings to life the daydream phantom, and is fantasy-based and unreal
Is based on mutual collaboration	Is competitive

Has conscious moral standards which are the result of profound inner awareness	Has unconscious, programmed and superficial moral standards and is fragile and rigid

Beyond this list, there are many other differences at deeper and more esoteric levels. This list only sums up some of the elements which enable us to distinguish genuine from false love. Nevertheless a relationship will not necessarily be false even if it does not include all the requisites listed above. Those requisites are meant as a sort of norm, and may be used to determine how closely a relationship approximates a true or an unreal one, according to the number of requisites fulfilled or left unfulfilled. For example, on a scale of 0 to 100, if a couple fulfills all the conditions in the left hand column, they would be given a hundred points; if they lacked all of them, they would get zero points, which would mean total falseness. Once one knows the extremes, then one can find the points in between.

Even though a love might be labeled false, it does not mean the relationship cannot evolve toward truth, for one cannot prescribe a remedy without first diagnosing the disease. Only with a diagnosis does an individual get the chance to improve. Recognizing the symptoms is not meant to label the "patient" untouchable or useless. It is a way to decide which remedy should be prescribed.

False love is mostly a product of ignorance, rather than a lack of the ability to love. This is why a couple should develop their intelligence, sense of responsibility, awareness and interest to the maximum in order to create the best conditions for a higher union through the knowledge they acquire. One must, with necessary openness and generosity, have a sense of self-criticism, deliberation and humbleness to acknowledge possible falseness or unreality in love. This scrutiny may be an open door to a stable marital life, happiness and a union beyond one's wildest dreams.

Acknowledging falseness in love should not bring separation, but should rather offer a chance to become truly united.

Here, an important point can be addressed; that of a significant age difference between the individuals in a couple and whether or not this is a barrier to true love. The Hermetic view and experience acknowledges that love easily goes beyond the barriers of chronological age, because what matters is psychological and spiritual age. In many marriages, there is an age gap of twenty or more years, yet these marriages are happy. The couple's qualities are often complementary. One party has experience, equilibrium and stability, while the other has enthusiasm and vitality. The most important element in establishing and maintaining a relationship of this type, is the union and correspondence of inner worlds, not the union of bodies alone. This type of relationship can be infinitely more solid and profound, because to a great extent, it disregards the physical and is based on more lasting and transcendental values, on spirituality and understanding. Physical beauty perishes and it is painful and menacing to depend exclusively on this asset. The situation of beautiful women who make their beauty their prime asset is a difficult one because beauty fades. They are left quite empty or perhaps dead to life, because they lack inner resources.

There are also many couples with great age differences whose relationship is not based on the true or profound, but on neurotic or compulsive needs. An example would be a person motivated by an Oedipus

Complex who really seeks a mother substitute, or a daughter in love with her father who has similar intentions. In any case, one cannot pass judgment because these couples, although they may not attain the very highest in love, may find happiness and companionship, and even if they are driven by compulsive needs, they may, at heart, lead a happy and productive life.

We recommend a flexible and reasonably tolerant attitude in judging the quality of love, because we realize that one cannot achieve the best without constant and progressive effort which might take years. The magnitude of this task should not daunt anyone, but be evaluated in relation to the reward the couple will gain when they have fulfilled it. The reward is the attainment of genuine love which will bring the couple a happiness that is beyond their expectations.

MORALS IN LOVE

A book on love must determine what moral and immoral standards of behavior are. It might seem as though everything has been said on this matter both by the law and by well known moral and religious precepts, however, we want to go further than what is already known, penetrating as deeply as possible into what the concepts "moral" and "immoral" really mean. We will go beyond the narrow and rigid limits of ordinary beliefs, and further than the conventional moral codes of the cultural legacy of humanity, which are blindly accepted by ordinary individuals. All societies are governed by certain moral precepts, but these differ considerably according to time and place. People memorize certain precepts, habits and taboos, and attempt to conform as faithfully as possible to these laws; or in certain cases they violate them and are consequently punished. Moral principles are mainly encouraged by the home, school, church, public opinion and the law.

What are morals? The word "moral" is derived from the latin *MOS*, which means custom or scale of values created by social habit. These are the norms which a certain nation, culture or society has come to consider as good, just and legal, because morality should be supported by the law. The law is an ensemble of obligatory norms, obligations which may be either juridical, moral or both at once. The basis for the law is to be found in the will of God, in the will of the legislator, in the majority consensus of society or in the demands of reason and common sense.

Through this analysis, we intend to arrive at a distinction between obligatory and conventional morals, which are those currently in practice throughout the world, and morals of an inner, individual nature, which are profoundly respectful to human legality. These morals are also based on natural legality, which is genuine, profound and real. There are several types of legality:

- Divine legality
- Human legality
- Natural legality
- Moral legality

In practice, moral rules are confused with religious precepts and juridical obligations, for acceptable norms of behavior form an ensemble of juridical and religious obligations which must be observed if one is to act morally. The person who does not adapt to these social values is considered immoral. People are usually governed by human morals, a mixture of juridical and religious mandates, as well as taboos and unwritten laws based on prevailing public opinion.

Love also has its foundation in human moral. Love depends on and accommodates itself to these human morals under penalty of general disapproval. Marriage as an institution is morally accepted, for it has been adapted to human legality, while concubinage is disapproved of because it does not have a juridical norm. In our study we will question the methods of applying the current moral system, not because we disagree with its content, but because its rules become unconscious messages which program people blindly, forcing these rules to be accepted as moral. Life would certainly be far worse if these rules did not exist, for then the human being's blind instincts would be unleashed.

What are the origins of moral and juridical rules? Why were they established? To answer these questions, we could conclude that the rules were established because it was understood that the human being was totally immoral unconsciously and instinctively and that it was necessary to program him in a pattern which would foster a stable social order. One wonders what would happen in the world if all laws and moral rules were abolished for a month? Under these conditions people would only show themselves as they really are; immoral. It is obvious that the human being's moral indoctrination is merely an ensemble of barriers and limits grafted into his brain, to control his "human animal." At heart, the "human animal" is still as bestial as he has always been. This is why morals are external; the individual is obliged to repress or conceal his true impulses, so as not to be rejected by society.

Nevertheless, the primitive man still prevails in his unconscious. It is here unconsciously that the individual violates all known rules; he kills, steals, destroys, deceives his wife, commits incest and gives free rein to all animal impulses. Moral principles only operate in the external world and do not modify his inner world. Although these mandates are appropriate, they only affect social welfare, not the individual's inner world. Thus we live in a more or less moral society, albeit made up of internally immoral individuals. Jesus referred to them as "whited sepulchres," to describe the phenomenon of the simultaneous existence of an external moral standard and internal decay.

Puritanism has often tried to establish mandates of

such overwhelming strength that they force the individual to keep to the straight and narrow path. This restriction has done no more than worsen the individual situation. The same has happened with the law, for the harshness of its sentences is meant not only to punish, but to prevent crime. All this has been set up to protect society; but who protects the individual? Who can help him acquire an inner morality so that he may become more spiritual? Only the individual himself can do this by understanding the phenomenon we are discussing. What needs to be determined is when a human being behaves in an integrally moral way and when he does not.

It appears that he fulfills integral morality when he strictly observes human, moral and religious law. However, this is not always the case because the spiritual merit of a human being's acts must be taken into account. To be moral means to think, to feel and to act in accordance with an inner notion inherent to the Ego, constituting an inner criterion or judgement of what is correct and incorrect. The Ego will recognize what is perfect or imperfect, false or true, deserving or undeserving. People do not behave morally out of an authentic inner motivation. They do so because of strong external pressure which comes from the realm of the law and social standards.

We must wonder if there is any spiritual merit in respecting the law when one cannot break it. Is the individual who does not steal or kill out of fear of punishment really moral? Human morals are incomplete because they disregard the *voluntary* acceptance of their norms by the individual. Thus we may speak only of "moral acts," but rarely of intentions. There is no inner guarantee for a person's moral acts; he respects legality because he has no other option, insured by the practice of society's system of reward and punishment.

This view does not pertain to everyone. There are people who behave correctly from inner mandates and not external ones. It is worth wondering though whether this inner impulse is the result of free will or the product of cultural programming. People normally act according to social decree. The "normal" individual practically ignores the acts of the Superior I and acts in accordance with the blind programming of learned behavior. Individuals generally lack true *inner morality* which is a product of *self-motivation*. There can exist *moral passion* which is passive, but a *true moral act* is very rare because it is born of the will.

Therefore there are three types of morality:
1. Social or external
2. Programmed and individual
3. Self-motivated and individual

And human beings can be divided into four groups:
1. The immoral ones who do not comply with the law.
2. Basically immoral ones, who comply with the law through fear.
3. Those who have internalized part of the social morals and comply with the norms, not out of fear, but out of an inner conviction that is conditioned and educated by the social message. In this group, respect for morals is only a conditioned reflex and not self-motivated.
4. Those who comply with the moral and juridical rules out of free inner motivation and not out of any sort of external coercion.

Profound meditation is required if one is to understand that true moral worth is not based on the power of the law, but on the individual's Ego, on his intimate, free conviction and desire to comply with norms which he himself has accepted as morally valid. Otherwise, the individual does not carry out a "moral action," but a "moral passion," that is, he gives himself passively to complying with certain dispositions in a blind and mechanical way without any understanding of what the rules mean in terms of value. There is no authentic morality without a true understanding of the importance and significance of these principles.

There are persons who, although immoral internally, carry out moral acts. Although this is certainly better than the reverse, this type of *external morality* lacks spiritual merit, which is not the general concern of society. The difference between internal and external morality is very important to the individual who wishes to attain a certain degree of spiritual and human perfection. Spiritual virtue alone allows the person, in the final analysis, to be accepted as a truly moral being and guarantees the soundness and permanence of his qualities. He will have a respectful attitude to the law which is voluntary and not compulsive. Even if the law has not established punishment for particular offenses, the moral person would still not commit these offenses because his notion of what is right is part of his very being. He acts not out of conditioning but out of choice.

This analysis draws an important distinction between *external* and *internal* morals. To be in possession of the external is no guarantee of inner morality, but inner morality is a guarantee of external morality. Such an individual sustains a self-generated inner moral conscience which is active and dynamic, not programmed and euphoric.

An interesting point to consider is that all who

observe the law are honest and moral in the eyes of society. However, what happens to those who break the law and are not caught and who keep up impeccable moral appearances even when they may have committed very serious crimes? In this case, when the individual is not only immoral but also a criminal, he retains his moral standing legally in society, but not before divine or natural law. Therefore, a person is only truly moral when he complies internally with the rules out of a love of truth, justice, respect for the natural and an understanding of the principle of cause and effect, not out of fear of punishment, compulsion, or conditioned reflex.

There may be legality without morality, or morality without legality. The philosopher, Kant, maintained that true morality is a function of awareness, including an awareness of legality. True morals should be independent of all fear, all hope and all external sources.

Considering these points, what could be the most moral act of a human being? Contrary to what may be assumed, the act does not involve charity, goodness or love, but centers on a person's capacity for self-control. In fact, the more self-control a person has, the more moral his inner world will become. True self-control means becoming more aware of and immune to passions. It does not mean the repression of instincts, emotions or thoughts.

To the extent that a man controls himself, he manages to separate himself from his animal side and raise himself above it. He becomes more highly conscious, which means he will no longer be passive, but self-motivated and self-generated. He will achieve an individuality that will allow him to modify his conduct thoughtfully, on the strength of his own standards formed from keen observation of reality. He will free himself from being an appendage of the social structure or a reflection of the collective impulses of the species. Self-control progressively leads the individual to attain free will and take responsibility for himself. Social morals are the collective's responsibility. For the individual this really means irresponsibility, since there is no single source that can be held accountable. *Inner morals* are the responsibility of the individual himself. To be moral means to take full individual responsibility and to make oneself responsible before Nature for one's own actions. Only a truly conscious person can do this. This is why the individual who lacks proper self-control, cannot act morally; he will be limited to blindly and unwittingly following the paths indicated by the majority.

If morals are social law, one should ask a vital question. What would have happened in the past if humanity had totally deviated from the right path and fallen into perverse or erroneous beliefs? Wouldn't malign forms of behavior be considered acceptable and acts of goodness and love a matter for reproach? No doubt only words would have been changed. Evil would have been called good and vice-versa. When we have no guidance, how are we to detect error? Only those individuals who have managed to have an awareness of *inner morals* would have recognized error and evil. This is the danger of collective behavior in man; pathological or immoral ways may inadvertently be viewed as normal or suitable. The acceptance of wrong values is quite plainly the reason why certain great civilizations decayed so dramatically. When collective values are distorted and there are no wise men possessing inner morality and an elevated state of consciousness, humanity goes on blindly without the orientation of a higher intelligence.

True wise men often exist, but because they commit the "sin" of thinking differently from the majority, they are thought to be mad or unworthy of trust and credibility. Unfortunately, the masses only accept suggestions and ideas from men of great personal prestige, often measured in financial or academic capital and not in terms of real wisdom. Someone with only a little bit of knowledge and inner awareness, a "semi-sage," may be infinitely more harmful to humanity than an ignorant man, because there is no guarantee what effect his personal acts may have when the concept of true wisdom has been distorted. Except in rare circumstances, there exist erudite men who understand only a tiny fraction of the pageant of life.

We want not only to attempt to rehabilitate love and morality, but also to rescue the spiritual values of humanity, which are caught up in a sea of materialism, having lost the path to evolution.

There is also a "dark side of moral conduct" and a "divine type of moral conduct," more closely related to natural law than to human law. So far, we have referred only briefly to natural legality. The subject of natural law is most important and is a concept which can be understood by comparing it with moral law.

Moral Law (Ethical):
May be violated; it is expressed in prescriptive language; it prevails in the realm of effects and results; it is the expression of an imperative that is of a valid and objective principle of universal legislation.

Natural Law (Scientific) :
Cannot be violated; it is expressed in expedient and practical language; it prevails in the realm of causes; it can be proved; it is the expression of the constant relationships observed in the phenomena of Nature.

We call the immutable principles of Nature, "natural law" and believe that these principles have their origin in the rules of the game set by the Creator of the Universe. These principles are constant, eternal and transcend good and evil. We have defined the dark side of love and morals as the natural corrupted or perverted. Man is a perverted being in the sense that he has abandoned his mere animal condition and upon beginning his path towards the opposite extreme of becoming a man, he lost the purity of the wild animal, without yet attaining human consciousness. He became corrupt in his "hybrid" existence and became unaware of what is just or incorrect. *Homo sapiens* is an animal onto which a divine principle was grafted. It was only to be expected that this revolutionary mixture lead first to chaos, caused by the desperate search for his own standards for which there was no precedent. The corruption under discussion is a phenomenon inherent in the anxious exploration and probing of *homo sapiens* for his own particular identity and destiny. This does not vindicate man's corrupt state however, for man has lost the right path to finding his own identity and evolution. The corruption which was first logical and natural is now the fruit of ignorance, negligence, irresponsibility and disorientation.

Despite the fact that this "hybrid" man lives in and by the grace of Nature, he does not respect Nature's laws, but attempts to impose his own will on them. His own will is often chaotic and arbitrary in its expression. This does not happen with the wild animal who exists harmoniously in accordance with the wisdom of Nature, respecting and complying with her laws. Consequently, the dark path may be defined as the natural corrupted, and the divine as the pure and natural. The path to human fulfillment lies in recovering the lost purity through the attainment of a truly human consciousness, devoting one's efforts toward keeping wise and harmonious contact with Mother Nature. This path will lead to constant progress and evolution.

Related to the subject of love and morals, let us briefly examine the problem of adultery, one of the most incendiary types of immorality in love.

What is adultery? The dictionary defines it as a "violation of conjugal fidelity," a violation of the marital obligation of faithfulness. But how are we to define what conjugal infidelity is? Does it perhaps refer to copulating with another individual who is not one's spouse? If it were only limited to this, we would have to conclude that animals constantly commit adultery, which is laughable and absurd.

Adultery is actually the disavowal of the spiritual commitment and not the sexual obligation. The spiritual commitment of love is what is worthwhile, not copulation. This is why it is unfair and misguided to circumscribe so-called adultery to an occasional change of sexual partner. If a union is indeed an inner relationship, then nobody is free from adultery. There is no man or woman who has not desired at some time or another, in his or her heart, contact with an individual other than the spouse. This is just as serious as copulation, perhaps even more so. Copulation expresses only a genital commitment, which may not affect the individual's inner world, whereas unsatisfied desire in love greatly affects the individual's inner world.

Again we can apply the distinction between inner and external morality, for it may be more immoral to commit oneself emotionally than genitally because, although sexual desire dies after coitus, emotion may have an infinitely longer existence. In practice, people swear "eternal love," but never promise "eternal copulation," for this in itself is devoid of any commitment to love. The problem lies in the fact that, as the sexual is considered dirty or tainted, it is assumed that the individual would commit a greater sin if he had coitus than if he intimately desired a love relationship of the emotional type. It is assumed that the sinful lies in breaking a pact of physical exclusivity and not in breaking the emotional bond.

One should handle the label of adulterer cautiously and consider that there are many facets to this issue. There is fidelity of the heart, of sex, of the mind and of the spirit. A person may be unfaithful at heart and sexually loyal, or he may commit physical adultery while he maintains emotional, mental and spiritual loyalty. This leads to the need to define what type of infidelity may be the most serious; spiritual or sexual.

Of course, the ideal would be to keep integral fidelity, that is, fidelity at all levels. Nevertheless, this is practically impossible considering the weaknesses and vicissitudes of the human being.

Considering adultery, one cannot establish a general norm but must judge each situation individually, trying to determine the degree or level of infidelity, particularly if that infidelity has harmed the spiritual contact of the parties involved or undermined their mutual trust. It is more threatening to a woman if her husband confesses that he is in love with another woman, even though he may never have touched the woman in question, than it is if he admits to having had a sexual dalliance of little consequence.

Although adultery is inexcusable, one should give equal attention to the survival or destruction of the spiritual ties between the couple. There are many marriages which have come to an oasis of calm and happiness after surviving the impact of adultery and others who have separated at the least threat of infidelity, which is usually a result of a lack of an authentic and profound spiritual bond. If these bonds are indeed strong, they should be able to withstand any crisis. This spiritual fidelity is really the basis of genuine loyalty.

Observe certain extremely puritanical people in their sexual habits. They manage to keep total physical chastity for years, either for religious or psychological reasons, but, at heart live through a hell of internal lechery and morbidity. Are they perhaps more moral and pure than others? Of course not. They lack inner morality. While they comply with a "sexual legality," they give free rein to their psychological immorality. Public opinion is often shocked to learn that one of these "pure" individuals is really quite depraved, even though he might have externally preserved a perfectly moral appearance.

To understand the difference between the concepts of "pure" and "impure" as applied to human beings is of crucial importance. This is a central part of the ethics of love. This is particularly important if an individual wishes to grow spiritually through love. The stereotype of purity is associated with a weakening of the physical body through fasting, penitence and abstention from sex, alcohol and tobacco. It is thought that a person becomes more spiritual in this way, perhaps because it is commonly thought that by starving the flesh, the spirit is strengthened, thereby purifying the individual. Without denying the benefits of asceticism, we do however deny the spiritual merit of this system unless it is accompanied by strict inner control and sublimation. That which the person abstains from doing physically, is not the only important thing. His inner attitude is more relevant. There is a type of inner chastity which reflects the purity to which a person who wishes to grow spiritually through love should aspire to and which is acquired through training and self-control. When the individual lends his higher consciousness and intelligence to his three vital centers, instinct, emotion and intellect, he closes the door to the type of "inorganic masturbation" which we have already discussed and which profoundly affects his inner balance.

"Purity" is an individual's degree of humanness, that is the extent to which a person approaches the human, the higher pole of evolution moving further from the animal. We have already mentioned the course which *homo sapiens* should follow toward his higher evolution and we have said that he has hardly begun his journey. To recover his original purity, he must rise along the path of evolution to attain "human purity." From the natural point of view, this is equivalent to the innocence of an animal now attired in the splendor of a higher human consciousness.

"Purity" is the degree of perfection attained by an individual in one's own species, that is, the magnitude of his approximation to the highest possibilities of that species.

Obviously any advance on the path of evolution is very slow and man may take thousands of years to approach the peak of his possibilities. In other works, we have referred to the possibility of the individual evolving, changing and becoming a "true mutant," thus bringing about a prodigious leap forward into the future. This is the aspiration and goal of authentic Hermetic schools from the remotest antiquity, and throughout the ages and many extraordinary personages reveal how successful such schools have been in their aim.

It is impossible to separate the issue of love from the individual himself, for true love is love between persons who are advanced from the spiritual point of view, while false love is the relationship between inferior beings on the ladder of evolution.

When the individual becomes "pure," that is, truly human, he leaves the species of *homo sapiens* forever and becomes a *Stellar Man*. This Hermetic expression defines the individual who transcends terrestrial knowledge to attain stellar wisdom. This true man possesses a genuinely sound morality which comes from his inner consciousness and not from imposed rules; he does good because he wishes to, and not out of obligation or for self-esteem. His purity does not depend on what he eats or what he does or does not do. He "only does what he should and abstains from what he should not," making decisions coming from his inner judgement. This profound type of wisdom is the result of his conscious spirituality. The spiritual person, the person whose spirit displays itself through his own brain, acts morally because he is the essence of morality itself; he will never act contrary to the highest universal ethics. This person however, may be misunderstood by those at a lower level on the path of evolution, for they will be unable to explain the actions and thoughts of the *Stellar Man*. They will attribute to him, their own distorted intentions thus projecting their imperfect human model onto that spiritual individual, seeking the reasons for his acts from the perspective of their own passionate and egotistical motives.

The truly moral person does not repress his libido, but sublimates it by stamping it with consciousness and intelligence so that it thus has no need to be controlled. By acquiring the notion of human intelligence, he rids himself of those impulses which come in conflict with the higher norms of ethical, human and natural legality. These forces are not extinguished, but become higher virtues, which reflect the essence of what sublimation is.

Regarding morality, certain questions arise: is it moral to condemn but to hide one's own faults? Is it moral to judge without knowing the whole truth of a matter? Is it permissible to harm one's neighbor by aggressive acts that will not be punished by human law, while avoiding all responsibility? Is it moral to try to obtain what one does not really deserve? Is it moral not to have a stable Ego, which is both mature and adult and which is responsible for the individual's actions?

One of the greatest types of immorality lies in the fact that people constantly change their "directing Ego," the controlling center of their psychological awareness, which directs psycho-biological unity. This situation is equivalent to a business issuing false documents because it has no legal representative. The ordinary human being lacks a representative stable individuality and therefore has no true basis for his actions; he is like a bounced check or paper money with no real backing. This situation is intrinsically immoral for it deceives those who trust unreliable people's words. The majority of human problems stem from these deceptive one's. When the "directing Ego" is expelled by a different individuality which totally discredits the former, one's word which at first seemed so fine, serious and responsible, has now lost all meaning. Is it by chance that all people lie? No. While they are for the most part, sincere with others, they deceive themselves because they lack a constant identity. The person who now denies what he promised an hour ago is not a liar; he is a different person who is unaware of his predecessor. This is a different moral situation, for the person is well-intentioned about his action or commitment, but is incapable of fulfilling it as he had formerly intended. This is the eternal story of many people who break their promises and who thwart their own and others' expectations because they do not possess the continuity of a stable and mature Superior I. This leads us to be indulgent with those who sometimes break promises to their family or who betray philosophical, ideological, friendship and love commitments without malice. One should not lose sight however, of the fact that these faults may at a given moment bring about very serious consequences for the promise breakers themselves, their relations, friends and colleagues.

In this case, a person can have an *inner morality*, with no fraudulent intentions, but because he lacks a higher intelligent foundation for his acts, emotions and thoughts, he fails to follow through on his commitments.

THE SUPERIOR COUPLE

To further clarify the concept of true love, the following characteristics show the relationship between two people of a higher consciousness, a superior couple, truly united by real love.

1. Developing a Fully Grown and Mature Ego

The crucial factor which allows love to really exist is the possession of a developed Ego, because when the Ego is weak, the individual is unable to love and seeks only to be loved in order to feed upon the energies of this affection. The first thing any person must do to attain true love is to work on knowing himself and to achieve a necessary degree of self-control, going beyond complexes and frustrations to reach a state of wakefulness and higher consciousness.

Only the possession of this adult and conscious Ego will allow a person to really love and to maintain the depth and continuity of his affections. There is no other way for a person to be responsible for his love, to give the other party what he has promised, and to guarantee the happiness and higher destiny of both partners. Furthermore, one of the real requisites of true love is also fulfilled; that is, that of each of the parties is constantly aware of his or her existence as a separate Ego. This awareness helps to maintain the person's individuality, which is absolutely necessary for the personal development of each party. Suitable polar distance is also maintained in this way.

2. *Communicating with One's Own Inner World*

Most people are not acquainted with the art of introspection and live constantly turned outward, so that they inevitably misplace their own Ego, losing their identity by fusing with the complex and ever changing outer world. There comes a moment when the individual does not know who he is, what motivates him, what really interests him and what his concept of life is at the level of his own Ego. He only knows the concepts and ideas which come from the external world, which his brain has submissively taken in and accepted. The inner world is the area of the Ego. It is the zone of the thinker (the one behind the thought) and not that of the thought; it is the part that belongs to the individual and, finally, it is what remains when all his social patterns have been removed and when he is stripped of all his masks. It may be argued that very little is left after this; this conclusion is correct. What remains is the material which makes up what the person really is and which forms the foundation for building a fully grown and mature Ego. To communicate with the inner world means to center one's consciousness on this Ego, to live with it, to perceive from it the more superficial layers of one's being in order to know who one is, what one is really worth, what place one has in life and what one really wants. To decide this, the individual needs to periodically be alone with himself in order to keep up a connection with the power center of the Ego, because contact with the outside world wears down this connection which is essential for communication and proper understanding of one's partner.

When the relationship between the sexes is limited to the external world of people, that is, what is alien to the Ego, there is a sort of negative predestination in one's life, as if "everything has already been written" and success or failure will depend only on the elements one already has, as if nothing could be changed or added.

3. Going Beyond Superficiality

There is nothing more harmful than judging one's potential partner on the strength of physical beauty, physical attraction, financial position or social lineage, for all these assets are alien to the being. Love is a relationship between two people and not between two ensembles of assets. Unfortunately, assets almost always take precedence in the process of judging people. Physical appearance, intelligence, material possessions, bank balance, popularity and the amount of power or influence the person has, are taken into account. Character, behavior, education, activities and ideas are also considered. None of the types of assets mentioned here however, make up the "being" of a person; they are only his assets. As it is obvious that one needs to communicate with the being before communicating with what this being possesses, it is clear that people get married to totally unknown individuals as far as their essence is concerned. This makes the reason for failure quite obvious. If we consider that "what is seen" of a person is not even a tiny part of his or her totality, we must realize that we receive a gift and see only the wrapping while we remain unaware of the contents. The marriage market is dominated by the attractive nature of the wrapping, which is one of the most important obstacles to be overcome when we approach a person who interests us.

We should use all possible means to get to know the real person who hides behind the mask. One can only get to know the inner being with great patience and emotional deliberation. This process is totally opposed to the sudden event love is thought to be. Only when we keep impersonal and neutral for a time about a person's physical image and emotional caresses, can we get a rough idea of the true nature involved. We recommend that our readers refrain from judging by apparent assets and take the necessary time to come to know the real ones. This process is facilitated by circumstantial proof. There are certain conflicts which force a person to display his true self because emotional pressure generally prevents him from concealing himself. The other interesting test comes from the evidence of power, when we place a person we wish to know in a situation of power so that he believes he has all the advantages and privileges. Nothing better reveals a human being than the time when he believes he has all the advantages on his side.

4. Knowing the Defense Mechanisms of the Ego

There are subconscious mechanisms which soothe the anxiety of the Ego by denying or distorting reality. They are familiar to anyone who has read anything about analysis and the important role of these mechanisms in a relationship is easy to understand. If each person in a relationship holds back from the other person, the partners will never come to terms with reality for they will not know how to grasp it. Because information on the defense mechanisms of the Ego is so widely available we shall only mention these mechanisms in passing. They are known as repression, projection, reaction formation, fixation and regression.

Repression is when an impulse from the subconscious is silenced, in order to suppress anxiety by falsifying reality or denying the existence of a threat.

Projection relieves the pressure of the Superior I (the inner censure), by attributing one's feelings to an external cause. "I hate him" becomes "he hates me." "My conscience hurts me" becomes "he annoys me." One attributes one's own aggressive impulses to other people.

Reaction Formation refers to the existence of instincts and types of behavior in opposite pairs: Life/Death, Love/Hate, Constructive/Destructive and Passive/Active tendencies. When a negative instinct, for example, hate, causes anxiety by exerting pressure on the Ego, the Ego may try to counterbalance it by concentrating on the opposite. This behavior is evident in feminine men who adopt rough, masculine manners, but who, by exaggerating them, become true caricatures.

Fixation: A human being develops throughout four stages: infancy, childhood, adolescence and adulthood. Fixation is the case of arrested psychological growth which most often occurs in infancy or childhood. This is a subconscious defense against the anxiety of taking the next step in growth. Why should a person fear growth? Perhaps he anticipates the danger of insecurity, failure or punishment. A person fixates on his mother because he remains psychologically united to her, like a small child, out of fear of loneliness and a desire to be protected.

Regression: This is a return to a former stage of development due to fear. Typical examples are: fear of authority, the dentist, attachment to the maternal image, etc. Normally these defenses are created when the Ego cannot develop itself properly. The Ego often does not develop because it wastes all its energies defending itself against real or imaginary dangers.

To summarize, the Ego attempts to reduce anxiety by: denying danger (repression), externalizing danger (projection), hiding the danger (reaction formation), remaining in the same state (fixation) and returning to a former state (regression).

A relationship between two weak Egos who resort to all these devices to distort reality cannot lead to anything genuine. Individuals in a partnership must analyze themselves in depth to understand to what extent these attitudes are present in their personalities.

5. *Loving Oneself*

The Christian maxim, "love thy neighbor as thyself," tells us that a person should not disregard his own self as far as love is concerned and that he should begin by loving himself. Through analyzing this saying, a person may understand that loving oneself is a prerequisite for loving one's neighbor; in other words, "you should love your neighbor as you already love yourself." People misinterpret the maxim and believe that loving oneself is synonymous with selfishness, a word which in practice has a negative connotation. Erich Fromm has studied this subject in depth and believes that, far from being identical, selfishness and love for oneself, are quite the opposite. The selfish individual does not love himself, but instead hates himself. "Really," says Fromm, "selfish people are not only incapable of loving others, but are also unable to love themselves." "It is easier to understand selfishness," he adds, "by comparing it with an intense concern for others, such as that which we find, for example, in an over-protective mother. While she consciously believes that she is extremely affectionate with her child, she really bears a deeply repressed hostility toward the object of her concern. Her exaggerated care does not correspond to excessive love for the child, but to the fact that she must compensate for her total inability to love him."

Furthermore, to love oneself consists of being loyal to oneself, which is the starting point for being able to love others. A person who is not true to himself, who constantly lies to himself and does not keep his own word, who lacks a sound ethical code, will really have great difficulty loving others. To love oneself means, in its highest sense, to be committed to the Superior I. This is the very opposite of selfishness which is centered in the Inferior I. Union with one's Superior I implies loyalty to oneself and love for others. Generally, those who hate themselves and cannot accept themselves as they are, are unable to love their partners, for they lack the ability to give, something which is indispensable to the science of loving.

6. *Loving One's Neighbor*

Loving one's neighbor teaches a person to understand people. It does not mean indiscriminate giving, which is lost if bestowed upon the wrong person. Loving blindly, deprives the giver of something valuable and also denies another worthier person of the chance to receive love. Interpreted rationally, it means "to do good, but take great care to whom." What is of concern in this instance is people's ability to comprehend their own motives. People must understand precisely what leads them to act one way or another; they must disregard the labels of "good" or "bad," focusing instead on whether behavior is born of ignorance, unawareness and/or irresponsibility; or whether it is a result of wisdom and a high level of consciousness and responsibility. In trying to understand others, we will gradually find it harder to judge them negatively, for we will clearly observe that they acted out of passion and in most cases were driven by compulsive forces beyond their will. Fear, pride, vanity and selfishness are no more than the expression of a person's inner insecurity and he subconsciously tries to reassure himself through misguided behavior. Each person has his own vision of reality and his own concepts. We cannot be content to approve of only those who think like ourselves and disqualify those who think differently. We must interpret "loving one's neighbor" as an exercise in mutual tolerance; training which makes the individual more likely to be successful in a relationship.

7. *Taking the Necessary Time to Understand One's Partner*

How long should one maintain a relationship with a person of the opposite sex before thinking of marriage? How can one know if one's partner is the right person? There are many cases of people who, although they have been married for twenty years or more, have suddenly felt, with the force of a revelation, that they did not even know the person who had accompanied them for so long, causing a disillusionment which plunged them into the depths of disorientation and bewilderment.

The process of getting to know one's partner has three clearly defined stages:
(i)   The stage prior to matrimony
(ii) The stage of testing one's judgment
(iii) The stage of consolidation

(i) *The Stage Prior to Matrimony* is the most important stage in establishing the rules of the game for the couple and it should receive careful planning. The main task during this period will be to decide whether the person we believe we love or with whom we wish to unite, is the right one. This is the time to judge our possible love and the compatibility with the other person. The decision must be made to take the plunge with the appropriate person.

The most important thing is to judge the person we are interested in objectively. We must avoid idealizing the other and we need to find out quite clearly if he or she sets in motion our dreams and unconscious hopes. If so, this is a clear danger signal coming from our daydream phantom, that creature who can wreck our true happiness. We should analyze the partner objectively and go further than the body, face and words, trying our utmost to penetrate the defenses behind which the real Ego is hidden. We should observe attentively everything the person says and not take what he says literally, but try to find the hidden meaning behind his words. This is what truly reveals the individual's hidden side. The most important thing is a firm, resolute attitude of "keeping our feet on the ground." We should consider whether we want to live with this person forever; whether we can manage to communicate properly, disregarding our illusory dreams; we should decide which things are not satisfactory about our partner and try to understand if these are related to our own failings or to those of the other person. We should realize that if we are friendly, affectionate and pleasant to other people, they will normally respond in the same way, and we shall only come to know them by observing their reactions when we behave rudely or inconsiderately. These tests, however tiresome they may be, may save us from making the wrong choice.

(ii) *The Stage of Testing Our Judgment:* This is the stage in which we must test whether we have made the right decision. We will only know if this is so after several years of marriage. Only after a certain amount of time will the partners reveal themselves sufficiently to know one another more deeply and to be able to decide whether there is true compatibility. In this process, there should be the deepest mutual concern, a sense of responsibility and an effort to make the companion happy, apart from understanding and respecting him or her. Without constant attention, concern, and without an effort of the will, love cannot be developed or deepened. We should avoid superficial judgments and try to understand the motives for our partner's actions. This is the only way to lead the relationship to deeper levels. Eventually there comes a moment when we are able to decide whether we have been successful in marriage or not. We should do this in the inner recesses of our soul to avoid being led into error through pressures from family, companions, social rules or self-love. It is important to have objectivity in judgement disregarding the above circumstances and to be able to discuss realistically if necessary, any problems which may arise.

(iii) *The Stage of Consolidation:* After having worked through both the previous stages, comes the time to lead the relationship to higher levels, because one is now sure of having chosen the right path in life. The main concern here is to establish broader and deeper channels of communication in order to have a relationship between two integral "individuals." This is the time to reap the best fruits of the union, for it is possible to attain peaks of peace and happiness such as one had never imagined possible.

The main thing to keep in mind is not to judge prematurely, nor superficially, the person we want for our partner, for each individual is an immense world which holds constant surprises in store for us. It is essential that we do our best to get to know our current or future companion as much as possible, and this process never ends.

8. Not Idealizing Our Counterpart

This work has referred to the serious dangers which await the person who unwittingly projects his daydream phantom onto his loved one. The person pins all of his or her illusions onto the loved one, projects his daydream phantom onto the chosen person. This type of relationship will be doomed to failure, because at heart the individual projecting the phantom loves his own reflection in a distorted way. In fact, the demands of the daydream phantom are impossible to fulfill because they are exaggerated and founded on illusion. This is precisely the problem; one partner demands of another what his own daydream phantom demands of him. The partners only find frustration, suffering and misfortune. It is so important not to idealize the person with whom we want to have a relationship, because it is the most direct way of projecting our daydream phantom onto the other person. One can only know genuine love over the "dead body" of the daydream phantom.

Not to idealize our partner means viewing our situation consciously and rationally, not with our heart or sex. It means discarding romanticism, illusions and self-serving lusts for power and influence. It means seeing our partner for who he or she is and not as we would like them to be, that is, to serve our own selfish purposes.

9. Presenting Oneself as One Really Is

The first concern of a person who wishes to love intelligently and scientifically is to act in a natural way, to show oneself as one really is, and to avoid projecting a false image onto the opposite sex. There are two beings within us: the one we really are and the one we would like to be. Generally, people display the image of what they would like to be and they act out a pattern alien to their real character, concealing their true personality. This causes unhappiness and misfortune, not only in love, but in life as a whole. The person does not experience life and love fully, but plays them out artificially and subjectively. There are many unhappy couples who because they do not experience their relationship in practice, simulate their relationships. It is quite easy to fake virtue and this is often done by a person who wishes to attract the opposite sex, although he should realize there will inevitably come a moment when he will be discovered. It is most important for one to be honest and show oneself as one is. Although this approach may seem to have its drawbacks, it will be of benefit in the long run, because this openness will become the strongest foundation of happiness in love. "Deceit breeds deceit" and "frankness encourages frankness."

The person who shows himself as he is, also encourages his partner to do the same and the relationship is thus entered upon by real and not fictitious beings. It necessarily requires courage and bravery to show oneself as one really is. It means confronting the world face to face, not hiding behind the barrier of a mask. For this reason many people find it very hard to act openly and naturally, even though they know that by pretending, they are shaping their own unhappiness. They will be exhausted; this process takes up an inordinate amount of energy. To be able to act naturally and to reveal oneself, fear of the other party must be absent, because where there is fear, there is no love; fear prevents one from being frank. The golden rule for a perfect relationship between a couple is to not be afraid of showing who one really is.

10. *Discarding Selfishness and Jealousy*

Many individuals are selfish because they have had little opportunity to worry about other people. They do not realize that they are prisoners of their own psychological limitations and that with enlightenment they could overcome their painful situation. A profound narcissism hides behind selfishness and basically reveals a lack of development of the Ego. This results in a fixation at an early age when the child is intrinsically selfish; his relationship with his mother is purely utilitarian because he only needs her to feed and care for him. Whenever a person tends to act very selfishly, one may assume that he is acting childishly and that even though he may be aware of his weakness, he is afraid of giving because he is frightened at not being able to replace what he must give up. For this reason, the safety valve of his selfish relationship with people only functions inward; he does no more than receive and accumulate. He not only expects to continuously receive from others, but also wants to do it scot-free. This type of psychological avarice produces emotional impotence because the person views love as experiencing the loss of his hidden treasure. Only with the passing of time does he discover that by not giving, except for few exceptions, he no longer receives and he is isolated from the world and people. This causes him a great anxiety which he tries to fight by absorbing new emotional input from others or by living through their affections. Only by understanding the phenomenon of his selfishness can the individual free himself from becoming an emotional parasite and be helped to emerge from a negative, pre-established situation. One can only love through the active notion of giving; one can only be successful by making the other person happy.

Jealousy is also a consequence of the same circumstance as selfishness, and although there are many different causes, they are nevertheless closely related to each other. An exaggerated attempt to monopolize or trap the other person as if he or she were the miser's pot of gold, makes the individual over-sensitive about his partner's freedom which he tries to curtail in order to control and dominate. The fear behind this behavior is as real as the fear of being the victim of a theft; just as the miser would be horrified at the thought of being robbed.

Selfishness is a serious obstacle towards acquiring the necessary empathy (the ability to put oneself emotionally in the other person's place) for a happy, amorous union.

11. Communicating with the Partner's Inner World

The importance of this communication on an individual and private basis was covered previously in the second point. However, once a lover learns to communicate with his own inner world, he should do the same with his loved one's in order to establish a truly profound union. Rather than contact at only the level of bodies, there should be a relationship between souls, which will allow the individual to know and be known. He may then decide what his companion really needs to develop herself, to perfect herself and to be happy. She for her part will perceive her man as he really is and will know how to support and help him in his own self-fulfillment. As a direct result of this communication, they will form a couple that functions on a much higher level than usual, thus complementing each other perfectly to make up a dynamic structure which will help them obtain the good things of life. The nature of the relationship between their inner worlds will make both know each other far more completely than they could through the spoken or written word, and each will know about the other what he might not even know about himself.

12. *Absence of Lying*

There are many forms of lying. All of them severely damage a couple's real chances of love, because essentially, lies are a means of manipulation, a way of taking advantage of the other party. Even though deceit takes on a variety of forms, there are two notable types of lying: one which comes from self-deceit and one which has its origins in fear. Self-deception makes one lie unwittingly, for the person really lies to himself. His false statements are not intentional but come from a sincere, though misguided, conviction. But this defense mechanism may become one of the main causes of a couple's falling apart, because the partner will never be able to carry out what he says he will do. Inevitably there will come a time when the partner apparently "changes his mind"; he will suddenly face reality and throw all previous plans and projects to the winds. He constantly contradicts himself and breaks his word in this way. There is no malice in it, only irresponsibility; a lack of a fully grown "directing Ego" which is both mature and responsible.

Even when no bad intentions exist, the consequences are just as ill-fated as if the person had deliberately and perversely planned everything. His companion may be traumatized by this process and believe that her partner acted in bad faith.

The other form of lying also occurs with the best of intentions and is not meant to hurt the partner. One partner fears there is a risk that the other will discover thoughts, feelings, or acts which could be considered offensive, lacking in love, aggressive or indifferent. The fear may be based on real facts which the individual wishes to hide from his companion, the intention being of not to worry or disappoint her, or to keep up a good image of himself. Sometimes, an intolerant and demanding person will provoke his partner into lying, because he does not want to see her unhappy and he tries to keep her happy. This practice only brings temporary success at the expense of tremendous harm in the long run, for deception and falseness are always found out, even though they may have been practiced as a sort of sentimental anesthesia.

We must eliminate the concept of "out of sight, out of mind" and insist, even though it may be painful, on speaking the naked truth. This is the foundation for the birth and development of true love, but this approach demands a mature and intelligent attitude from both parties. We must realize that it is fatal to be misunderstood when we are sincere, because this encourages future lies to protect ourselves from the backlash of scenes and verbal aggression. We must bear in mind that if we wish to truly know our companion, we must reward and not punish him or her. If not, we run the risk of slipping into permanent lack of communication.

13. *Loving the Other Person as He Is*

This means simply to not complain about the other person's character and to consider that if we have committed ourselves to another, it is to love that other person as he or she is and not to want our partner to serve our own purposes. Therefore, it is essential to help our companion overcome certain defects or problems and it is also advisable to point them out at the right moment and to help the partner change positively. It is not wise to accept forms of behavior which are useful to our own purposes and to reject those which go against our desires. There are people who, having accepted those parts of their companions which are in their interests, later disregard them and devote their efforts to destructive criticism of those behaviors which differ from their selfish aims. In view of this we must understand that our counterpart is a person, not a tool for our own purposes and, as an autonomous being, has the full right to enjoy his or her own opinions, tastes, sympathies, antipathies, types of behavior and points of view, all of which we must respect. This obviously does not mean that if we honestly think that he or she is wrong it would not be right to show our disagreement openly. This should be based on logical and intelligent reasoning and not on capricious, irrational or whimsical arguments. There are people who, out of habit, disapprove of everything that differs from their own personal frame of reference and who lack the tolerance necessary for unbiased analysis of other people's ideas. We should avoid this at all costs, especially because some individuals go to the extreme of wanting their companions to be duplicates of themselves. Even if this were possible, such duplication would be a diabolical invention liable to cancel and deny the progress that comes through growth and evolution.

Each person must show himself as he really is in order to work together in building both a mutual and individual future. It is common for men and women to try to force their partners to change, to drop their own ideas and to adopt theirs. When this endeavor is not successful, the partner who is trying to impose his ideas on the other, expresses his disagreement or slyly argues that his counterpart does not love him.

The wish for harmony is quite understandable, but it is unacceptable to try to achieve this through the absorption and fusion of the other person into oneself, for this means the death of love.

14. *Letting Go of Exploitation*
Exploitation in love means using the other party as a tool to achieve one's own ends, without taking into consideration at all the fulfillment of the other being's goals. The exploiter uses the other person as a tool, without feeling any real love at heart. This is not only a form of vampirism in which one person feeds on the vital forces of the other, but is also a form of corrupt behavior and immorality. It represents the development and survival of one being at the price of the other's extinction. Macho behavior, matriarchal behavior or sadistic behavior have led many couples into this exploitive state.

One should study a person's psyche in great depth in order to understand the true motives for such behavior. Exploitation is a danger signal for those who unwittingly fall into it and it should be considered just as immoral, if not more so, as theft, fraud, or murder. A lack of exploitation means that each person can develop just as he or she is and not as the other might wish in order to serve his own ends; it means respect for one's partner's individual liberty and implies tolerance and understanding.

We should also point out that whoever allows

himself to be exploited voluntarily is just as guilty or immoral as the other, even though he may be accepting this situation out of fear, coercion or threats.

15. *Letting Go of Illusion*

Unfortunately, there are many who spend their whole lives chasing illusory phantoms, seeking things that are worth nothing in themselves, but which are only important because they bring social recognition. In a consumer society, it is quite normal for a married couple to direct all their efforts to acquiring material goods which may bring the illusion of happiness and social recognition, rather than real happiness in love. Many of the goods available to the human being become power symbols and their worth lies in the image which the person manages to project through them to the world. A luxurious car, a fur coat or valuable jewels, all have the same meaning as tribal ornaments do in primitive societies. They symbolize the power an individual has attained. Medals which generally lack any objective value also symbolize achievement or social recognition, for example.

It is pathetic to see how the majority of modern married couples pursue the possession of these power symbols, while they do not nurture the love that could be their most prized possession. In the face of ignorance or the apparent lack of true love, this pursuit of possessions can be an attempt to create a suitable substitute, binding the couple through obligations and the joint ownership of material goods. Social climbing becomes the main activity, absorbing all the couple's energies. This illusory ascent never ends, and as a result, there is not the slightest opportunity for the birth of love.

These considerations are only for those who really wish to have true love. Those who do not mind playing out a parody all their lives have no reason to bother with this task.

If a couple gives priority to attaining true love first, they will later have sufficient time to also raise their economic and social standards if they so wish.

16. *Preoccupation With Giving Before Receiving*

We have said that one of the main characteristics of love is its active or giving nature. When this condition is not fulfilled and a person only wishes to receive, he becomes incapable of loving. Real giving does not imply "I'll give to you, if you give to me," but rather, "I'll give to you without expecting anything in return."

How many lovers are able to give without expecting anything in return? Unrequieted love is by no means pleasant and giving without expecting anything in return does not imply that a lover should practice a form of emotional masochism, but that he or she should avoid a materialistic approach to love. A person either does or does not love and love cannot depend on how much is given in exchange, although there should be a balance of giving and receiving in a healthy and positive relationship. This process should be born of an individual act of free will and not be a product of demand. It is realistic to anticipate that the act of giving will inspire a similar attitude in one's partner, even when this may take some time to develop. However, in order for this to happen, there should be an active initial impulse from the person who loves, which will light the fire of desire. Love is often not immediately returned but, as the days go by, a suitable balance is established. This will not happen if the initiator of the relationship demands some sort of correspondence before continuing in his giving attitude. No love will flourish if both parties have the same demanding attitude. Love can never be an obligation, but a voluntary act of giving oneself; one cannot expect to possess, but only to give oneself in the legitimate hope of being loved in return. The imbalance lies in expecting that the act of giving oneself to someone obligates the other to give something of equivalent value.

Some partners bitterly reproach their loved one when the other person changes his or her mind and does not wish to continue the relationship; these partners feel cheated, as if they had paid a fee for a faulty or undelivered article.

17. *Sharing Responsibilities*

The most common and harmful error in relationships is the effort to pin the blame on one or the other when something goes wrong. Behind this behavior lies the purpose of designating only one of the persons as responsible, while the other remains clear of all guilt. Interminable and bitter arguments arise in the face of conflict in which each tries to save himself by sacrificing the other. These attitudes have the hidden purpose of making the other party feel guilty. The individual therefore improves his position in the sense that he can thus impose his own will and control the situation to his favor.

This does not mean that one should not point out the other person's faults when one sincerely believes them to exist, but simply that it is not honest to take advantage of the situation nor to use it to shirk responsibility. The most suitable way to analyze problems is to share responsibilities, to take into account the errors of the couple's faults and not to focus on who may have behaved mistakenly. Thus, a mistake on the part of a woman will also be her husband's responsibility and vice-versa. It is as if a person were to say, "I am responsible for my mistakes and for my partner's, too."

A married man or woman may feel frightened by this system, especially if the spouse is really careless, irresponsible or not very intelligent. This would mean taking on the burden of a volume of imperfections greater than one's own. Love is like this; everything should be shared, and the concerned individual would have no other course but to make the spouse aware of carelessness or lack of concern. He must point out the need for striking a balance, unless he prefers separation which is a superficial and unsatisfactory solution.

This is the main problem of unequal matches, that is of unions in which one of the partners exceeds the other in his level of development. Therefore, one partner will be obliged to burden himself with a disproportionate amount of deadweight. This inequality is not determined by university degrees, wealth, physical assets, or chronological age, but rather as a matter of consciousness, maturity, awareness and a degree of evolution. The person who takes advantage in a relationship, exploiting the other person, will nevertheless get his dues, as karma escapes no one.

18. *Proper Balance Between Strength and Beauty*

In universal Hermetic symbology, a woman represents beauty and a man strength. Life is upheld by these two pillars. When either of the parties does not respect the role he or she has been given by Nature, the balance is upset and it is very hard to attain happiness. But, what do beauty and strength mean? These concepts do not refer to physical beauty or muscular strength, but to the transcendent concept of inner beauty and psychological and spiritual strength. Woman's beauty should be shown through her feelings, thoughts, words and deeds, in order to establish an harmonious rhythm with the laws of Nature. Woman's beauty means inner loveliness or the focusing of her conceiving feminine power on the aesthetic perfection of her invisible children. It also means harmony, equilibrium, naturalness, spontaneity, happiness, optimism, perfection, love, vitality, intuition and tenderness.

Man's strength refers, above all, to his intelligence, consciousness, spiritual power, psychic and mental soundness.

When inner balance is lacking, men become neurotic, aggressive, effeminate, chauvinistic or hysterical, while women become too authoritarian, domineering and masculine.

One can usually observe in a sexual relationship how a man's feelings of inferiority lead him to attempt to show himself to be very strong and capable, thus hindering tenderness and naturalness. During sex, such a man acts rapidly, mechanically and reaches orgasm almost at once.

Above all else, a woman seeks tenderness, affection, strength and understanding. If she does not find these qualities, she is sometimes obliged to adopt attitudes which really correspond to a man's. In general terms, we could say that men most need sensitivity and intuition; while women need greater emotional control and the elevation of their objective reasoning ability to control and channel their femininity towards their joint and personal goals. To form a couple of quality, the man should be constant and steadfast, conscious and intelligent, tender and intuitive, while the woman should be intelligent and understanding, spontaneous and capable of reasoning, gentle and loving and in possession of her emotions and words.

19. Self-Control, Discipline and Will Power

The practice of true love is not simple and mastery in this science comes through adequate training. The only way a person can achieve this goal is through the training and control of himself, for love is inseparable from the individual. Only by reaching a certain level of self-control, discipline and will power can one work consciously to overcome the serious difficulties which will stand inevitably in one's way. Only by using one's energies correctly will a person make the constant effort to understand and offer a partner happiness. The practice of love needs continuous care, for it is like an exotic plant that needs extra special attention.

Each of the partners should do their utmost, with intelligence, will power and consistency, to make the other person happy. This means tolerating and understanding the other's faults, supporting them in their failures and weaknesses. It also means enlightening the other in the fields or subjects which one has mastered, but the other has not. One should lavish tenderness on the other and one must have infinite patience. One should not let oneself be defeated by boredom or tedium. One should know how to criticize objectively and put up with criticism with intelligence and equanimity. One should watch over the other party's happiness above one's own and know when to accompany the other and when to leave the other alone. One should allow for the partner's free individual development. One should be frank and honest even to one's own detriment, and should understand and support the other in all ways. This also implies respect for the inner sanctuary of the other's soul, which is the individual's private place of refuge wherein nobody can enter; the oasis where he or she recovers the forces spent in the battle of life. One should respect this privacy and understand that every human being has the right to preserve this sacred place, which is one's ultimate refuge. One should not interfere with what happens there, except with the permission or invitation of the other person.

20. Fidelity

This characteristic refers more than anything to faith in oneself, for when this condition is fulfilled, all other aspects of fidelity are also fulfilled. To be true to oneself means loyalty to one's own moral principles, as we explained in the chapter on morality. It means that the person becomes indissolubly united to his Superior I, and that he can do nothing that runs counter to his inner codes. A couple's happiness depends first of all on loyalty to oneself, which will bring about the voluntary commitment to honesty and frankness with one's spouse, regardless of the results. When this first obligation is fulfilled, fidelity is born spontaneously. Above all it depends on spiritual loyalty and all it implies.

Viewed as the highest type of morality, fidelity, if it is to be genuine, will be the inner attitude of a person, not just an external facade. Love and sexuality cannot become an obligation, for this would be more immoral than any other type of immorality. This would mean enslaving a human being through the power of law and social opinion, to force the person to share a life with someone he might find repulsive or unpleasant. The person would undergo the dishonor and defilement of lending the use of his penis or of her vagina to someone who is hateful or repulsive.

On the contrary, there are individuals who build up a web of lies to hide the fact that they cheat on their spouses and this deceit paradoxically allows society, the individual and the spouse to remain reassured and satisfied. In other words, people will respect social or external morality, while they violate all the rules of individual, natural and divine morality. In this way, they fall into the hypocritical conduct that is the very opposite of fidelity.

THE HERMETIC COUPLE

This chapter will briefly touch on the subject of a couple, perfected in a higher union. In this type of union, the couple would have been initiated in Hermetic science and would have carried out a considerable part of the training.

We will first look at what could be the highest achievement of a union of love. In its highest expression a man and a woman are united beyond time and distance and the sexual act would not be absolutely necessary for their union, provided we accept that intercourse may be carried out at the level of the mind.

The Hermetic couple possesses many qualities identical or similar to those described in the last chapter; qualities which have been elevated to their total fulfillment. At the Hermetic level, love occurs only to the extent that both people realize a truly effective development of their own Egos, followed by the stages of maturity and plenitude.

The couple will have covered much ground, first attaining a high state of watchfulness, overcoming the type of sleep-walking automatism which rules ordinary people. They will have controlled themselves to gain full dominion over their instincts, emotions and thoughts, having defeated selfishness, vanity, pride and jealousy and having shaped themselves to be able to form the mental ovoid. In sum, they will have attained the knowledge and control of their own physical instruments, which would then allow them a higher form of relationship that, apart from leading them to true happiness, would also guide them to ever increasing advancement on the path of spiritual evolution.

Seven points of the Hermetic couple's love may be revealed here. These following points involve esoteric practices that consolidate their union on a higher plane and which ensure their happiness and evolution:

1. A Man Projects His Femininity onto the Woman and a Woman Projects Her Masculinity onto the Man

In the beginning, we mentioned that a man has a feminine side and that a woman has a masculine side. The problem for the balance of the sexes lies in the percentage of the opposite sex which we all have. In a sense, this prevents each sex from reaching a perfected state. The feminine element makes a man weak and makes him to be ruled by passion; the masculine makes a woman domineering, hysterical and unfeminine.

In the Hermetic couple a woman must renounce all the masculine part of herself to her companion and, in turn, accept the feminine element which her man must give her. This is how they come to perfect integral masculinity and femininity, which, as will be understood from the teachings of previous pages, leads to the *greatest possible polar distance between the couple*. This is how the active and passive poles achieve their maximum tension and consequently, their highest degree of attraction. Through this process, a powerful vital force is also generated which allows the couple to renew and regenerate themselves constantly. If the active or masculine force possesses a certain amount of passive energy, it cannot be placed at the extreme of the positive pole, but can only approach it. If the same thing happens with the negative pole, we are faced with the situation in which the potentiality of both poles is diminished, and therefore these poles could not generate their fullest potency, as would happen if they were perfectly defined in their essential polar nature.

This is one of the great differences between an ordinary couple and a Hermetic one; the first lacks the correct polar distance, while the second has perfect tension between the two poles which among other things, ensures adequate vitality. How can these misplaced masculine and feminine elements be reciprocally transferred, as we mentioned? This can only be achieved when the awareness of both partners leads them to understand that in true marriage, the other person is the "alter ego" of oneself. This happens when a person learns how to unfold him or herself in his companion, which is a task for advanced disciples. This does not come about suddenly, but gradually and progressively. Preparation for it consists of first achieving perfect harmony and understanding between the partners in a couple.

2. *Adopting Natural Roles*

As we have mentioned, a woman incarnates Nature, while a man represents the Spirit. There is a great difference between playing these roles unconsciously and doing the same consciously. A couple should act responsibly and wisely in the same way as the heavens and the earth should be joined in a creative embrace in order to reconquer the lost Paradise.

When we state that a woman is Nature, we say so in the broadest sense of the word. This is why her path to spiritual evolution is so different from a man's. Only when she manages to master the force of Nature in her interior, will she be projected to a different cosmic dimension. She will move from being a woman to becoming the queen of Nature.

A man can only learn the mysteries of Nature when he comes to a full understanding of the feminine soul. This explains the uselessness of those who attempt spiritual development in isolation, cut off from Nature. They can never attain true wisdom in this way. A woman needs a man to raise her to the heaven of the spirit, for he is the spiritual energy which comes from heaven to earth. There is no heaven for woman without a man; for man, there is no wisdom or Paradise without a woman. This concept will of course lack all meaning for unawakened couples or those who seek only the momentary pleasure of the body at the expense of the soul.

A woman reaches her maximum cosmic fulfillment in giving her soul to the man, a goal she unwittingly pursues all her life. In fact, in the Hermetic couple the woman must give her soul to her man to receive from him in turn the fire of heaven, his spiritual virile power. This exchange will lead them to a relationship impossible to describe to non-initiates as it takes the woman to heaven and allows the man to penetrate the mysteries of Nature.

Every woman, whether she is a Hermeticist or not, intimately desires to find a man worthy of giving her soul to, but she very rarely finds him. Apart from implying higher spiritual fulfillment, there are only very few males who possess heavenly spiritual fire, the fire which Prometheus is said to have stolen in myth. However, when a woman does not find the right man, she should take a less ambitious path and be content with what is also an enormous advancement, that is, mastering Nature within herself, a circumstance which will also allow her to attain a higher evolution.

3. *Fusion into a Third Being*

The ordinary couple attempts to fuse into one single being and seeks to stop existing individually in order to make up a unity. What may at first sight seem a highly desirable goal really becomes the death of love, for it means uniting opposite poles in a middle ground which kills the attraction. Certainly, the partners should unite as intimately as possible and achieve a common identity, but how can they do this without extinguishing the tension created by polar distance? This can only be achieved by fusion into a third being. This refers to the hidden child in which part of a man and a woman are fused without either one losing their own individuality. By keeping their individuality, they make up an androgynous being which gives them perfect fusion and adequate polarity. Duality does not become unity, but trinity. This type of occult hermaphroditism offers the couple the power to contemplate their own intellect from the opposite point of view, from the other side of the coin. Men and women alone are only able to see half of reality because their intelligence is conditioned by their sexual gender. Only by integrating in the unity born of the trinity can they manage to complete their view. This does not occur when ordinary couples fuse together. Each partner is impotent to understand the other party and to reveal him or herself.

4. *Regaining the Hidden Paradise*

Through their integral relationship, the Hermetic couple can enjoy the hidden Paradise of Adam and Eve. In this Eden, they can acquire the power to create everything. This does not free them from the Law of Cause and Effect but, on the contrary, makes them more responsible. The power to create refers to the intelligent use of Hermetic principles, not to the ability to materialize things from nothing. One does not have to give up expectations of material advancement, but one should aspire to the wise, responsible channeling of one's own resources. These principles stress that a Hermeticist cannot go against the laws of Nature but should always respect them. No one is above the laws of Nature. One may only utilize the higher laws as opposed to inferior ones by obeying the rules of the game.

5. The Creation of Gods

The mystery of theurgy shows how it is possible for the human being to create gods. We have already discussed at length the opposite, negative pole of this practice in the dangerous play of human passions with the creation of magnetic demons. The Hermetic couple may consciously direct their generating power and have invisible children who are truly gods born of the higher spiritual principles and not of the individual's animal nature. These hidden children are the couple's spiritual offspring which not only make up their descendants but also the "divine family." They are also the elements which protect and help them to attain their perfect evolution.

6. Mental Coitus

The Hermetic couple has normal sexual relations, although of an infinitely higher quality than ordinary ones. Sex is not only an instrument of gratification for them, but a means of rising to higher states of consciousness. There is a Hindu word which has no equivalent in English which illustrates our explanation. It is the term "samadhi" which means a state of divine ecstasy. It is precisely this state which one attains through mental coitus, in a relationship between the magnetic sexualities united to the evolved minds of the partners. From the point of view of ordinary people they may misunderstand this concept of "mental coitus" assuming it to mean that a man and a woman must concentrate on imagining that they are participating in the sexual act, even though they are physically separated. It is quite different, however, because the mental is not synonymous with the intellectual or imaginative. In Hermeticism, the word "mind" has a different meaning than the usual one and here refers rather to the formation of a "magnetic ovoid," made up of conscious energy of a high vibration. Mental coitus is a state of profound enjoyment which can only be imagined by understanding that the principles of sensual pleasure which govern the material world hold no sway in the spiritual one. Spiritual enjoyment is far more intense and refined than the sensual, but may only be experienced by those who have managed to become truly spiritual, manifesting their spirit through their own brains. Mental coitus is more of a state of consciousness than a practice designed for obtaining pleasure.

7. Creating a Private Sanctuary in the Home

For the Hermetic couple, the home should be a place in which they are armed against any inferior vibrations. It should be the refuge which protects them from both visible and invisible enemies; the sanctuary in which they can shelter themselves from the evils of corrupt beings.

There is nothing more offensive to corrupt beings than the contemplation of the peace and happiness in true love. Just as a red cape taunts the bull in the ring, goodness, love, peace and spirituality arouse the hate and ferocity of the demons who dwell in the realm of inferior energy. They will always attack those who represent the opposite of their own dark condition. Just by coming into contact with the great mass of humanity, a person is contaminated with all kinds of negative vibrations which are the product of people's animal passions. This is why monks who wish to purify themselves to be worthy of divine grace remove themselves from all contact with the world and retire to monasteries.

The Hermetic path follows a different course. It does not advocate this type of seclusion. On the contrary, it insists on an active relationship with one's environment, this being the only way to understand the human soul and to not shirk social responsibilities. Nevertheless, in the course of every-day events, the individual loses energy and becomes contaminated with negative states. Upon his return home, through the re-concentration on himself in the pure environment of his sanctuary, an individual can recover the lost energy and keep himself protected.

The couple's harmonious vibrations will offer strong protective magnetic radiation for the home against destructive influences and the home will become a place of calm, peace, beauty, harmony, spirituality and protection. The legendary *Shangri-La*, a mythical place where the most profound beauty, peace and happiness reigned, is only a symbol of the sacred space which couples may create in their home, independently of the material comforts they might enjoy. Love and happiness can only grow and develop properly in a place where the warmth of true humanity reigns, protected against the perversity of alien influences.

The type of union achieved by a Hermetic couple goes beyond any known concept. It is not due to fantasy, but to the real and concrete nature of the results they obtained. Life is like a large garden in which the most desirable fruits are within our reach, but people usually receive only those which fall by chance on their heads.

Hermetic love is immortal. It withstands the passing

of death and survives the destruction of the physical body. It extends to that world which begins where illusions and dreams end, beyond life and death, beyond good and evil or beyond pleasure and pain. Love is the fruit from the tree of the science of good and evil, to which God referred when He said: "if ye eat of this fruit, ye shall become as gods."

ADDENDUM

FALLACIES ABOUT LOVE, SEX AND MARRIAGE

People often have false expectations about love, sex and marriage, and these expectations are simply reflections of current social patterns. These misconceptions include the following most common expectations and ideas.

FALLACIES ABOUT LOVE:
1. Love is easy, spontaneous and everybody is prepared for it.
2. Passion and jealousy are gauges for real love.
3. Love is a feeling that resides in the heart.
4. Everyone has a right to obtain happiness in love.
5. Love should be selfish.
6. Luck and happiness in love depend exclusively on finding the right person.
7. Love should be an explosive and overwhelming experience.
8. Love should be blind, without involvement of the power of reason.
9. Love should be like a novel, romantic and fantastic.
10. Love is dependent on physical beauty.
11. Love depends on sexual union.
12. Love never knows any type of discord.
13. Love is a cure for loneliness, failure and anxiety.
14. The feeling of euphoria is a sign of true love.
15. Falling in love is destined to be a positive and desirable experience.

16. One partner should give all his time and devotion to the other.
17. One is capable of fulfilling all the needs of the other.
18. Love is something which will fill one's life completely.
19. Love will be the most important thing in life.
20. Love centers exclusively on personal gratification and reproduction.
21. Love requires no will power or discipline.
22. One person should possess the other person.
23. Love may be stimulated, activated or conditioned by emotional, economic or sexual incentives.
24. Love will allow a person to fulfill all his illusions and desires.

FALLACIES ABOUT SEX:
1. Sex is sinful.
2. Sex should either be repressed or given free rein.
3. Sex is expressed only through the genitals.
4. Satisfaction depends on the frequency of coitus.
5. Sexual affinity should exist from the beginning of a relationship.
6. Sexual coincidence is synonymous with love.
7. Marriage is the seal of approval or permission for sexual relationships.
8. Sex is filthy.
9. All sexual experience will be marvelous, fulfilling all expectations, when in fact the result may be disappointing.
10. If a person has any objections to the sexual act, these will disappear after marriage.
11. The sexual act takes away something one had before. The loss is irreversible. In reality there is no loss but rather an exchange.
12. Sexual relationships are signs of maturity and the ability to take decisive action.
13. A woman's satisfaction depends on the size of the male organ.

14. Sexual excitement in a woman should be centered in her physical organs.
15. Virility is expressed by sexual potency.
16. Frigidity is just a problem of feminine puritanism.
17. A woman's femininity is proven by the number of orgasms she reaches.
18. Coitus is necessarily an expression of animal behavior.
19. Sexual attraction will last forever.
20. Sexual chastity is a guarantee of purity.
21. Sexual chastity is essential for attaining spirituality.
22. Contraceptives are evil.

FALLACIES ABOUT MARRIAGE:
1. Marriage is a requisite goal in life.
2. Marriage will allow young people to enter into the world of adults.
3. Marriage will necessarily be pleasant and sweet.
4. A person achieves stability through marriage.
5. Marriage must last forever.
6. Marriage means possessing and taking over the other person.
7. Marriage automatically means happiness and security.
8. Marriage must necessarily result in the birth of children.
9. Marriage is an annoying obligation.
10. One loses and should lose, freedom with marriage.
11. One's marriage will be different and not include the mistakes made in other marriages.
12. Marriage will solve or compensate for one's personal problems.
13. A spouse will spend his or her life constantly and solely devoted to the other.
14. Marriage is a solution for loneliness, anxiety, or depression.
15. Marital union and stability is based on sexual expression.
16. The longer the time spent together in daily life, the

closer the marriage will be.

17. The spouse's time belongs to other.
18. Momentary disinterest is a sign of lack of love.
19. Sleeping in separate beds harms the relationship or shows lack of interest.
20. Inner affection is always in proportion to physical caresses.
21. Marriage is the means of obtaining the things one lacks.
22. Fidelity only consists of sexual exclusivity.
23. Children can save the love of a marriage.
24. Success in marriage should be measured by economic power, number of children, social position or material possessions.
25. One should put up with anything in marriage in order to avoid separation or divorce.

WORDS TO THOSE SUFFERING

FOR A LOST LOVE

Many people, when they have found a great love, lose it for any number of reasons. This experience can be traumatic and can lead to tremendous inner crises. Some people even commit suicide or murder, and the world thinks that they must have loved to an extreme degree to have taken their own or another's life as a result of losing the object of their affection.

We must look at the distinct difference between the natural and pathological effects of a disappointment in love because so many people suffer over a lost love. Certain feelings, such as sadness or loneliness, are normal and these responses often help the person who experiences them to mature. The pathological experience is of concern though, for this reaction causes the most harm to a person and is what one must learn to avoid or counteract.

This experience is suffered by all people for whom love means not only pleasure, but also narcissistic gratification. The force of love maintains and reinforces narcissism. Through narcissism, an individual keeps up his self-esteem, adoring and caressing himself, forming the nucleus of his psychic life and his directing Ego. A narcissistic person believes that everything has been created for his own satisfaction and that the whole world revolves around him. Narcissism has its origins in infancy when a child discovers that all his needs can be immediately satisfied by the mother. He thinks that she and the world at large exist only to serve him. Later, when his mother spoils him and over-protects him, he acquires the feeling of omnipotence upon which narcissism is founded. When he becomes an adult, he realizes that he is not omnipotent, but this understanding does not dispel the complex. The complex is fixed at an unconscious level in infancy and the individual must resort to external reinforcements to raise his self-esteem through a "narcissistic supply line." For the narcissist, love may become the most powerful supply line, causing a "pathological" reaction to disappointment in love. A pathological reaction is produced not only when love has brought disappointment, but also when love has brought pleasure. By losing the "loved one," the individual feels that he has really lost his life. This profound feeling does not come from having lost someone dear, but from the fact that he can no longer count upon the "narcissistic fuel" which love had given him.

Imagine the individual who, like a deflated balloon, constantly needs people of the opposite sex to "inflate him," and that this process must be repeated regularly. When the other party refuses to continue "inflating him," this person feels empty and that he has died, when all he really needs is the volume of air which made him feel important. This analogy symbolizes the process of narcissistic disappointment in love. The person feels as if he were dying, or at least wishes to, because, deprived of the support of love, he feels insignificant and worthless. It is not true that he suffers for love; his pain is due to the sudden lack of support to which he had become accustomed. This is evident when we witness how easily a "love object" can be replaced when another of an equivalent ability to give comes along. Suffering in love is therefore a relative matter because it is not easy to determine the line between true love and narcissism. The narcissist cannot suffer the loss of something he has never really had. The loss represents the dispelling of a pleasant illusion or the shrinking of self-esteem.

The only sensible solution lies in truly understanding what has happened and in seeking the support of inner values, not external ones. When a person lacks a developed Ego which is both strong and mature, he seeks support in external ways. He subconsciously perceives his own weakness, and identifies himself with the object of his love; not to give love, but to feed upon the other's strength.

Love between two people possessing very weak Egos is no more than a sad game which arises when together they pursue in the other, elements each lacks, a search inevitably ending in the disillusionment of two beings who have nothing to offer one another but their own bodies. To be able to love, one must eliminate narcissism at all costs because it causes one to perceive as truth only those things which exist within oneself, thus discounting the reality of the external world. The narcissist evaluates life and people solely for his or her personal usefulness. Narcissism noticeably distorts reality and keeps the individual a prisoner in the depths of his own person so that he is unable to communicate with people. The experience of disappointment in love as well as the tremendous suffering resulting from the frustration of losing a narcissistic support system, imprisons the person in pain. He feels self-pity, remaining submerged in his own world and not experiencing external reality. The experience of disappointment in love is so difficult for such people, unless they quickly find an adequate substitute. The loss of self-esteem not only represents a far too serious threat to them, but is also an unbearable existence.

Those who react more normally, on the contrary, adapt with relative speed to disappointment in love unless that lover were of a genuine and higher type in which case it would be very difficult to fill the gap left by the loss. Depending on the couple's state of spiritual advancement however, the death of one of the parties does not necessarily cut off the relationship which continues eternally.

CLUES TO DETECT

NARCISSISM IN LOVE

Several danger signals can alert us to the presence of the element of narcissism in a relationship. The most common of these signals are the following:

1. A person needs to be constantly praised.
2. He has low resistance to frustration.
3. He lacks the equanimity to accept criticism.
4. He is needy and demanding.
5. He demands total devotion from his partner.
6. He is extremely jealous.
7. His judgements are lacking in objectivity.
8. He has a feeling of omnipotence.
9. He is overly vain and proud.

Erich Fromm provides the following example of a narcissistic distortion of reality:

"A woman called the doctor telling him that she wished to visit him at his office that afternoon. The doctor replied that he had no time that day, but that he could see her the following day. The woman's answer was: "But, doctor, I only live five minutes away from your office." She could not comprehend that just because the distance between them was short, did not mean that he would have the time to see her. She experienced the situation narcissistically. Because she would save time, he must also save time. The only reality for her, was herself."

We conclude that the narcissist has an inability to objectively appreciate external reality because he projects his own inner world onto it. Faced with disappointments in love, he has only two alternatives: seek a substitute who will once more "inflate the balloon" which would bring momentary relief for his anxiety, or else set about facing the reality of his own condition as a weak, childish person, lacking inner strength. He should not be depressed by this latter alternative, but should instead consider facing reality as the essential condition which would lead him to true development and strength. In fact, as long as a person does not acknowledge or accept his own weakness, it will be impossible for him to become strong, for this can only occur by having a clear idea of his situation. There is no cure without prior awareness of the disease.

For narcissists, who experience unbalanced reactions to a stimulus and for those with normal reactions, learning and comprehending the science of love is invaluable in the search for happiness and success.

THE DANGERS OF

LEARNING THE SCIENCE OF LOVE

The science of love must be tailored to the individual, because it involves training a person to love with the same care and skill as playing an instrument. A human being produces a melody of love through a union of body and mind. Furthermore, attaining this knowledge alone is not enough for practical fulfillment in love. A person requires a being of the opposite sex with similar needs and goals who also knows and practices wisdom in love. This could happen either of two ways: individuals who will know the science of love and lack a partner and individuals who are married or who already have a partner and must now learn the science of love.

Those who already know the science of love will need to guide their future partners, helping them to also acquire wisdom in love. They must unite in marriage only when the chosen partner has done a sufficient and profound self-examination and study in the science of love, which can then be completed in the course of their life together. Those wise in the science of love will infinitely increase their chances of reaching true happiness and fulfillment. For those who already have a partner, there is a risk however, that their efforts to achieve true love may find no response in their partners. The absence of responses in the other partner could be due to a lack of cultural exposure, a lack of interest, or simply a lack of care. As a person gains knowledge of the science of love, he feels needs which become more elevated and broader from the perspective of human and spiritual sensitivity. His motivation may profoundly change from having gained access to a richer, more elevated and complete reality.

If his companion does not advance due to inability or lack of interest, there comes a distancing between them caused by the remarkable difference in their states of consciousness because even though one of them is elevated and active, the other remains static. This distancing may bring about a lack of communication just as distinct as that between a literate and an illiterate person. One of the partners could be faced with giving up his chances of growth, so that both would remain united in ignorance, because the alternative would perhaps be too dangerous to marital stability. If only one of the partners reaches his full potential and wisdom in love, while the other remains limited to demanding satisfaction of personal fantasies or expressing the behavior of the corrupt side of love, there will be no chance of the couple's advancement.

These risks are why this knowledge should be handled with infinite patience, concern, and although it may seem redundant, with great love. The principal aim of this knowledge is to unite a couple in true love, so that they may find real happiness, strengthen family and home ties, and contribute to a more humane, spiritual and conscious world.

The aim is for the couple to attain a union of such strength, permanence and soundness as only authentic love can offer. In the search for this unity, the person who is already married and who attains the knowledge of love, should give his or her spouse all the opportunities possible to gradually achieve the established goals. On the path to achieving the most perfect union, their shield should be patience and tolerance.

When a couple arrives simultaneously to this knowledge of love and possesses the same level of dedication and involvement, their advancement will be swift and more fruitful. With their resolve, they will undoubtedly arrive at their happy and prosperous goal.

GLOSSARY

ALTER EGO

It is an aspect of the personality which acts as a comparison, confidante, opposite or counterpart to the individual and is linked to the Ego's perception of itself, its desires, fantasies and dreams. It is free of the domination and imprint of the social program or conscience by remaining silent or hidden until it reveals itself as a result of the action of a catalyst, such as alcohol, drugs, stress, etc. or by projection onto other individuals. This process is not to be confused with repression.

CEREBRAL INTELLIGENCE

It is the functioning of the brain for absorbing and processing "information" which becomes incorporated and remains in the brain through the process known as "memorization," this memory being based on already programmed "points of reference." Because the processing of any information is controlled by the individual "points of reference" which are already there and are not new, it does not allow the possibility of any experience outside of its realm and it denies the possibility of new and fresh perspectives, selecting what is useful and what is not. This selective process is not based on anything objective, but on the subjective "points of reference."

DIVINE SPARK MANIFESTED THROUGH ONE'S BRAIN

The Divine Spark exists in a latent state within the individual already, but the development of the will and the formation of the mind permits the divine spark or spirit to express itself through the individual in his acts which are in alignment with the purposes of the All.

EGO

It is the psychological part of the person, through which the personality observes itself and through which it chooses what positions to take with reference to external reality. The personality depends upon and lives through it. In conclusion, the Ego, psychologically, is that part of the personality which dictates the norms of behavior of the person.

EMOTIONS

Whereas feeling is the response to stimuli, emotion is the subjective response to feeling, involving physiological changes, such as sweaty palms, increased heart beat, release of adrenaline, cold feet etc., as a preparation for action. Some emotions are love, fear, hate, anger, envy, hysteria, jealousy and compassion.

ESOTERIC

This term refers to a deeper layer of existence and comprehension, only understood by a limited number of individuals. All existence and understanding has layers, some of whose surface meaning is apparent to the masses, and still some, whose deeper and profound truths require a higher level of consciousness in order to be comprehended. All religions and philosophies have a branch of teaching for the masses, and at the same time, there exists an inner core of the same teaching on a deeper and more profound level, such as Kabbala's relationship to Judaism, Sufism to Islam, and Esoteric Christianity to Christianity. Esoteric does not only refer to the religious or philosophical, as there are esoteric meanings in all things. It is the hidden level, not open to the "naked eye."

FEELING

The ability to perceive internal and external stimuli; an awareness, state or disposition.

As a noun, it is an impression and intuitive awareness or aptitude in response to stimuli.

GENDER

It is the existence of masculine and feminine, or positive and negative, visible or invisible in all things in the Universe.
(see Sex)

HERMES TRISMEGISTUS

Ancient Egyptian Sage and author, considered the central figure of Esoteric Wisdom, whose teachings may be found at the source of all esoteric teachings of every culture and religion. His life work was focused on the direction of "the planting the great Seed-Truth" which has grown and blossomed so that all contemporary, religious and philosophical teachings can be traced back to him.

HERMETIC

Pertaining to Hermes Trismegistus, the works ascribed to him and the science that developed from his Teachings which are sealed and protected. As an adjective, the word "hermetic" not only refers to something which is sealed and airtight, but it also refers to more profound levels of meaning, not always apparent by normal methods, observation and reasoning.

HUMAN-ANIMAL CONDITIONS

The presence of the unconscious bestial or animal characteristics in the human being describes the human-animal condition the author frequently speaks of.

ID

It is the part of the personality whose actions are motivated by instinctual impulses and demands for immediate gratification of primitive needs.

INCARNATE

The embodiment of spirit in human form or thoughts and ideas manifested in the material.

INTEGRAL INTELLIGENCE

The physical, mental, psychic and spiritual elements of one's being, united in one complete intelligence with all the elements harmoniously functioning together.

LIBIDO

Life energy which symbolizes the strength and force of life; it represents the generative driving force of life itself which is part of everything.

MAGNETIC OVOID

When a couple is formed, they create through their union, a productive, vibratory field surrounding both which metaphorically takes on the shape of an egg. Once again, the quality of the vibrations depends on the level of development of the partners. This field can be perceived by others from the outside and when it is very strong, other people cannot enter into it.

Going one step further, when true love exists in a couple, the matrimonial aura or matrimonial ovoid can be achieved. It is an "occult," or "mental child" of both mates, a positive and a magnetic closed field which joins, harmonizes and protects the couple, making the marriage truly "established" according to the laws of Nature. Couples who lack this occult child of love are joined solely by passions, personal convenience, loneliness, habit or social convention.

MIND

Just as "cerebral intelligence" is the product of the brain and is unconscious intelligence, without internal sense, so "mental intelligence" is a product of the mind and has the characteristic of being conscious. The mind is formed from the three vital sources, that is from the brain (intelligence), heart (feelings), sex (instinct). Through a perfect equilibrium between the three vital centers and the individual's own efforts and discipline that he must accomplish, the individual gradually leads to the formation of the mind. The mind or super-brain permits the evolved individual to reach wisdom,which is beyond good and evil and is eternal and is contrasted to the limited and temporal characteristics of cerebral intelligence.

NARCISSISM

Excessive love and affection is totally centered upon oneself, instead of flowing towards other people or the world outside of oneself. A narcissist is one whose affections are perverse and distorted because of the belief that the world and people exist only to serve him. The narcissist does not love himself, and in order to cover up his guilt in this regard, prefers to project his hate to the whole world.

OCCULTISM

True occultism is the study of man and the laws of Nature, and the way in which these act and influence man. It is called occultism because it is hidden from those passionate beings who are slaves to their material desires. To be privy to this science is dependent on the level of consciousness of the individual which makes him worthy of instruction. Its main objective is the liberation of the human being, liberation from ignorance, pain, bestiality, lies, destiny and death, in order to some day change and create a new world of responsible men entirely conscious of their human quality. It teaches how one can live wisely by correctly using the forces of Nature.

PLATONIC CONCEPTS

Aspects in relationships based on the philosophy of Plato in which emphasis is placed on the ideal or spiritual elements over and above the physical and sexual.

REINCARNATE

Nothing dies; nothing is lost in the Universe. All is transformed and passes into another state of existence, which can easily be observed in Nature by the recurrent cycles of life. Just as ice changes into water and water into steam, it is nonetheless constant, only changing its form. Death is but a transformation, which is only birth into another life for the spirit. Man has a body, which ages and eventually dies, and a spirit, which is perpetually young and immortal, being part of God who is eternal. Reincarnation is the doctrine which states that the spirit, in order to attain perfection, must dwell within many bodies to acquire different experiences which are necessary for its evolution.

ROSACRUCIANISM

During the course of history, Hermetic Science adopted many names, such as Freemasonry, Initiates, Mysticism etc., but remained constant in its internal nature which was to give man access to a new and higher conscious awareness through which he is able to know himself and comprehend the laws of Nature, to be able to transform his human-animal condition using the forces of Nature. The Rosacrucian Order is an eternal fraternity made up of individuals who have access to a certain knowledge, known as occultism, after an arduous process of spiritual development. A real Rosacrucian is defined by the way he lives, his manner of speech, and his actions, not by means of documents, signs, words or proofs of accumulation of information. There are many usurpers and pseudo-Rosacrucian orders who endeavor to prove their legitimacy. The true Rosacrucian order however, continues to exist imperceptibly and silently.

SEVEN PRINCIPLES OF HERMETIC SCIENCE

1. *MIND:* "All is mind, the Universe is Mental."

2. *CORRESPONDENCE:* "As it is below, so it is above."

3. *VIBRATION:* "Nothing is stationary; everything moves, everything vibrates."

4. *POLARITY:* "Everything is dual; everything has two poles; everything has its pair of opposites; like and unlike are the same;

opposites are identical in nature but different in degree; extremes meet; all truth is semi-truth; all paradoxes can be reconciled."

5. *RHYTHM:* "Everything flows out and in; everything rises and falls; the swing of the pendulum is manifested in everything and the measure of the swing to the right is the measure of the swing to the left and rhythm is the compensation."

6. *CAUSE AND EFFECT:* "Every cause has its effect. Every effect has its cause. Everything happens according to the Law. Chance is but a name for the Law not recognized. There are many planes of causation, but none escape this law."

7. *GENDER:* "Gender is in everything. Everything has its masculine and feminine principles. It is manifested on all planes." (For more detailed information - see The Stellar Man by the same author)

SEX

Sex is the physical manifestation of gender. It is the distinction between male and female, positive and negative. Although everything in Nature has elements from both male and female, sex identifies the predominant characteristics, the outer raiment. Behavior is not necessarily in accordance with the outer appearance of sex. (See Gender)

SOUL

The soul is the intelligent, animal part of the primordial component of the individual, which is a combination of four intelligences; the intelligence of the respiratory apparatus, the intelligence of the digestive apparatus, the intelligence of the circulatory apparatus, the intelligence of the procreative apparatus, which are traditionally represented by the four natural elements of air, earth, water and fire.

The soul is given to every human by Nature at birth through the four elementary intelligences located in the digestive, circulatory, respiratory and procreative systems. It is not yet imbued with a higher consciousness and intelligence of its own. It has no leader and it moves forward without the addition of its will, functioning only as a result of its inherent characteristics which pertain to the collective animal soul. The soul is the bed, or soil on which the spirit can place its seed and grow.

The ultimate goal consists of the wedding of the spirit and the soul. When the soul acquires consciousness and spirit, the human being can act at will with the forces of Nature. The soul that is freed from the emotional and base passions is the protecting shield of the human being.

SPIRIT

The Sun by its nature irradiates millions of particles of light and heat, maintaining or sustaining life. Like the Sun, God or spirit emits and bestows particles of himself within each individual, each one of these particles, termed the "divine spark," being equivalent to the spirit of each man. Man therefore, is a spirit incarnated in a body.

The spirit and the soul seek each other out like a man and a woman seek one another out. All human beings have a spirit and a soul. But human beings could be unaware of either. Only through knowledge and education of one's soul, can one's spirit which is already there, shine through. To clean one's soul, enables one's spirit to act without the limitations of the corporeal, to move closer and fuse with God.

SUBLIMATION

The transformation or modification of an instinctive impulse. The manifestation of the impulse is not left entirely in the hands of the instinct, but is governed by the will or Superior I. Sublimation of the libido is the positive and creative channeling of the life force. Sublimation means bowing to the demands of the spirit, by dominating the demands of the personality or the beast.

SUPER EGO

It is the psychological part of the person which contains the learned and programmed sense of right and wrong. This right and wrong is arbitrary and is incorporated through the cultural and familiar programming. It is mainly unconscious.

ABOUT THE AUTHOR

John Baines, (literary pseudonym of Dario Salas Sommer), is the contemporary philosopher, founder and director of the Dario Salas Institute for Hermetic Science. From an early age he has given his heart and soul to the study and dissemination of a practical philosophy based on the esoteric principles of Hermes Trismegistus. As a man he encompasses the universal qualities of true humanness by actively promoting the individual development of men and women. His literary career began with the publication of **The Secret Science**, which introduces the neophyte to a body of work which expounds upon the inner world of man and his relationship to his environment. His unique perspective unites contemporary psychological practice with ancient philosophical wisdom. Further books in his series are intended to enrich and harmonize man's understanding of himself and his relation to all. The publication of **The Science of Love** is the natural progression of the ideas set forth in all his works, because through studying the relationships between men and women, the author brings the vast expanse of this wisdom onto a tangible and operative level.